1 MONTH OF
FREE
READING

at
www.ForgottenBooks.com

By purchasing this book you are eligible for one month membership to ForgottenBooks.com, giving you unlimited access to our entire collection of over 1,000,000 titles via our web site and mobile apps.

To claim your free month visit:

www.forgottenbooks.com/free1204579

ISBN 978-0-331-51731-6
PIBN 11204579

This book is a reproduction of an important historical work. Forgotten Books uses state-of-the-art technology to digitally reconstruct the work, preserving the original format whilst repairing imperfections present in the aged copy. In rare cases, an imperfection in the original, such as a blemish or missing page, may be replicated in our edition. We do, however, repair the vast majority of imperfections successfully; any imperfections that remain are intentionally left to preserve the state of such historical works.

THE

CHARTER

OF

council

THE CITY OF BOSTON,

AND

ORDINANCES MADE AND ESTABLISHED

BY THE

MAYOR, ALDERMEN, AND COMMON COUNCIL,

WITH SUCH ACTS OF THE

LEGISLATURE OF MASSACHUSETTS,

AS RELATE TO THE

𝔊𝔬𝔟𝔢𝔯𝔫𝔪𝔢𝔫𝔱 𝔬𝔣 𝔰𝔞𝔦𝔡 ℭ𝔦𝔱𝔶.

COMPILED AND ARRANGED IN PURSUANCE OF AN ORDER OF
THE CITY COUNCIL.

BOSTON:
TRUE AND GREENE,—CITY PRINTERS.
....
1827.

1852. Nov 29
Gift of
Edward R Andrews,
of the Senior Class,
from Boston

CHARTER.

===

Commonwealth of Massachusetts.

AN ACT

Establishing the City of Boston.

Sec. 1. *BE it enacted by the Senate and House of Representatives, in General Court assembled, and by the authority of the same,* That the inhabitants of the Town of Boston, for all purposes, for which towns are by law incorporated, in this Commonwealth, shall continue to be one body politic, in fact and in name, under the style and denomination of the City of Boston ; and as such, shall have, exercise, and enjoy, all the rights, immunities, powers and privileges, and shall be subject to all the duties and obligations, now incumbent upon and appertaining to said town, as a municipal corporation. And the administration of all the fiscal, prudential, and municipal concerns of said city, with the conduct and government thereof, shall be vested in one principal officer, to be styled the Mayor ; one select Council, consisting of eight persons, to be denominated the Board of Aldermen ; and one more numerous Council, to consist of forty eight persons, to be denominated the Common Council ; which Boards in their joint capacity, shall be denominated the City Council, together with such other Board of Officers, as are herein after specified.

Title.

General powers.

City Officers.

Sec. 2. *Be it further enacted,* That it shall be the duty of the Selectmen of Boston, as soon as may be, after the passing of this act, to cause a new division of the said town to be made into twelve wards,

Wards.

in such manner as to include an equal number of inhabitants in each ward, as nearly as conveniently may be, consistently with well defined limits to each ward ; including in such computation of numbers of inhabitants, persons of all descriptions, and taking the last census, made under the authority of the United States as a basis for such computation. And it shall be

Computation of numbers.

in the power of the City Council, herein after mentioned, from time to time, not oftener than once in ten years, to alter such division of wards, in such a manner as to preserve, as nearly as may be, an equal number of inhabitants in each ward.

SEC. 3. *Be it further enacted,* That on the second Monday of April, annually, the citizens of said city, qualified to vote in city affairs, shall meet together, within their respective wards, at such time and place,

Election of City Officers.

as the Mayor and Aldermen may, by their warrant, direct and appoint ;—and the said citizens shall then choose by ballot, one Warden and one Clerk, who shall be a resident in said ward, who shall hold their offices for one year, and until others shall be appointed in their stead. And it shall be the duty of such Warden to preside at all meetings of the citizens of such ward, to preserve order therein ;—and it shall be the duty of such Clerk, to make a fair and true

Duty of Wardens and Clerks.

record, and keep an exact journal of all the acts and votes of the citizens, at such ward meetings ;—to deliver over such records and journals, together with all other documents and papers held by him, in said capacity, to his successor in such office. And if, at the opening of any annual meeting, the Warden of such ward should not be present, the Clerk of such ward shall call the citizens to order, and preside at such meeting, until a Warden shall be chosen by ballot. And if, at any other meeting, the Warden shall be absent, the Clerk in such case, shall so preside, until a Moderator, or Warden, *pro tempore,* shall be chosen ; which may be done by nomination

Inspectors.

and hand-vote, if the Clerk so direct. At such meeting also, five Inspectors of Elections shall be chosen, for such ward, being residents therein, by ballot, to hold their offices for one year. And it shall be the duty of the Warden and Inspectors, in

each ward, to receive, sort, count and declare all
votes, at all elections within such ward. And the
Warden, Clerk, and Inspectors, so chosen, shall, respectively, be under oath, faithfully and impartially
to discharge their several duties, relative to elections ;
which oath may be administered by the Clerk of such
ward, to the Warden, and by the latter, to the Clerk
and Inspectors, or by any Justice of the Peace of
the County of Suffolk ; and a certificate of such oaths
having been administered, ahall be entered in the record or journal, to be kept by the Clerk of such ward.

Sec. 4. *Be it further enacted,* That, the warden,
or other presiding officer, of such ward meeting, shall
have full power and authority to preserve order and
decorum therein, and to repress all riotous, tumultuous, and disorderly conduct therein ; and for that
purpose, to call to his aid, any Constable, or other
peace officer, and also to command the aid and assistance of any citizen or citizens, who may be present ;
and any peace officer, or other citizen, neglecting or refusing to afford such aid, shall be taken and deemed to
be guilty of a misdemeanor. And such Warden shall
also have power and authority, by warrant under his
hand, to cause any person or persons, who shall be guilty of any riotous, tumultuous, or disorderly conduct at
such meeting, to be taken into custody, and restrained ;
Provided however, that such restraint shall not continue after the adjournment or dissolution of such
meeting ; *and provided, further,* that the person, so
guilty of such disorderly conduct, shall be liable notwithstanding such restraint, to be prosecuted and punished, in the same manner, as if such arrest had not
been made.

Sec. 5. *Be it further enacted,* That the citizens
of said city, qualified to vote in city affairs, at their
respective ward meetings, to be held on the second
Monday in April, annually, shall be called upon to
give in their votes for one able and discreet person,
being an inhabitant of the city, to be Mayor of said
city, for the term of one year. And all the votes so
given in each ward, being sorted, counted, and declared by the Warden and Inspectors of Elections,
shall be recorded at large, by the Clerk, in open ward

Returns of votes.

meeting; and in making such declaration and record, the whole number of votes or ballots, given in, shall be distinctly stated, together with the name of every person voted for, and the number of votes given for each person respectively; such numbers to be expressed in words at length : and a transcript of such record, certified and authenticated by the Warden, Clerk, and a majority of the Inspectors of Elections for each ward, shall forthwith be transmitted or delivered by such Ward Clerk, to the Clerk, of the city. And it shall be the duty of the City Clerk, forthwith to enter such returns, or a plain and intelligible abstract of them, as they are successively received, upon the journal of the proceedings of the Mayor and Aldermen, or some other book to be kept for that purpose. And it shall be the duty of the Mayor and Aldermen to meet together, within two days after such election,

Examination of votes.

and to examine and compare all the said returns, and to ascertain whether any person has a majority of all the votes given for Mayor : And in case a majority is so given, it shall be their duty to give notice thereof, in writing, to the person thus elected, and also to make the same known to the inhabitants of said city. But if, on such an examination, no person appears to have a majority of all the votes given for Mayor, the Mayor and Aldermen, for the time being, shall issue

Continued Elections.

their warrants for meetings of the citizens of the respective wards, for the choice of a Mayor, at such time and place, as they shall judge most convenient : And the same proceedings shall be had, in all respects, as are herein before directed, until a Mayor shall be chosen by a majority of all the voters, voting at such election. And in case of the decease, inability, or absence of the Mayor and the same being declared, and a vote passed by the Aldermen and Common Council, respectively, declaring such cause,

Vacancies to be supplied.

and the expediency of electing a Mayor, for the time being, to supply the vacancy thus occasioned, it shall be lawful for the Aldermen and Common Council to meet in convention, and elect a Mayor to hold the said office, until such occasion shall be removed, or until a new election.

SEC. 6. *Be it further enacted,* That the citizens in their respective ward meetings, to be held on the second Monday of April, annually, shall be called upon to give in their votes for eight persons, being inhabitants of said city, to constitute the Board of Aldermen, for the ensuing year ; and all the votes so given, being sorted, counted, and declared by the Warden and Inspectors, shall be recorded at large, by the Clerk, in open ward meeting ; and in making such declaration and record, the whole number of votes or ballots given in, shall be particularly stated, together with the name of every person voted for, and the number of votes given for each person ; and a transcript of such record, certified by the Warden and Clerk, and a majority of the Inspectors of each ward, shall, by the said Clerk, within two days, be transmitted to the City Clerk ; whereupon the same proceedings shall be had, to ascertain and determine the persons chosen as Aldermen, as are herein before directed, in regard to the choice of Mayor, and for a new election, in case of the whole number required, not being chosen at the first election. And each Alderman, so chosen, shall be duly notified in writing, of his election, by the Mayor and Aldermen for the time being.

Board of Aldermen.

Mode of Election

SEC. 7. *Be it further enacted,* That the citizens of each ward, qualified to vote as aforesaid, at their respective ward meetings, to be held on the second Monday of April, annually, shall be called upon to give in their votes for four able and discreet men, being inhabitants of said ward, to be members of the Common Council; and all the votes given in as aforesaid, in each ward, and being sorted, counted, and declared, by the Warden and Inspectors, if it appear that four persons have a majority of all the votes given in at such election, a public declaration thereof, with the names of the persons so chosen, shall be made in open ward meeting, and the same shall be entered at large, by the Clerk of such ward, in his journal, stating particularly, the whole number of votes given in ; the number necessary to make a choice ; and the number actually given for each of the persons, so declared to be chosen. But, in case four

Common Council.

Mode of conducting election.

persons are not chosen at the first ballot, a new ballot shall be opened for a number of Common Councilmen, sufficient to complete the number of four; and the same proceedings shall be had, as before directed, until the number of four shall be duly chosen; *Provided, however,* that if the said elections cannot conveniently be completed on such day, the same may be adjourned to another day, for that purpose, not longer distant than three days. And each of the persons so chosen, as a member of the Common Council, in each ward, shall, within two days of his election, be furnished with a certificate thereof, signed by the Warden, Clerk, and a majority of the Inspectors of such ward; which certificate shall be presumptive evidence of the title of such person to a seat in the Common Council; but such Council, however, shall have authority to decide ultimately, upon all questions relative to the qualifications, elections, and returns of its members.

Adjournment of meeting.

Authority of the Common Council

SEC. 8. *Be it further enacted,* That every male citizen of twenty one years of age and upwards, excepting paupers, and persons under guardianship, who shall have resided within the Commonwealth one year, and within the city six months next preceding any meeting of the citizens, either in wards, or in general meeting, for municipal purposes, and who shall have paid by himself or his parent, master or guardian, any state or county tax, which, within two years next preceding such meeting, shall have been assessed upon him, in any town or district in this Commonwealth, and also every citizen who shall be, by law, exempted from taxation, and who shall be in all other respects, qualified as above mentioned, shall have a right to vote at such meeting, and no other person shall be entitled to vote at such meeting.

Qualification of Electors.

Exempts.

SEC. 9. *Be it further enacted,* That the Mayor, Aldermen, and Common Councilmen, chosen as aforesaid, shall enter on the duties of their respective offices on the first day of May, in each year, unless the same happen on a Sunday; and in that event, on the day following; and before entering on the duties of their offices, shall respectively, be sworn by taking the oath of allegiance and oath of office, pre- scribed in the constitution of this Commonwealth, and an oath to support the constitution of the United States.   And such oaths may be administered to the Mayor elect, by any one of the Justices of the Su- preme Judicial Court, or any Judge of any Court of Record, commissioned to hold any such Court, with- in the said city, or by any Justice of the Peace for the County of Suffolk.   And such oaths shall and may be administered to the Aldermen and members of the Common Council, by the Mayor, being him- self first sworn as aforesaid : and a certificate of such oaths having been taken, shall be entered in the jour- nal of the Mayor and Aldermen, and of the Common Council, respectively, by their respective Clerks.

Oath of office.

SEC. 10.   *Be it further enacted,* That the Mayor and Aldermen, thus chosen and qualified, shall com- pose one Board, and shall sit and act together as one body, at all meetings, of which the Mayor, if present, shall preside ; but in his absence, the Board may elect a Chairman for the time being.   The said Board, to- gether with the Common Council, in convention, shall have power to choose a Clerk, who shall be sworn to the faithful discharge of the duties of his office, who shall be chosen for the term of one year, and until another person is duly chosen to succeed him ; re- movable however, at the pleasure of the Mayor and Aldermen, who shall be denominated the Clerk of the City ; and whose duty it shall be, to keep a jour- nal of the acts and proceedings of the said Board, composed of the Mayor and Aldermen ; to sign all warrants issued by them, and to do such other acts, in his said capacity, as may, lawfully and reasonably, be required of him ; and to deliver over all journals, books, papers, and documents, entrusted to him as such clerk, to his successor in office, immediately upon such successor being chosen and qualified as aforesaid, or whenever he may be thereto required by the said Mayor and Aldermen.   And the City Clerk thus cho- sen and qualified, shall have all the powers, and per- form all the duties, now by law, belonging to the Town Clerk of the Town of Boston, as if the same were par- ticularly and fully enumerated, except in cases where it is otherwise expressly provided.

Mayor and Alder- men to act as one body.

General Powers.

Duties of Clerk.

2

Sec. 11. *Be it further enacted*, That the persons so chosen and qualified, as members of the Common **CommonCouncil.** Council of the said city, shall sit and act together as a separate body, distinct from that of the Mayor and Aldermen, except in those cases in which the two bodies are to meet in convention ;—and the said Council shall have power, from time to time, to choose one **General powers.** of their own members to preside over their deliberations, and to preserve order therein ; and also to **Choice of Clerk.** choose a Clerk, who shall be under oath, faithfully to discharge the duties of his office, who shall hold such office during the pleasure of said Council ; and whose duty it shall be, to attend said Council, when the same is in session, to keep a journal of its acts, votes, and proceedings, and to perform such other services in said capacity, as said council may require. All sit- **Duties of Clerk.** tings of the Common Council shall be public ; also all sittings of the Mayor and Aldermen, when they are not engaged in executive business. Twenty five members of the Common Council shall constitute a quorum for the transaction of business.

Sec. 12. *Be it further enacted*, That the Mayor of the said city, thus chosen and qualified, shall be taken and deemed to be the chief executive officer of said corporation ; and he shall be compensated for his services by a salary, to be fixed by the Board of **Compensation of** Aldermen and Common Council, in City Council con- **the Mayor.** vened, payable at stated periods ; which salary shall not exceed the sum of five thousand dollars annually, and he shall receive no other compensation or emoluments whatever ; and no regulations, enlarging or diminishing such compensation, shall be made, to take effect until the expiration of the year for which the Mayor then in office, shall have been elected. And it shall be the duty of the Mayor, to be vigilant and active at all times, in causing the laws for the government of said city, to be duly executed and put in force ; to inspect the conduct of all subordinate officers in the government thereof, and as far as in his power, to cause all negligence, carelessness, and positive violations of duty to be duly prosecuted and punished. He shall have power, whenever in his judgment, the good of said city may require it, to summon meetings of the Board of Aldermen and Common Council, or either · of them, although the meeting of said Boards, or either of them, may stand adjourned to a more distant day. And it shall be the duty of the Mayor, from time to time, to communicate to both branches of the City Council, all such information, and recommend all such measures as may tend to the improvement of the finances, the police, health, security, cleanliness, comfort and ornament of the said city.

SEC. 13. *Be it further enacted,* That the administration of police, together with the executive powers of the said corporation generally, together also, with all the powers heretofore vested in the Selectmen of the Town of Boston, either by the general laws of this Commonwealth, by particular laws, relative to the powers and duties of said Selectmen, or by the usages, votes, or by-laws of said town, shall be, and hereby are vested in the Mayor and Aldermen, as hereby constituted, as fully and amply, as if the same were herein specially enumerated. And further, the said Mayor and Aldermen shall have full and exclusive power to grant licenses to innholders, victuallers, retailers, and confectioners, within the said city, in all cases wherein the Court of Sessions for the County of Suffolk, on the recommendation of the Selectmen of Boston, have heretofore been authorized to grant such licenses ; and in granting such licenses, it shall be lawful for the said Mayor and Aldermen, to annex thereto, such reasonable conditions, in regard to time, places, and other circumstances, under which such license shall be acted upon, as, in their judgement, the peace, quiet, and good order of the city may require : Also, to take bonds of all persons so licensed, in reasonable sums, and with sufficient sureties, conditioned for a faithful compliance with the terms of their said licenses, and of all laws and regulations respecting such licensed houses : And said Mayor and Aldermen, after the granting of any such license, shall have power to revoke or suspend the same, if in their judgment the order and welfare of the said city shall require it. And any person or persons who shall presume to exercise either of the said employments, within said city, without having first obtained a license therefor, or in any manner contrary to the terms of said license, or after the same shall have been revoked or suspended, such person or persons shall be Forfeitures liable to the same penalties and forfeitures, and to be prosecuted for in the same manner, as now by law provided, in case of exercising either of said employments without license from the Court of Sessions, for the County of Suffolk; and shall also be taken and deemed to have forfeited their bonds, respectively given aforesaid, upon which suits may be instituted, against such licensed persons or their sureties, at the discretion of said Mayor and Aldermen, and in such manner as they may direct, for the purpose of enforcing such forfeiture : *Provided, however,* that all innholders, retailers, confectioners, and victuallers, shall, on being licensed as aforesaid, pay the same sum now required by law ; which sum shall be accounted for in the same way and manner as is now by law required.

SEC. 14. *Be it further enacted,* That the Mayor and Aldermen shall have power to license all theatrical exhibitions and all public shows, and all exhibitions of whatever name or nature, to which admission is obtained on payment of money, on such terms and conditions as to them may seem just and reasonable ; and to regulate the same, from time to time, in such manner as to them may appear necessary to preserve order and decorum, and to prevent the in-
Licenses for public exhibitions. terruption of peace and quiet. And any person or persons who shall set forth, establish or promote any such exhibition or show, or publish, or advertise the same or otherwise aid or assist therein without a license so obtained as aforesaid, or contrary to the terms or conditions of such license, or whilst the same is suspended, or after the same is revoked, by said Mayor and Aldermen, shall be liable to such forfeiture as the City Council may, by any by-law made for that purpose, prescribe.

SEC. 15. *Be it further enacted,* That all other powers now by law vested in the Town of Boston, or in the inhabitants thereof, as a municipal corporation, shall be, and hereby are vested in the Mayor and Aldermen, and Common Council of the said city, to be exercised by concurrent vote, each Board as hereby constituted having a negative upon the other. More especially they shall have power to make all such needful and salutary by-laws, as towns by the laws of By-Laws. this commonwealth have power to make and establish, and to annex penalties not exceeding twenty dollars for the breach thereof, which by-laws shall take effect and be in force, from and after the times therein respectively limited, without the sanction or confirmation of any court, or other authority whatsoever ; *provided*, that such by-laws shall not be repugnant to the Constitution and laws of this Commonwealth : *And, provided, also,* that the same shall be Proviso. liable to be annulled by the Legislature thereof. The said City Council shall also have power, from time to time, to lay and assess taxes for all purposes for which towns are, by law, required or authorized to assess Assessment of and grant money, and also for all purposes for which Taxes. county taxes may be levied and assessed, whenever the city shall, alone, compose one county : *Provided*, Proviso. *however*, that in the assessment and apportionment of all such taxes upon the polls and estates of all persons liable to contribute thereto, the same rules and regulations shall be observed as are now established by the laws of this Commonwealth, or may be hereafter enacted, relative to the assessment and apportionment of town taxes.

The said City Council shall also have power to provide for the assessment and collection of such Collection of Taxes. taxes, and to make appropriations of all public monies, and provide for the disbursement thereof, and take suitable measures to ensure a just and prompt account thereof; and for these purposes, may either elect such Assessors, and Assistant Assessors, as may Assessors to be chosen. be needful, or provide for the appointment or election of the same, or any of them, by the Mayor and Aldermen, or by the citizens, as in their judgment, may be most conducive to the public good, and may also require of all persons entrusted with the collection, custody, or disbursement of public monies, such bonds with such conditions and such sureties, as the case may, in their judgments require.

SEC. 16. *Be it further enacted,* That the said City

Council shall have power, and they are hereby authorized to provide for the appointment or election of all necessary officers, for the good government of said city, not otherwise provided for ; to prescribe their **City Officers.** duties, and fix their compensation, and to choose a Register of Deeds, whenever the city shall compose one county. The City Council, also, shall have the care and superintendence of the public buildings, and the care, custody and management of all the property of the city, with power to lease or sell the same, **Public Buildings.** (except the Common and Faneuil Hall,) with power also to purchase property, real or personal, in the name, and for the use of the city, whenever its interest or convenience may, in their judgment, require it.

SEC. 17. *Be it further enacted,* That all the power and authority now by law, vested in the Board of Health for the Town of Boston, relative to the quarantine of vessels, and relative to every other subject whatsoever, shall be, and the same is hereby transferred to, and vested in the said City Council, to be carried into execution by the appointment of Health **Health Commissioners.** Commissioners, or in such other manner as the health, cleanliness, comfort and order of said city may in their judgment, require, subject to such alterations as the Legislature may from time to time adopt.

SEC. 18. *Be it further enacted,* That the Mayor and Aldermen of said city, and the said Common Council shall, as soon as conveniently may be, after their annual organization, meet together in convention, and elect some suitable and trustworthy person, to **City Treasurer.** be the treasurer of said city.

SEC. 19. *Be it further enacted,* That the citizens, at their respective ward meetings, to be held on the second Monday of April, annually, shall elect, by ballot, a number of persons, to be determined by the City Council, but not less than three in each ward, to **Firewards.** be Firewards of said city, who together shall constitute the Board of Firewards for said city, and shall have all the powers, and be subject to all the duties, now by law appertaining to the Firewards of the Town of Boston, until the same shall be altered or qualified by the Legislature. And the said citizens shall, at the same time, and in like manner, elect one person in each ward, to be an Overseer of the Poor; and Overseers of the Poor. the persons thus chosen shall, together, cons'itute the Board of Overseers for said city, and shall have all the powers, and be subject to all the duties, now by law, appertaining to the Overseers of the Poor for the Town of Boston, until the same shall be altered or qualified by the Legislature. And the said citizens shall, at the same time, and in like manner, elect one person in each ward, to be a member of School Committees. the School Committee, for the said city; and the persons so chosen, shall, jointly with the Mayor and Aldermen, constitute the School Committee for the said city, and have the care and superintendence of the public schools.

SEC. 20. *Be it further enacted*, That all Boards and Officers, acting under the authority of the said corporation, and entrusted with the expenditure of public money, shall be accountable therefor, to the City Council, in such manner as they may direct. Accountability. And it shall be the duty of the City Council, to publish and distribute, annually, for the information of the citizens, a particular statement of the receipts and expenditures of all public monies, and a particular Annual Financial Statements. statement of all city property.

SEC. 21. *Be it further enacted*, That in all cases, in which appointments to office, are directed to be made by the Mayor and Aldermen, the Mayor shall have the exclusive power of nomination; such nomina- Nominations. tion however, being subject to be confirmed or rejected, by the Board of Aldermen: *Provided, however*, that no Proviso. person shall be eligible to any office, the salary of which is payable out of the city treasury, who at the time of his appointment, shall be a member either of the Board of Aldermen or Common Council.

SEC. 22. *Be it further enacted*, That it shall be the duty of the two branches of the City Council, in the month of May, in each year, after their annual organization, to meet in convention, and determine the number of Representatives, which it may be ex- State Representatives. pedient for the corporation to send to the General Court in such year, within its constitutional limits, and to publish such determination, which shall be conclusive;—and the number thus determined, shall be specified in the warrant calling a meeting for the election of Representatives: and neither the Mayor, nor any Alderman, or Members of the Common Council, shall, at the same time, hold any other office under the City Government.

SEC. 23. *Be it further enacted,* That all elections for Governor, Lieutenant Governor, Senators, Representatives, Representatives to Congress, and all other officers who are to be chosen and voted for by the people, shall be held at meetings of the citizens, qualified to vote in such elections, in their respective

Ward Meetings for the choice of National & State Officers.

wards, at the time fixed by law for those elections respectively. And at such meetings, all the votes given in, being collected, sorted, counted, and declared, by the Inspectors of Elections, in each ward, it shall be the duty of the Clerk of such ward to make a true record of the same, specifying therein the whole number of ballots given in, the name of each person voted for, and the number of votes for each, expressed in words at length. And a transcript of such record, certified by the Warden, Clerk, and a majority of the Inspectors of Elections in such ward, shall forthwith be transmitted or delivered by each Ward Clerk to the Clerk of the City. And it shall be the duty of the City Clerk forthwith to enter such returns, or a plain and intelligible abstract of them, as they are successively received, in the journals of the proceedings of the Mayor and Aldermen, or in some other book kept for that purpose. And it shall be the duty of the Mayor and Aldermen to meet together within two days after every such election, and examine and compare all the said returns, and there-

Examination and return of votes.

upon to make out a certificate of the result of such election, to be signed by the Mayor and a majority of the Aldermen, and also by the City Clerk, which shall be transmitted, delivered, or returned, in the same manner as similar returns are by law directed to be made by the Selectmen of towns; and such certificates and returns shall have the same force and effect in all respects, as like returns of similar elections made by the Selectmen of towns. And in all elections for Representatives to the General Court, in case the whole number proposed to be elected, shall not be chosen by a majority of the votes legally returned, the Mayor and Aldermen shall forthwith issue their warrant for a new election ; and the same proceedings shall be had in all respects, as are herein before directed, until the whole number shall be elected. *Provided, however,* that it shall be the duty of the Selectmen of the said Town of Boston, within twelve days from the passing of this **act,** to call a meeting of the qualified voters of the said town, to give in their ballots on the following question : Shall the elections for State and United States Officers, be holden in general meeting ? And it shall be the duty of the Selectmen to preside at the said meeting, to receive, sort, count, and declare the votes given in, and to forward a certificate of the result to the Secretary of the Commonwealth, and publish the same in two or more of the newspapers printed in Boston ;—and if a majority of the votes so given in, shall be in the negative, then the provisions of the preceding part of this section, shall regulate the said elections in wards—but if a majority of the votes given in as aforesaid, shall be in the affirmative, then the said elections for State and United States Officers, shall be holden in the manner prescribed by the constitution and laws of the Commonwealth, with the exception that the Mayor and Aldermen and City Clerk shall perform the duties now required by law, to be performed by the Selectmen and Town Clerk.

SEC. 24. *Be it further enacted,* That prior to every election of city officers, or of any officer or officers, under the government of the United States, or of this Commonwealth, it shall be the duty of said Mayor and Aldermen to make out lists of all the citizens of each ward, qualified to vote in such election, in the manner in which Selectmen and Assessors of towns are required to make out similar lists of voters, and for that purpose they shall have free access to the Assessors' books and lists, and be entitled to the aid and assistance of all Assessors, Assistant Assessors, and other officers of said city. And it shall be the duty of said Mayor and Aldermen to deliver such list of the voters in each ward, so prepared and corrected, to the Clerk of said ward, to be used by the

Margin notes: Conditional Elections. Proviso. Contingent clause. Ward Lists.

3

Warden and Inspectors thereof, at such election ; and no person shall be entitled to vote at such elec-

tion, whose name is not borne on such list. And to prevent all frauds and mistakes in such elections, it shall be the duty of the Inspectors in each ward, to take care that no person shall vote at such election, whose name is not so borne on the list of voters, and

to cause a mark to be placed against the name of each voter, on such list, at the time of giving in his vote.

SEC. 25. *Be it further enacted,* That general meetings of the citizens qualified to vote in city affairs, may from time to time, be held, to consult upon the common good, to give instructions to their Representatives, and to take all lawful measures to obtain a redress of any grievances, according to the right secured to the people by the Constitution of

this Commonwealth. And such meetings shall, and may be, duly warned by the Mayor and Aldermen, upon the requisition of fifty qualified voters of said city.

SEC. 26. *Be it further enacted,* That all warrants for the meetings of the citizens, for municipal purposes, to be had either in general meetings or in wards,

shall be issued by the Mayor and Aldermen, and shall be in such form, and shall be served, executed, and returned, at such time, and in such manner, as the City Council may, by any by-law, direct and appoint.

SEC. 27. *Be it further enacted,* That for the purpose of organizing the system of government hereby established, and putting the same into operation in the first instance, the Selectmen of the Town of Boston, for the time being, shall seasonably, before the sec-

ond Monday of April next, issue their warrants for calling meetings of the said citizens, in their respective wards, qualified to vote as aforesaid, at such place and hour as they shall think expedient, for the purpose of choosing a Warden, Clerk, and five Inspectors of Elections ; and also, to give in their votes for a Mayor and eight Aldermen for said city, and four Common Councilmen, three Firewards, one Overseer of the Poor, and one Member of the School

Committee, for each ward ;—and the transcripts of the records of each ward, specifying the votes given for Mayor and Aldermen, Firewards, Overseers, and Members of the School Committee, certified by the Warden, Clerk, and a majority of the Inspectors of such ward shall, at said first election, be returned to Return of votes. the said Selectmen of the Town of Boston, whose duty it shall be, to examine and compare the same. And in case said elections shall not be complete at the first election, then to issue a new warrant, until such election shall be completed, and to give notice thereof, in the manner berein before directed to the several persons elected. And at said first meeting, the Clerk of each ward, under the present organization, shall call the citizens to order, and preside until a Warden shall be chosen ; and at said first meeting, a list of voters in each ward, prepared and corrected by the Selectmen of the Town of Boston, for the time being, shall be delivered to the Clerk of each ward, to be used as herein before directed.

SEC. 28. *Be it further enacted*, That so much of the act heretofore passed, relative to the establishment of a Board of Health for the Town of Boston, as provides for the choice of Members of the said Board, and so much of the several acts relative to the assessment and collection of taxes within the Town of Boston, as provides for the election of Assistant Assessors, also all such acts and parts of acts, as come within the purview of this act, and which are inconsistent with, or repugnant to the provisions of this act, shall be, and the same are hereby repealed. Repeal of act.

SEC. 29. And whereas by the laws of this Commonwealth, towns are authorized and required to hold their annual meetings, some time in the months of March or April, in each year, for the choice of town officers ; and whereas such meeting in the month of March, in the present year, for the Town of Boston, would be useless and unnecessarily burthensome—Therefore,

Be it further enacted, That the annual town meetings in the months of March or April, be suspended, March meetings. deferred. and all town officers now in office, shall hold their places until this act shall go into operation.

Legislative control.

SEC. 30. *Be it further enacted,* That nothing in this act contained, shall be so construed as to restrain or prevent the Legislature from amending or altering the same, whenever they shall deem it expedient.

Conditional clause.

SEC. 31. *Be it further enacted,* That this act shall be void, unless the inhabitants of the Town of Boston, at a legal town meeting, called for that purpose, shall, by a written vote, determine to adopt the same within twelve days.

[Approved by the Governor, Feb. 23, 1822.]

———

At a legal meeting, of the freeholders and other inhabitants of the town of Boston, holden at Faneuil Hall, on Monday the 4th day of March, A. D. 1822.

This meeting was called in conformity to the 23d and 21st sections of an act, entitled " An act to establish the city of Boston," passed on the 23d day of February, 1822.

The Selectmen presiding, the Chairman submitted the following questions to the qualified voters of the town, and requested them to write yes, or no against each question.

1st Question. Will you accept the Charter granted by the Legislature, entitled " An act to establish the City of Boston ?"

2d Question. Shall the elections for State and United States Officers be holden in general meeting?

Voted, That the Poll be closed at 3 o'clock.

At the close of the Poll it appeared that the whole number of ballots given in the first question was

4678

———

viz. Yeas, 2797
     Nays, 1881——4678
     Majority 916 for accepting the Charter.

The whole number of votes given in on the second question was   4700

viz. Yeas, 1887   ———
     Nays, 2813——-4700

Majority 926 against electing State and United States Officers in general Meeting.

The state of the votes was declared by the Chairmen of the Selectmen, and then the meeting was dissolved.

Attest, **THO'S CLARK**, *Town Clerk*.

A true Copy from Record.

Attest, **S. F. M'CLEARY**, *City Clerk*.

AN ACT

Concerning Surveyors of Highways in Boston.

Be it enacted by the Senate and House of Representatives in General Court assembled, and by authority of the same, That the City Council of the city of Boston shall have the power and authority of electing, if they see fit, the Mayor and Aldermen of said city, Surveyors of Highways for said city, any thing in the act establishing the city of Boston to the contrary notwithstanding.

City Council to elect Mayor &c.

[Approved by the Governor, June 10th, 1823.]

AN ACT

Concerning the Regulation of the House of Correction in the City of Boston, and concerning the Form of Actions commenced under the By-laws of said city, and providing for filling vacancies in the Board of Aldermen.

SEC. 6. *Be it further enacted,* That in case of the death or resignation of any member of the Board of Aldermen, the citizens of Boston shall have power to fill such vacancy at any regular meeting that may thereafter be convened for that purpose.

[Approved by the Governor, June 12th, 1824.]

AN ACT,

In further addition to an Act, entitled " An Act establishing the City of Boston."

Time of electing City Officers altered.

SEC. 1. *Be it enacted by the Senate and House of Representatives, in General Court assembled, and by the authority of the same,* That the election of the Mayor, Aldermen, and Common Councilmen, and such other officers of the City of Boston, as are now by law to be Chosen on the second Monday in April, annually, shall in future be made on the second Monday in December, annually, and the said officers so chosen shall hold their respective offices for the same term of time, and the same proceedings shall be had in relation to such elections as is provided in and by the Act, entitled, " An Act establishing the city of Boston," to which this is in addition : *Provided nevertheless,* That the next choice of the said city officers shall be made at such time, and in such manner, as are prescribed in and by the Act aforesaid, and the officers so elected shall severally hold their offices until the first Monday of January next, any thing in this act to the contrary notwithstanding.

Time of entering on duty of the of the City Officers fixed.

SEC. 2. *Be it further enacted,* That the officers chosen under and by virtue of this Act, shall enter on the duties of their respective offices on the first Monday of January in each year, and shall be liable to all the duties and restrictions, and shall exercise all the powers to which the said officers are respectively subject or entitled, under and by virtue of the Act to which this is in addition, and of all other Acts in relation to this subject matter.

This act to be adopted by the City.

SEC. 3. *Be it further enacted,* That this act shall be void, unless the inhabitants of the City of Boston, at any general meeting duly warned by public notice, of at least fourteen days, by the Mayor and Aldermen, shall, within sixty days from the passing hereof, by written vote, adopt the same.

Repealing clause.

SEC. 4. *Be it further enacted,* That all the provisions of the Act to which this is in addition, or of any other Act inconsistent with the provisions of this Act, shall be, and hereby are repealed.

[Approved by the Governor, January 27, 1825.]

———

At a general meeting of the inhabitants of the City of Boston, held at Faneuil Hall, on the 25th day of February Anno Domini 1825.

The meeting was called for the purpose of giving in the written votes upon the adoption of the Act of the Legislature, entitled " An Act in further addition to an Act entitled an Act establishing the city of Boston,"

Voted, That the poll be closed at one o'clock, P. M.

At the close of the Poll it appeared that the whole number of ballots given in was   102

viz. Yeas,   100   —-
      Nays,   2—102

So the same was decided in the affirmative.

A true Copy from Record,

        Attest, S. F. M'CLEARY, *City Clerk*.

Accounts and Accountability in Expenditures.—Auditor.

CHAP. I.

An ordinance establishing a system of accountability in the Expenditures of the City.

Sec. 1. *Be it ordained by the Mayor, Aldermen and Common Council of the City of Boston, in City Council assembled,* That from and after the end of the present Municipal year, there shall be appointed in the month of January annually by ballot in each board of the City Council, a joint committee of accounts, to consist of two on the part of the board of Aldermen, and three on the part of the Common Council, whose duty it shall be to meet once a month, and as much oftener as they may deem expedient.

Sec. 2. *Be it further ordained,* That from and after the end of the present municipal year, there shall be appointed, in the month of May annually, by concurrent ballot in each board, one able and discreet person, to be styled, Auditor of Accounts ; who shall continue in office until removed, or a successor be appointed ; who shall receive such compensation for his service as the City Council shall authorize and establish, and who shall be removable at all times, at the pleasure of the City Council ; who shall be sworn to the faithful discharge of the duties of his office, and give bond with surety or sureties, to be approved by the Mayor and Aldermen, in the penal sum of five thousand dollars, for the faithful discharge of said duties, the true accounting for and payment over, of all monies which shall come into his hands, and the delivery over to his successor or the Mayor and Aldermen of all the books, accounts, papers and other documents and property, which shall belong to said office ; and in case said office should become vacant by death, resignation or other-

Commitee of Accounts appointed.

Manner in which money is to be drawn out of the Treasury.

wise, a successor shall forthwith, and in like manner
be appointed, who shall continue in office until the
appointment of a successor.

SEC. 3. *Be it further ordained*, That no monies
shall be paid out of the City Treasury (except in
the cases hereinafter provided) unless the expenditure, or the terms of the contract, shall be vouched
by the chairman of the committee of the board under whose authority it has been authorized or made ;
nor unless the same shall be examined by the auditor, be approved by the committee of accounts, and
be drawn for by the Mayor.   And it shall be the duty of the Mayor, to compare such expenditures with
the general appropriations made for the various objects, and require the auditor to make an exhibit of
the state of such appropriations, monthly, to the City
Council : *Provided*, that in all cases where it is necessary for money to be paid in advance, for contracts made or for work begun, but not completed,
the Mayor may upon being satisfied of such necessity, draw upon the City Treasurer, for the
amount thus necessary to be advanced ; which draft
shall be paid by the City Treasurer, provided the same
be countersigned by the Auditor ; and it shall be the
duty of the Auditor to countersign all such drafts, not
exceeding three hundred dollars, and to charge the
same to the proper person and account ; but the said
Auditor shall not countersign any such draft for any
sum exceeding three hundred dollars, without the direction of the Committee of accounts.

Manner in which money is to be drawn out of the Treasury.

SEC. 4. *Be it further ordained*, That it shall be
the duty of the Committee of accounts to direct the
Auditor, as to the manner in which the books, records and papers belonging to his department shall be
kept, and the mode in which all bills and accounts
against the City, shall be certified or vouched ; and,
at least, once in every month, to examine, and if they
see fit, to pass, all bills and accounts against the City,
which shall be certified by the Auditor.

Committee of accounts to direct the manner of keeping Auditor's books,

SEC. 5. *Be it further ordained*, That it shall be
the duty of the Auditor to keep in a neat methodical
style and manner, a complete set of books, under the

Auditor's duty as to keeping his books.

4

direction of the Committee of accounts ; wherein shall be stated among other things, the appropriation for each distinct object of expenditure, to the end that whenever the appropriations for the specific objects shall have been expended, he shall immediately com-

His duty in examining accounts, &c.

municate the same to the City Council, that they may be apprised of the fact ; and either make a further appropriation, or withold further expenditure for such object or objects as they may deem expedient : The Auditor shall also receive all bills and accounts from persons having demands against the City : examine them in detail ; cast up the same ; and have them filed and entered in books, in such manner and form as the Committee of accounts shall order and direct.   And when the Auditor shall have any doubt concerning the correctness of any such bill or account presented against the City, he shall not enter the same in a book until he shall have exhibited the same, with his objections, to the Committee of accounts at their next meeting, for their consideration and final decision.   And it shall also be the duty of the Auditor to render any other services, from time to time, as the City Council, or the Committee of accounts, shall direct.

Sec. 6. *Be it further ordained,* That it shall be

Auditor's duty as to receiving and paying money.

the duty of the Auditor, to receive all monies collected by the City Clerk, the City Marshall, the Clerk of the Market, the weighers of hay, or any other officer, who is or may be authorized to collect any monies belonging to the City, the Collector and Treasurer excepted : and it shall be the duty of all such officers (the Collector and Treasurer excepted) to pay over to the Auditor from time to time, all monies which they shall receive belonging to the City : and it shall also be the duty of the Auditor to pay over to the Treasurer, at least once in every week, all the monies in his hands belonging to the City, and take his receipt therefor.   He shall open an account with the Treasurer of the City, wherein he shall charge him with the whole amount of taxes placed in his, the said Treasurer's, hands for collection ; also the whole amount in detail, of all bonds, notes, mortgages, leases, rents and interest receivable : and pay over and charge him with all monies he may receive belonging to the City, in order that the value and description of all personal property belonging to the City, may at any time be known, at his office; and from and after the end of the present municipal year, the said auditor shall in the month of February annually make and lay before the City Council an estimate of the amount of money necessary to be raised for the expenditure of the ensuing year, under the respective heads of appropriation; and shall on or before, the fifteenth of the month of May, annually make and lay before the City Council a statement of all receipts and expenditures of the past year, giving in detail the amount of appropriation and expenditure, for each specific object.

SEC. 7. *Be it further ordained*, That the City Treasurer shall make up his annual accounts to the thirtieth of April; and the Financial year shall henceforth begin on the first day of May, and end on the thirtieth day of April in each year.

Treasurer to make up his accounts.

SEC. 8. *Be it further ordained*, That from and after the commencement of the next municipal year, an ordinance of the City Council made and passed on the second day of August, in the year of our Lord one thousand eight hundred and twenty-four, entitled " An ordinance establishing a system of accountability in the expenditures of the City ;" and another ordinance, made and passed on the twelfth day of May, in the year of our Lord one thousand eight hundred and twenty-five, entitled, " An ordinance in addition to, and to amend an ordinance entitled an ordinance establishing a system of accountability on the expenditures of the City," shall cease to operate, and the same, from and after the commencement of the said next municipal year, are hereby repealed, provided, that nothing contained in this ordinance shall impair the validity or effect of any bond or bonds given by the Auditor of accounts to the City.

Former ordinances repealed.

[Passed Dec. 22, 1825.]

ACTIONS.—See Suits at Law, Chap. 43,—and By-Laws, Chap. XI.

CHAP. II.

Assessors and Assessments.

ACTS OF THE LEGISLATURE.

An act regulating the collection of taxes in the Town of Boston, and providing for the appointment of Constables in the said town.

Rendered inoperative by the 13th section of the City Charter.

SEC. 1. *Be it enacted by the Senate and House of Representatives in General Court assembled, and by the authority of the same,* That the Selectmen of the Town of Boston, be, and they are hereby empowered to appoint annually, such a number of persons as Constables in the said town, as the public service may require; and the said Constables, so appointed, shall give bonds to the Treasurer of the Town of Boston, in such sums, and on such conditions, as the said Selectmen shall think proper, for the faithful performance of the duties of their office; and the Constables so appointed by the Selectmen, shall have the same powers as are by law vested in Constables chosen by the towns in this Commonwealth.

See City Charter Sec. 15, for the new mode of appointing assessors and assistant assessors.

SEC. 2. *Be it further enacted,* That the inhabitants of the Town of Boston, shall assemble annually on the first Wednesday in April, in their respective wards, and shall then choose and appoint two persons in each of their respective wards, to assist the assessors in taking a list of the polls, in estimating the value of their personal property, and in appraising the value of all real estates in their own wards; and the twenty-four persons thus chosen, shall meet and appoint three persons whom they shall judge best qualified to serve the town in the office of Assessors, the ensuing year; which assessors shall have the same powers as are vested by law in assessors chosen by other towns in this Commonwealth; and in case of the death or resignation of any person so chosen in either of the wards, the clerk of such ward is empowered and directed to call a new meeting of the ward to choose a suitable person to supply the place of the person so dead or declining to serve.

SEC. 3. *Be it further enacted*, That the Treasurer of the Town of Boston, shall be the Collector of taxes in the said town, and shall be and hereby is empowered, to substitute and appoint under him, such and so many deputies or assistants, as the service may be found to require, who shall give bonds for the faithful discharge of their duty, in such sums and with such sureties as the Selectmen of said town shall think proper ; and the said Collector, and his deputy or deputies, shall have the same powers as are vested by law in collectors of taxes chosen by other towns in this Commonwealth.

Town Treasurer to be Collector of taxes.

SEC. 4. *Be it further enacted*, That all such inhabitants of the said Town of Boston, who shall voluntarily pay to the said town Collector or his deputy, within thirty days next after the delivery of their tax bills, the amount of their respective taxes, shall be entitled to an abatement of *five per centum* on the amount of their said taxes ; and such inhabitants of said town who shall voluntarily pay their said taxes to the said Collector, or his deputy, within sixty days after the delivery of their tax bills, shall be entitled to an abatement of *three per centum* on the amount of their said taxes ; and all such of said Inhabitants who shall so pay to the said Collector or his deputy, within one hundred and twenty days, next after the delivery of their tax bills, shall be entitled to an abatement of *two per centum* on the amount of their said taxes.

This Section is repealed, see Statute of 1811, at p. 32.

[Passed June 18, 1802.]

An Act in addition to an Act entitled "An Act regulating the collection of taxes in the Town of Boston, and providing for the appointment of Constables in the said town.

SEC. 1. *Be it enacted by the Senate and House of Representatives in General Court assembled, and by the authority of the same,* That the Treasurer of said Town of Boston, his deputy or deputies, shall be empowered to collect all such taxes as may be outstanding and uncollected, at the time of his being chosen to the office of Treasurer ; such Treasurer and his deputies first giving bonds for the faithful discharge of their duty, in such sums and with such sureties as the Selectmen of said town shall think proper.

Treasurer to collect taxes outstanding at the time of his election.

a 10/10/4 &
at Charter — Sect. 15

To issue warrants to his deputy.

SEC. 2. *Be it further enacted*, That the said Treasurer may issue his warrant to his deputy or deputies, for the collecting and gathering in such part of the rates or assessments as, in his discretion he shall think proper to commit to such deputy or deputies ; which warrant shall be in the same tenor with the warrant prescribed to be issued by the Selectmen or Assessors, for the collecting and gathering in of the state rates or assessments, *mutatis mutandis*.

[Passed June 18, 1803.]   .

An act in addition to an act entitled ·" An act regulating the collection of taxes in the Town of Boston, and providing for the appointment of Constables in the said town."

See provincial Statute of June 12th, 1762, 3 vol. special laws app. 19.

SEC. 1. *Be it enacted by the Senate and House of Representatives in General Court assembled, and by the authority of the same*, That the Treasurer and Collector of the Town of Boston, be, and he hereby is authorized to issue his warrant to the Sheriff of the County of Suffolk, his deputy, or to any constable of the Town of Boston, directing them to distrain the persons or property of any person or persons, who may be delinquent in the payment of taxes, after the time has expired, that is or may be fixed for payment, by any vote of said town. Which warrants shall be of the same tenor with the warrant prescribed to be issued by Selectmen or Assessors for the collecting or gathering in of the state rates or assessments, *mutatis mutandis*. And the said officers shall make a return of their warrants with their doings thereon, to the said Treasurer and Collector within thirty days from the date thereof : *Provided, however*, That nothing in this act shall prevent the said Treasurer and Collector, whenever there may be a probability of losing a tax, from distraining the person or property of any individual, before the expiration of the time fixed by the votes of said town.

Treasurer authorized in case of delinquents.

Proviso.

Sec. 2. *Be it further enacted,* That it shall be the duty of said officers, to execute all warrants they may receive from said Treasurer and Collector, pursue the same process in distraining the persons or property of delinquents, as collectors of taxes are now authorized by law to do and perform ; and for collecting the sum of money due on said warrant, receive the fees that are allowed by law for levying executions in personal actions : *Provided, however,* before the said officers shall serve any warrant, they shall deliver to the delinquent, or leave at his or her usual place of abode, a summons from said Treasurer and Collector, stating the amount due ; and that unless the same is paid within ten days from the time of leaving said summons into the town Treasury, with twenty cents for said summons, his or her property will be distrained according to law.

Duty of civil officers.

Proviso.

Sec. 3. *Be it further enacted,* That the Constables of the Town of Boston, in addition to the usual condition of their bonds, shall also be bound to the faithful execution of all warrants committed to them by the Treasurer and Collector of said town.

[Passed March 12, 1808.]

An act in addition to the several Laws regulating elections.

Be it enacted by the Senate and House of Representatives in General Court assembled, and by the authority of the same, That the assistant Assessors in any town wherein such officers are, or may by law be chosen, shall, before entering the duties of their respective offices, be sworn to the faithful discharge thereof, and shall have the same powers, and they are hereby required to perform the same duties in their several wards, in collecting and making lists of all such inhabitants as are qualified to vote in any election, and also of all ratable polls, as assessors are by law required to do and perform.

See 1813, chap. 68—as to duty of. assessors at Elections.

[Passed March 6, 1810.]

An act to repeal part of an act entitled " An act regulating the collection of taxes in the Town of Boston, and providing for the appointment of Constables in the said town."

Be it enacted by the Senate and House of Representatives in General Court assembled, and by the authority of the same, That the fourth section of the act, passed the eighteenth of June, one thousand eight hundred and two, entitled " An act regulating the collection of taxes in the Town of Boston, and providing for the appointment of Constables in the said town," which allows a discount on the payment of taxes within certain periods, be and the same is hereby repealed.

See 1821, ch. 110 Sect. 15.

[Passed June 22, 1811.]

ORDINANCES OF THE CITY.

An Ordinance upon the subject of Taxes on real Estates.

SEC. 1. *Be it ordained by the Mayor, Aldermen, and Common Council of the City of Boston, in City Council assembled,* That the Assessors of the City of Boston, be, and they hereby are required to assess upon the owners of real estates within the City of Boston, the amount of taxes for which such estates may be respectively taxed ; *Provided,* that in cases where the assessors may think it to be more for the public interest to assess the tenant or occupant instead of the owner, they may so assess ; *Provided also,* that nothing in this ordinance contained, shall affect the rights which owners and tenants may have be-

Owners to be assessed.

Proviso,

tween themselves respectively, by reason of any contract or agreement between them.

SEC. 2. *Be it further ordained*, That no abatement shall be made of any tax assessed, except by the assent of the permanent assessors, and the Assistant Assessors in convention; and that every applicant for abatement shall state his claim in writing, and subscribe the same with his name, and address the claim to the assessors.

Repealed, see post. p. 34.

SEC. 3. *Be it further ordained*, That no sum of money shall be assessed on the inhabitants of this City, in order to provide for the deficiences which may afterward arise from abatements, but that the abatements which shall be allowed in the present year, shall be stated by the assessors; and their statement shall contain the names of all persons whose taxes have been abated, in whole or in part, and the amount originally assessed, the amount of abatement, and the causes of abatement; and this statement shall be laid before the City Council, to the end that such order may be taken to supply the deficit occasioned by abatements as the City Council may see fit.

Repealed, see post. p. 34.

[Passed July 8, 1822.]

An Ordinance in addition to an Ordinance upon the subject of taxes on real estates, and for repealing the second and third sections thereof.

SEC. 1. *Be it ordained by the Mayor, Aldermen, and Common Council of the City of Boston, in City Council assembled*, That the permanent assessors may transfer the amounts of taxes assessed on real estate, not owned at the time of assessment by the person or persons charged with such taxes, to the person or persons by whom the same may have been owned at the time of such assessment;—that they may abate all taxes for the payment of which, the person or persons assessed are not legally liable by reason of non residence;—and may abate poll taxes in all cases where they are satisfied that the individual assessed is unable, or not legally liable, to pay the same.

Assessors may transfer taxes.

May abate.

SEC. 2. *Be it further ordained*, That in all cases where a tax does not exceed the sum of sixteen dollars, the same or any part thereof may be abated:

Taxes may be abated.

5

Proviso.

Provided, that a majority of the permanent Assessors, and both the Assistant Assessors who reside in the same ward with the person or persons applying for relief, are first fully satisfied that such person or persons are rated more than his or their proportion of the taxes ;—or are unable from old age, infirmity, or poverty to pay the tax assessed against him or them. But no abatement (unless for reasons stated in the first section of this ordinance) shall be made of any tax where the same exceecs the sum of sixteen dollars, except by the assent of a majority of the permanent assessors, and Assistant Assessors, from the several wards of the City, expressed and declared in convention. And every applicant for abatements, shall state his claim in writing and subscribe the same with his name and address the same to the permanent assessors.

Abatements, reasons to be stated.

SEC. 3. *Be it further ordained*, That all abatements which shall be allowed in the present year, shall be recorded by the permanent assessors, and the record thereof shall contain the names of all persons whose taxes shall be abated in whole or in part, and the amount originally assessed, and the amount of abatements ;—and that all the reasons for abatement, shall be stated on the said record, against the name of each person whose tax shall be abated ; and that this record shall be laid before the City Government, as soon as may be, and before the election of assessors for the ensuing year.

Former Ordinance repealed.

SEC. 4. *Be it further ordained*, That the second and third sections of an ordinance passed on the eighth day of July, A. D. one thousand eight hundred and twenty-two, on the subject of taxes on real estate, be, and the same are hereby repealed.

[Passed June 18, 1823.]

CHAP. III.

Auction.

ACTS OF THE LEGISLATURE.

An Act in addition to the several Acts, regulating the sale of goods by public Auction.

SEC. 1. *Be it enacted by the Senate and House of Representatives in General Court assembled and by the authority of the same,* That in all licenses granted to any person to sell goods and chattels by public Auction or out cry, within the Town of Boston, in the County of Suffolk, it shall, and may be lawful for the Selectmen of the said Town of Boston, or the major part of them, granting such license, to annex thereto, such conditions, limitations and restrictions, respecting the place or places, in said town, at, and within which the person so licensed, shall, and may be allowed and authorized to sell goods and chattels by public auction or out cry, as shall appear to them to be needful and expedient for the public welfare. And any person who shall sell any goods or chattels whatsoever, by public auction or out cry, at any place within the said Town of Boston, contrary to the conditions, limitations or restrictions, contained in, or annexed to such license, shall be liable and subject to the same penalties and forfeitures, to be prosecuted for and recovered in the same manner, as if such person had sold such goods or chattels, by auction or out cry, without any license whatever.

SEC. 2. *Be it further enacted,* That the owner, tenant or occupant of any house or store, having the actual possession and controul of the same, who shall allow or permit any person, licensed as aforesaid, to sell any goods or chattels by public auction or out cry, in his said house or store, or in any apartment or yard appurtenant to the same, contrary to the conditions, limitations or restrictions, annexed to the license of such person, shall be liable and subject to the same penalties and forfeitures, to be prosecuted

Limitations and restrictions.

Mayor and Aldermen.

Householders liable to a fine.

See Statute 1795, Chap. 8.

for and recovered in the same manner, as if such owner, occupant or tenant, had knowingly allowed or permitted any unlicensed person, to sell any goods or chattels, by public auction, or out cry, in his said house and store, or in any apartment or yard appurtenant thereto.

Sec. 3. *Be it further enacted*, That the law of this Commonwealth, which was passed on the fifteenth day of June, in the year of our Lord one thousand eight hundred and fifteen, entitled " An Act, in addition to an Act, entitled an Act to regulate the sale of goods at public vendue, and to repeal all laws heretofore made for that purpose, shall not apply or be enforced within the Town of Boston ; and the same so far as it respects said town, is hereby repealed.

Former acts repealed.

Statute 1815, Chap. 29.

[Passed February 21, 1820.]

See Statute 1822, Chap. 87.—Tax on auctions and general regulations. See also Statute 1795, Chap. 8—penalty for selling without license, and mode of recovering it. Also, 1814, Chap. 46—penalties recovered by indictment, another additional act 1815, Chap. 29—repealed as to Boston.

See also two statutes passed Feb. 26, 1825. Chap. 129 & 147.

CHAP. IV.

Bird Island.

ACT OF THE LEGISLATURE.

An Act for the preservation of Bird Island, in Boston Harbour.

Be it enacted by the Senate and House of Representatives in General Court assembled and by the authority of the same, That from and after the passing of this act, no earth or stones shall be taken from the Island, called Bird Island, in Boston Harbour, in the County of Suffolk, without license, first had and obtained of the Selectmen of the said Town of Boston, for that purpose, in writing, by the person taking the same, specifying the quantity allowed to be removed, and the object of removing it. And every person, who, without permission obtained as aforesaid, shall remove any earth or stones from the said Island, in any boat, or in any ship or vessel whatsoever, shall forfeit and pay for each offence, the sum of twenty dollars to the use of said town, by an action of debt, in any Court proper to try the same.

See Statute 1821, Chap. 110, Sect. 13—by which Powers of Selectmen are transferred to Mayor and Aldermen.

[Passed June 12, 1818.]

CHAP. V.

Boats and Lighters.

ACTS OF THE LEGISLATURE.

An Act respecting Boats and Lighters employed in transporting stones, gravel or sand, within this Commonwealth.

SEC. 1. *Be it enacted by the Senate and House of Representatives in General Court assembled and by the authority of the same,* That every boat or lighter, employed in transporting stones, gravel or sand, within this Commonwealth, shall be marked, at Lightwater mark ; and at least, at five other places, with the figures four, twelve, sixteen, twenty-four and thirty, legibly made, on the stem and sternposts thereof ; which figures shall express the weight such boat or lighter is capable of carrying, when the lower part of the respective numbers shall touch the water in which the said boat or lighter shall float. And every person who shall use or employ any boat or lighter, for the purpose of transporting stones, gravel or sand, as aforesaid, which shall not be marked as in this act is provided, shall forfeit and pay the sum of *fifty dollars,* to be recovered by an action of the case, in any Court proper to try the same, by any person who shall sue therefor. And any person who shall put or cause to be put, on any boat or lighter as aforesaid, any false marks as aforesaid, shall be subject to the like penalty, to be recovered in like manner.

SEC. 2. *Be it further enacted,* That it shall be the duty of the Selectmen in any town where boats and lighters are owned, which may be employed in transporting stones, gravel or sand, as contemplated in this act, to appoint annually, in the months of April or May, some suitable person to ascertain the capacities of all such boats and lighters, and mark the same as is prescribed in this act ; who shall be under oath faithfully to perform the duty as herein discribed.

[Passed March 7, 1801.]

An act in addition to an act, entitled "An act respecting Boats and Lighters, employed in transporting stones, gravel or sand, within this Commonwealth.

SEC. 1. *Be it enacted by the Senate and House of Representatives in General Court assembled and by the authority of the same*, That the marks by an act, entitled "An act respecting boats and lighters, employed in transporting stones, gravel or sand, within this Commonwealth," directed to be made on boats and lighters, expressive of the weights, such boats and lighters are capable of carrying, shall hereafter be inspected once every year; and whenever such mark shall be found to be illegible, the same shall be renewed. *Marks to be renewed.*

SEC. 2. *Be it further enacted*, That whenever the Inspector shall be of opinion, that the burthen or capacity of any such boat or lighter shall have been diminished, or increased by any repairs made on the same, or otherwise, it shall be his duty forthwith to ascertain anew, the capacities of such boats or lighters, and to mark the same accordingly. *Duty of Inspector.*

SEC. 3 *Be it further enacted*, That the Selectmen of towns in which boats or lighters used for the aforesaid purposes are owned, be, and they hereby are empowered, and it shall be their duty, to regulate the amount of fees which may be demanded by the Inspector of boats and lighters, of the owners thereof, for the performance of the duties imposed on him by this act, and that to which this is an addition. *Inspectors fees regulated.*

[Passed June 15, 1815.]

CHAP. VI.

Boundary Line.

ACTS OF THE LEGISLATURE.

An act for altering part of the boundary line between the Towns of Boston and Roxbury, and for ratifying an agreement made between the said towns for that purpose.

Whereas, that part of the boundary line between the Towns of Boston and Roxbury, which crosseth *Lambs Meadow,* so called, is nearly obliterated, and the Selectmen of said towns have petitioned this court, that a new direct line may be established in lieu thereof, agreeably to a plan mutually agreed on by the said towns; and it appearing reasonable that said agreement should be ratified and confirmed:

Line confirmed. SEC. 1. *Be it enacted by the Senate and House of Representatives in General Court assembled and by the authority of the same,* That the agreement entered into, between the Towns of Boston and Roxbury, for altering that part of the boundary line between the said towns, which crosseth *Lambs Meadow,* so called, be, and the same is hereby ratified and confirmed.

Manner in which line to be run in future. SEC. 2. *Be it further enacted, by the authority aforesaid,* That a line in lieu of the aforesaid obliterated boundary line, shall in all future perambulations thereof, be run in the following manner, that is to say, by a straight line in the same direction with the present line from the road leading from Boston to Roxbury, from the most easterly boundary marked stone in the said *Lambs Meadow,* one chain and forty-one links; thence turning and running north fifty-eight degrees east, by a straight line across the said meadow, until it strikes the ancient boundary mark in *Lambs Dam,* so called.

[Passed April 30, 1787.]

See Records of Boston, for 1788, where the line is established by agreement of the Selectmen of both towns.

An act relative to the boundary lines of the City of Boston, and the town of Brookline.

SEC. 1. *Be it enacted by the Senate and House of Representatives in General Court assembled and by the authority of the same,* That the agreement made by and between the Mayor and Aldermen, of the City of Boston, for and in behalf of said City, and the Selectmen of the Town of Brookline, in behalf of said town, relative to the boundary lines between the said City and town, be and the same hereby is ratified and confirmed, and that henceforth the boundary lines between the said City and town shall be as follows, viz. beginning at a point marked (*a*) on a plan drawn by S. P. Fuller, 1123 feet distant westerly from the westerly side of the filling sluices of the Boston and Roxbury mill dam ; thence running northwesterly from the said point (*a*) at an angle of 115 degrees from the mill dam, until it strikes the centre of the channel of Charles River, and also running from the said point (*a*) southerly, at an angle of 103 degrees, forty minutes, until it strikes the centre of the channel of Muddy River, at a point where the respective boundaries of Boston, Brookline and Roxbury meet each other. Boundary described.

SEC. 2. *Be it further enacted,* That the boundary lines between the Counties respectively of Suffolk and Norfolk, so far as they are affected by this act, shall hereafter conform to the said boundary lines between the said City and town, and the same are declared and established to be the boundary lines between the said Counties respectively, any thing in any former act to the contrary notwithstanding : *Provided, however,* That the several laws regulating the erection of buildings, within the City of Boston, shall not extend to the land hereby transferred from the said Town of Brookline, to the said City. Proviso.

[Passed Feb. 22, 1825.]

6

Chelsea — East Boston —

CHAP. VII.

ACTS OF THE LEGISLATURE.

An act for regulating the manufacture and sale of Bread.

To be sold by weight.

SEC. 1. *Be it enacted by the Senate and House of Representatives in General Court assembled and by the authority of the same,* That from and after the first day of April next, all soft bread, whether baked in loaves or biscuit, which shall be exposed to sale by any baker, or other person, shall be sold by weight.

Weights and marks directed.

Penalty for selling without.

SEC. 2. *Be it further enacted by the authority aforesaid,* That all soft biscuit, which shall hereafter be offered for sale, shall weigh *four* or *eight* ounces, and be marked with the initial of the Baker's christian name, and his surname at length, and the weight of the biscuit; and all loaves of soft bread, shall be of some one of the following weights, viz : *one pound, two, three or four pounds,* and be marked with the weight of the loaf, and the maker's name ; and if any Baker or other person, shall offer or expose to sale, any soft bread or biscuit, which shall not severally be marked, and conform to one of the weights before mentioned, every such person, so offending, shall forfeit and pay the sum of eight dollars, to be recovered by action of debt before any Justice of the peace within and for the County where such offence shall happen, by any person who shall sue for the same, together with legal costs; one half of the penalty aforesaid, to be for the use of the person who prosecutes, and the other half to the use of the poor of the town, where such offence may be committed.

Former laws repealed. 1798, ch. 67.

SEC. 3. *Be it further enacted,* That all laws heretofore made for regulating the assize of bread, be, and hereby are repealed, from and after the first day of April next, excepting so far as relates to the recovery of any forfeiture, fine or penalty incurred, or which may be incurred previous to that time, by a breach of any said Laws.

[Passed March 7, 1801.]

CHAP. VIII.

ᴀ ᴄᴛ ᴀᴘᴘ. 10. 1737   ᴄᴏᴍ. ₁ ₛᴄ. ₓᴿ⁻
Feb. 28. 1577

ACTS OF THE LEGISLATURE.

An act to secure the Town of Boston from damage by fire.

SEC. 1. *Be it enacted by the Senate and House of Representatives, in General Court assembled, and by the authority of the same*, That from and after the passing of this act, no house or building of any kind whatsoever, which shall be more than ten feet high from the ground to the highest point of the roof thereof, shall be erected or built within the town of Boston, unless all the external sides and ends thereof, shall be built or composed of brick or stone ; except so much as may be necessary for doors and windows, and unless the roofs of all such houses or buildings shall be intirely covered with slate, tile or some incombustible composition ; and the gutters secured effectually against fire ; and no brick or stone wall shall be deemed sufficient, within the meaning of this act, unless the same shall be at least twelve inches thick in the lower story ; and eight inches thick above the lower story ; and all additions, which shall be made to houses or buildings already erected, and all houses or buildings which shall be erected on old foundations, in part or in whole, shall be deemed and considered within the restrictions and regulations of this act : *Provided, nevertheless*, that upon any wharf, marsh or other place, where no sufficient foundations can be obtained, without unreasonable expense, on permission of the firewards of said town, or the major part of them, in writing, wooden houses or buildings, of not more than two stories high, may be erected, which shall be covered on all sides with slate, tile, or lime mortar, and filled in with bricks laid in mortar, and the roofs and gutters shall be secured as before directed.

SEC. 2. *Be it further enacted*, That in all cases where one dwelling house, ware house, store, mill, stable, or other building, above ten feet high, is separated

Marginal notes:

Houses of wood not to exceed ten feet in height.

Suspended as to South Boston, see post.

Altered to 16 feet see post.

Further altered to 16 feet 2 story buildings, see post.

Proviso.

prevention of fire —

from another dwelling house, or ware house or store
or mill, or stable, or other building, above ten feet high,
by a partition, such partition shall be built of stone or
brick, and shall be twelve inches thick in the lower
story and eight inches thick above the lower story ;
and shall be built up as far as may be necessary, in
order to cover or cap the same with flat stones above
the roof ; and such wall shall be entirely covered or
capped with flat stones, at least two inches in thickness

above the roof ; and every person offending against
this section, shall forfeit and pay a sum not exceeding
one hundred dollars, nor less than fifty dollars.

SEC. 3. *Be it further enacted,* That no wooden

building more than ten feet high, shall be removed
from any part of the town of Boston to any other
place within the same town, without permission of the
firewards of said town, or the major part of them,
under such restrictions and provisions as they shall
prescribe, nor shall any wooden building heretofore
erected within the said town, and not now used as a
dwelling house, be hereafter occupied as a dwelling
house, or for any other purpose than that to which it
is now applied, without the permission of the firewards, as aforesaid.

SEC. 4. *Be it further enacted,* That every person
who shall erect or add to, or cause to be erected or
added to, any building in said town of Boston, contrary to the true intent and meaning of this act, and
every person owning such building so unlawfully erected, and any person who shall remove or alter, or
cause to be removed or altered, any building as aforesaid, and every person who shall hereafter use and
occupy as and for a dwelling house, any wooden building, heretofore erected within the said town, and
not now used or intended for a dwelling house, or
shall convert the same to any other purpose than that

to which it is now applied, without permission first had
and obtained from the firewards of said town, or the
major part of them ; every person in eitherwise so
offending, shall forfeit and pay a fine not less than
fifty dollars, nor more than five hundred dollars, according to the nature and aggravation of the offence.

SEC. 5. *Be it further enacted*, That in addition to the fines above mentioned, there shall be laid and assessed upon every house or other building, which shall be erected contrary to the true intent and meaning of this act, the sum of fifty dollars annually, and every year, until such building or addition thereto, shall be effectually secured against fire, and made to conform to the provisions of this act. And it shall be the duty of the Firewards of the said town of Boston, to return to the assessors of said town annually, a list of all such houses or other buildings erected contrary to the provisions of this act, together with attested copies of the record of the conviction of any person or persons for such offence ; and thereupon it shall be the duty of the said assessors, to assess upon the owner or owners of the said building or buildings, the sum of fifty dollars, for each and every successive year thereafter, until said house or building shall be made conformable to the provisions of this act, which sum shall be payable by the person or persons by whom said house or building shall be owned ; and shall be collected in the same manner as other taxes are collected : *Provided, nevertheless*, that no such house or building shall be subjected to such annual tax, until an attested copy of said conviction, shall have been duly recorded in the office of Register of deeds for the county of Suffolk, whose duty it shall be to receive and record the same.

Fines and penalties.

Proviso.

SEC. 6. *Be it further enacted*, That if any person or persons shall, within the said town of Boston, roast, or cause to be roasted, any cocoa, for the purpose of manufacturing the same into chocolate, in any building whatever, excepting such as may or shall be licensed for that purpose, by the major part of the Firewards of the town aforesaid, he, she or they, shall forfeit and pay for every such offence, a sum not exceeding five hundred dollars, nor less than two hundred dollars.

No cocoa to be roasted without license.

SEC. 7. *Be it further enacted*, That all houses or buildings within the said town of Boston, which have been, or which shall hereafter be, erected in the manner prescribed in this act, and which are now or which may hereafter be covered with slate, tile, or

Covering of houses.

other incombustible composition, shall continue to be so covered with slate, tile or other incombustible composition, and shall be kept effectually secured against fire, in manner as is herein before described. And if any person or persons, being owner or proprietor of any house or other building, or having authority, or whose duty it shall be to repair the same, shall hereafter suffer his, her or their house, or other building, to remain in whole or in part uncovered with slate, tile, or other incombustible composition for the space of thirty days, after he, she, or they, shall have been notified to repair or cover the same by the Firewards of the town of Boston, he, she, or they shall forfeit and pay, for such offence, a sum, not exceeding one hundred dollars, nor less than twenty dollars ; and shall be subject to a like fine for every thirty days afterwards that such house or building shall be by him, her, or them, suffered to remain so uncovered, in the manner required by this act.

SEC. 8. *Be it further enacted*, That whenever any house or other building within the said town of Boston, hereafter erected, shall be found to have been erected contrary to the provisions of this act, the owner or owners of such house or building, or other person lawfully holden to keep the same in repair, shall be held and required to alter and make such house or building to conform to the provisions of this act. And any person or persons as aforesaid, who shall suffer his, her, or their house, or other building, to be and remain not conformable to the provisions of this act, for the space of thirty days, after he, she, or they shall have been notified by the Firewards of the said town thereof, shall forfeit and pay for such offence, a sum not exceeding one hundred dollars, nor less than twenty dollars, and shall be subject to a like fine for every thirty days afterwards, that such house or building shall be by him, her or them suffered to remain out of repair, and exposed to fire as aforesaid, and not conformable to the provisions of this act.

SEC. 9. *Be it further enacted*, That every Tar kettle, which shall be made use of in said town for the purpose of boiling tar, for the use of any ropewalk, and every kettle, boiler, or copper, for the use

Penalties for neglect of repairs.

Tar kettles to be secured.

of any caulker, graver, ship carpenter, tallow chandler, soap boiler, painter or other like artificer, shall be so fixed as to prevent all communication whatsoever between the contents of such kettle, boiler, or copper and the fire. And that the fire-place under every such tar or other kettle, boiler, or copper, shall be constructed with an arch built over the same and secured by an iron door, in such manner as to enclose the fire therein; and every person who shall erect any tar kettle or other kettle, boiler, or copper, or use the same for any or either of the purposes aforesaid, contrary to the provisions of this act, shall for every such offence, forfeit and pay a sum not exceeding three hundred dollars, nor less than fifty dollars, according to the degree and aggravation of the same.

SEC. 10. *Be it further enacted*, That every person who shall carry any fire through the streets, lanes, or on any wharves in said town, except in some covered vessel, or who shall kindle a fire in any of the places aforesaid, without the permission therefor in writing, of one or more of the firewards of said town, or shall smoke or have in his or her possession, any lighted pipe or cigar, in any street, lane or passage way, or on any wharf in said town, shall forfeit and pay for each and every offence, the sum of two dollars, to be recovered of the person so offending, or of his parent, guardian, master or mistress. *Penalty for carrying fire in the streets.*

SEC. 11. *Be it further enacted*, That if any person shall have in his or her possession, in any rope walk, or in any barn or stable within said town, any fire, lighted pipe or cigar, lighted candle, or lamp, except such candle or lamp is kept in a secure lantern, the person so offending shall forfeit and pay for each offence, a sum not exceeding one hundred dollars nor less than twenty dollars. *Penalties for exposing fire in barns, &c.*

SEC. 12. *Be it further enacted*, That all and any of the penalties which are given in and by this act, or in and by a certain act, made and passed on the fifteenth day of June, in the year of our Lord one thousand eight hundred and sixteen, entitled "An Act regulating the storage, safe keeping and transportation of Gun powder in the town of Boston," may be recovered by indictment, information or complaint in *Recovery of fines*

any court proper to try the same ; and in such indictment, information or complaint, it shall not be necessary to set forth any more of said acts, than so
much thereof as relates to, and is necessary, truly and
substantially to describe the offence alleged to have
been committed.   And it shall be the duty of each
and every fireward in the town of Boston, and they
and each of them are hereby required to enquire after all offences which shall come to their knowledge,
and which shall be committed against the true intent
and meaning of this act, and shall cause the same to
be duly prosecuted.

Duties and au-
thorities of fire
wards.

SEC. 13. *Be it further enacted*, That it shall be lawful for any one or more of the firewards of said town to
require and compel the assistance of all or any of the inhabitants of said town, and any other person, who shall
be present as spectators of any fire ; and in any suit
or prosecution therefor, it shall be lawful for them to
plead the general issue, and give this act in evidence ;
and if any person shall disobey the lawful and reasonable command of any Fireward or Firewards, to
aid in extinguishing such fire, or in rescuing property
from destruction thereby, such person, so offending,
shall be liable to a fine not exceeding twenty dollars,
to be recovered in manner aforesaid.

Repeal of former
acts.

SEC. 14. *Be it further enacted*, That all acts heretofore passed to secure the town of Boston from damage by fire, be, and the same are hereby repealed,
excepting that such parts thereof, as may be necessary to recover all fines and penalties incurred upon
the acts aforesaid, shall still remain in full force for
that purpose.

Distribution of
fines.

SEC. 15. *Be it further enacted*, That all the fines,
penalties and assessments, which shall be recovered
by force of this act, shall accrue and enure, one half
to the use of the poor of the town of Boston, to be
paid to the overseers of the poor thereof, and the other
half to the Firewards of said town : *Provided, however*, that whenever in the trial of any prosecution under
this act, any one or more of the said Firewards shall
be sworn and examined as a witness, or as witnesses
therein, record thereof shall be made in Court, and
the whole fine or penalty in such case, shall enure to

the use of the poor of the town of Boston, and be paid to the overseers of the poor thereof as aforesaid.

[Passed Feb. 23, 1818.]

An act partially to suspend the operation of an act to secure the town of Boston from damage by fire.

Be it enacted by the Senate and House of Representatives in General Court assembled, and by the authority of the same, That the operation of all laws now in force, which restrain the erecting and placing of wooden buildings in the town of Boston of more than ten feet in height from the ground to the highest point in the roof thereof, be, and the same are hereby suspended, so far as they respect any house, or other building, which may be erected or placed in that part of the town of Boston called South Boston, and which was heretofore set off from the town of Dorchester, for and during the term of five years from the passing of this act. *Provided however,* that such suspension and exemption, shall not be deemed to extend to any house or building of any kind, to be erected or placed within that part of the town of Boston aforesaid, called South Boston, which shall be more than thirty feet high from the ground to the highest part thereof, or more than forty feet square, or within fifty feet of any other house or other building. And the operation of the laws aforesaid, hereby partially suspended, and all penalties, forfeitures and disabilities thereby imposed, and every clause and provision thereof, shall have the like force and effect, in regard to all houses and other buildings, erected or placed in said South Boston, in any manner not conformable to the conditions and provisions of this act, and in regard to all persons who may be amenable therefor, as if this act had not been passed.

Suspension of law.

Proviso.

Limitation of power.

Penalties.

[Passed June 16, 1821.]

7

An act regulating the building with wood within the
town of Boston.

SEC. 1. *Be it enacted by the Senate and House of
Representatives in General Court assembled, and by
the authority of the same,* That from and after the
passing of this act, it shall be lawful to build houses,
or other buildings of wood within the town of Boston,
Dimensions of wooden buildings. the posts whereof, measuring from the bottom of the
lower sill to the top of the plate, shall not exceed ten
feet, and the pitch of the roof thereof, not to exceed
one third pitch : *Provided,* that such roof be of a
regular slope from the plate to the top thereof, and
that no window or windows shall be erected or made
on the sloping part of the roof of such house or build-
Proviso. ing : *And provided, also,* that in no case shall any
such house or building exceed sixteen feet in measure from the ground to the highest point in the roof.
SEC 2. *Be it further enacted,* That so much of
Part of former laws repealed. the laws heretofore passed, as are inconsistent with
the provisions of this act, be and the same are here-
by repealed.

[Passed June 16, 1821.]

An act to provide for the erection of Two Story Wood-
en Buildings in the City of Boston.

SEC. 1. *Be it enacted by the Senate and House of
Representatives in General Court assembled, and by
the authority of the same,* That from and after the
Two story wood-en buildings may be erected. passing of this act, it shall be lawful to erect, within
the city of Boston, two story wooden buildings, to
be used for dwelling houses, and for no other purpose,
except for such purposes as may be approbated by
the Firewards of said city of Boston, of the following description, to wit : the posts to be not more than
eighteen feet, the roof to be of a regular pitch of one
third ; the bottom of the sills to be elevated not ex-

ceeding eighteen inches above the level of the street, or above the point where such level shall be determined on by the city authorities ; such buildings in no case to be more than thirty feet in height from the bottom of the sill, to the highest point of the roof ; and in no case to be more than forty by twenty-five feet on the ground : the roof to be slated, and to have at least one window or scuttle in the same.

SEC. 2. *Be it further enacted,* that whenever two or more buildings as aforesaid shall be joined together, there shall be a partition wall of brick, at least **Brick partition walls.** eight inches in thickness, to extend in height at least to an even surface with the under side of the slating of the roof ; and whenever any such building shall be erected within five feet of the boundary line of the owner or owners of the land on which it may be built, unless such boundary line be on the highway, it shall have a brick wall of like thickness on the side so adjoining : *Provided,* that no two story wooden buildings provided for in this act, shall be erected within ten feet of each other, unless one of them have a brick wall on the side next adjoining, of the dimensions aforesaid.

SEC. 3. *Be it further enacted,* That whenever any out buildings shall be connected with the dwelling houses provided for in this act, of more than eleven **Slated roofs** feet in height, the roof of such out buildings shall be covered with slate.

SEC. 4. *Be it further enacted,* That from and after the passing of this act, no wooden building shall be erected within the city of Boston, except in that **Restrictions.** part called South Boston, in a range of more than fifty feet extent, without the intervention of a brick partition wall, of at least eight inches in thickness, such wall to extend six inches at least above the surface of the roof ; and no wooden buildings shall be placed within four feet of each other, unless the wall of one of them so adjoining, be of brick or stone, of the thickness aforesaid.

SEC. 5. *Be it further enacted,* That any person who shall be convicted, in due course of law, of violating any of the provisions of this act, either by himself or agent, shall forfeit and pay for each and every such violation, not less than fifty, nor more than five hundred dollars; which penalty he shall

pay annually, until such building shall be removed or constructed according to law; one half of said penalty to enure and be paid to the person who shall complain or sue for the same, and the other half to said city of Boston; the same to be recovered by action of the case, or by indictment.

SEC. 6. *Be it further enacted,* That all laws now in force, so far as they are inconsistent with the pro-

visions of this act, be, and the same are hereby repealed.

[Passed June 15, 1822.]

An act to prevent Livery Stables being erected in certain places in the town of Boston.

SEC. 1. *Be it enacted by the Senate and House of Representatives in General Court assembled, and by the authority of the same,* That from and after the

passing of this act no building shall be erected within the town of Boston, and used and improved as a Stable for the taking in and keeping horses or chaises or other carriages, upon hire or to let, commonly called Livery Stables, within one hundred and seventy feet of any church or meeting house erected for

the public worship of God : *Provided, however,* that this act shall not be so construed, as to prevent the finishing of any Stable which has been in part erected, if the completion thereof shall be approved by the Selectmen of the town of Boston.

SEC. 2. *Be it further enacted,* That for any offence against the provisions of this act, the owner or owners, keeper or keepers of such building, shall for-

feit and pay the sum of one hundred dollars for every calender month during which the same shall be so used and improved to be recovered by action of debt, one half thereof to enure for the use of the poor of the town of Boston, the other half thereof to him or them who shall sue for the same.

[Passed Feb. 28, 1811.]

An act for the more effectually preventing of trespasses in divers cases.

SEC. 4. *And be it further enacted by the authority aforesaid,* That when any trespasses shall be committed on any buildings or inclosures belonging to any county, town, or parish, the county, town, and parish treasurer, for the time being, shall be, and hereby are severally authorized, to sue for the damage done to the public buildings or inclosures of their county, town or parish respectively ; and where any public buildings are owned partly by the town, and partly by the county, in that case the county or town treasurer, whoever may first institute an action, may prosecute for damages thus sustained : *Provided, nevertheless,* that nothing in this act shall prohibit any surveyor of highways moving any incumbrances in any public way, nor be construed to prevent any prosecution for theft where a theft is committed.

Trespasses committed on any public buildings, damages how recovered.

2. Geo. I. ch : 2

Proviso.

[Passed Nov. 23, 1785.

See statute of March 4, 1805, authorizing selectmen to remove buildings, in streets.—see streets post.

ORDINANCES OF THE CITY.

An ordinance authorizing the numbering of buildings within the City of Boston.

Be it ordained by the Mayor, Aldermen and Common Council of the City of Boston, in City Council assembled, That the Mayor and Aldermen shall have power, (provided it can be done without expense to the city) to cause numbers of regular series, to be affixed to, or inscribed on, all dwelling houses and other buildings erected or fronting on any street, lane, alley, or public court within the city of Boston, at their discretion ; and shall also have power to determine the form, size, and material of such numbers and the mode, place, succession and order, of inscribing or affixing them on their respective houses or other buildings.

[Passed June 28, 1824.]

An ordinance to prevent the defacing or other injuries to buildings, fences and other property.

See statute 1785, chap. 28.

Be it ordained by the Mayor, Aldermen, and Common Council of the City of Boston, in City Council assembled, That any person or persons, who shall be guilty of defacing any building or buildings, fence, sign, or other property, standing upon or fronting any of the streets or other public places in the city by cutting, breaking, daubing with paint, or in any other way defacing or injuring the same, shall upon conviction thereof pay a fine not exceeding twenty dollars, and that the order of the City Council made and passed on the twenty second day of July, in the year of our Lord, one thousand eight hundred and twenty two, be and the same hereby is repealed.

[Passed Dec. 19, 1825.]

An ordinance directing that when buildings are to be erected, notice thereof shall be given to the City authorities. *Meeting &c*

Be it ordained by the Mayor, Aldermen and Common Council of the City of Boston, in City Council assembled, That hereafter all persons, intending to erect any building or buildings of any description, any part of which is to be placed upon or within ten feet of any of the public streets, squares, alleys or lanes of the city, the person or persons, so intending to erect any such buildings, shall before he, or they proceed to build and erect the same, or to lay the foundation thereof, give notice in writing of such their intention to the Surveyors of Highways, fifteen days at least before doing any act for carrying such their intent into execution, in order that any encroachment or any other injury or inconvenience to the said public streets, squares, lanes or alleys, which might otherwise happen, may be thereby prevented, and in default thereof, that the city be considered as discharged from all damages of any nature whatsoever, resulting from the failure to give notice as above provided, particularly from all such damages or expenses as have been enhanced or occasioned by reason of any thing done previously to, or without such notice.

[Passed Dec. 27, 1826.]

CHAP. IX.

Extract from the Statute of 1785, Chapter 75, Sec. 7.

See statute 1821, chap. 110. sec. 16, which together with the section here inserted contains the general powers of the city government as to the enactment of by-laws.

Be it further enacted, by the authority aforesaid, That the freeholders, and other inhabitants of each respective town, qualified as aforesaid, at the annual meeting for the choice of town officers, or at any other town meeting, regularly warned, may, and they are hereby empowered to make and agree upon such necessary Rules, Orders and By-laws, for the directing, managing and ordering the prudential affairs of such town, as they shall judge most conducive to the peace, welfare and good order thereof ; and to annex penalties for the observance of the same, not exceeding thirty shillings for one offence ; to enure to such uses as they shall therein direct : *Provided,* they be not repugnant to the general laws of the government, and provided also, such Orders and By-laws, shall have the approbation of the Court of General Sessions of the peace of the same County.

1801, chap. 62.

An act for carrying into execution, more effectually, the By-laws of the several towns within this Commonwealth.

Be it enacted by the Senate and House of Representatives in General Court assembled, and by the authority of the same, That from and after the passing of this act, all fines and forfeitures, accruing for the breach of any by-law in any town within this Commonwealth, may be prosecuted for, and recovered before any Justice of the Peace in the town or county where the offence shall be committed, by complaint or information, in the same way and manner other criminal offences are now prosecuted before the Justices of the Peace within this Commonwealth.

[Passed March 3, 1802.]

Extract from an act in further addition to an act, entitled "An Act for the due regulation of Weights and Measures," and for the more easy recovery of fines and penalties within the town of Boston, in the County of Suffolk.

SEC. 3. *Be it further enacted*, that all fines, forfeitures, and penalties accruing within the said town of Boston, under this act, or for the breach of any By-law of the said town, which is now in force, or which may hereafter be duly enacted and made, may be recovered by indictment, information or complaint, in the name of the Commonwealth, in any court competent to try the same; and all fines so recovered and paid, shall be appropriated to the uses for which the same are now by law ordered to be applied : reserving, however, in all cases, to the party complained of and prosecuted, the right of appeal to the next Municipal Court, in the town of Boston, from the Judgment and sentence of any Justice of the peace; in which case the Judgment of the said Municipal Court shall be final; and to the next Supreme Judicial Court, to be holden within the County of Suffolk, and for the Counties of Suffolk and Nantucket, from the Judgment of the Municipal Court where the indictment or information originated in the same; such party recognizing with sufficient surety or sureties, to the satisfaction of the Court, to enter and prosecute his, her or their said appeal, and to abide the final Judgment thereon.

SEC. 4. *Be it further enacted*, That when any person, who, upon a conviction before a Justice of the peace, for any offence mentioned in this act, or for the

breach of any By-law of the town of Boston, shall be
sentenced to pay a fine, and shall not appeal from said
Judgment, or if upon claiming an appeal, shall fail
to recognize as aforesaid, and upon not paying the
fines and costs so assessed upon him, shall be committed to prison, there to remain until he or she shall
pay such fines and costs, or be otherwise discharged
according to law ; such persons shall not be holden
in prison for a longer term than ten days ; and at the
expiration of that term, the keeper of the said Gaol is
hereby authorized to release such person from confinement.*

See title"Weights
and Measures."

Shall not appeal
from judgment.

[Passed June 17, 1817.]

1824, Chap. 28.

Extract from a Statute of 1824, Chap. 28, entitled
" An Act concerning the regulation of the House
of Correction in the City of Boston ; and concerning the form of actions commenced under the By-
laws of said City ; and providing for filling Vacancies in the board of Aldermen."

SEC. 5. *Be it further enacted,* That in all prosecutions by complaint before the Police Court for the
City of Boston founded on the special Acts of the
Legislature, the By-laws of the town of Boston, or
the Ordinances or By-laws of the City of Boston, it
shall be sufficient to set forth in such complaint, the
offence fully and plainly, substantially and formally ;
and in such complaint it shall not be necessary to set
forth such special Act, By-law, Ordinance or any part
thereof.

---

* The 7th section of the act to which this is an addition, is repealed so far as
it relates to the town of Boston. See Sec. 6, of this act.

An ordinance to continue in force the By-laws and Orders of the town of Boston.

Be it ordained by the Mayor, Aldermen, and Common Council of the City of Boston, in City Council assembled, That all the By-laws and Orders of the town of Boston which were in force on the thirtieth day of April, in the year of our Lord one thousand eight hundred and twenty-two, shall be, and they are hereby declared to be of force in the City of Boston.

[Passed May 2, 1822.]

An ordinance directing the manner in which fines and penalties shall be recovered.

SEC. 1. *Be it ordained by the Mayor, Aldermen, and Common Council of the City of Boston, in City Council assembled,* That all fines and penalties for the violation of any of the ordinances of the City Council, or any of the orders of the Mayor and Aldermen, when recovered shall enure to the use of the City, and shall be paid into the City Treasury, except in those cases where it may be otherwise directed and provided by the acts of the Legislature, or the ordinances of the City Council.

SEC. 2. *Be it further ordained,* That it shall be the duty of the City Marshall, and of all other officers of the City to take notice of the complaints of all persons for violation of all acts, ordinances, and orders aforesaid, which affect the particular department of such officers, and to cause all prosecutions to be instituted and pursued which may be necessary to enforce obedience to the acts, orders, and ordinances aforesaid.

See title "Marshal of the City."

[Passed Dec. 22, 1825.]

An ordinance directing the manner in which the Ordinances of the City Council, and the Orders of the Mayor and Aldermen shall be promulgated.

Be it ordained by the Mayor, Aldermen, and Common Council of the City of Boston, in City Council assembled, That all the ordinances of the City Council, and all the orders of the Mayor and Aldermen, shall be published and promulgated by inserting the same two weeks successively in the newspapers printed by the printer for the Commonwealth for the time being, and in such other of the newspapers published and printed within the City as the Mayor and Aldermen shall from time to time, and at their discretion designate and appoint.

[Passed Dec. 19, 1825.]

CHAP. X.

ACTS OF THE LEGISLATURE.

An act for regulating Hackney Carriages in the town of Boston, and to repeal an act heretofore made for that purpose.

SEC. 1. *Be it enacted by the Senate and House of Representatives in General Court assembled, and by the authority of the same,* That no person or persons shall be permitted to set up, or employ any Coach, Chariot, Coachee, or other Carriage in the town of Boston, for the purpose of conveying persons for hire, until the owner thereof shall obtain a license for that purpose, in writing, from the major part of the selectmen of said town ; which license shall be and remain in full force for one year from the date of it, unless sooner revoked or annulled by said selectmen, or the major part of them ; and the said selectmen are hereby authorized to grant licenses for such number of hackney coaches and carriages, and to make such rules and regulations for the standing of said carriages in the different streets of said town, as they shall judge proper, and the same to change and vary, as occasion may require.

Carriages to be licensed.

Carriages to be numbered.

SEC. 2. *Be it further enacted,* That the selectmen of said town be, and they are hereby authorized and directed, to cause all such hackney carriages to be numbered and registered in a book to be kept by the town Clerk for that purpose : and the number of each carriage shall be fixed upon the same, in such conspicuous place or places as the said selectmen shall direct. And the fees for each license, to be paid by the person receiving the same, shall be one dollar.

SEC. 3. *Be it further enacted,* That any person who shall set up, or use any hackney carriage for the purpose aforesaid, without having obtained a license from the said selectmen, or who, having obtained such license, shall continue to keep and use such carriage after the same license shall be revoked, annulled, or become void according to this act, shall forfeit and pay for every time such carriage shall be used, a sum not exceeding four dollars. And every such hackney carriage that shall be found standing or plying in any street or highway contrary to the regulations of the said selectmen, or without its number painted on it as aforesaid, or after the license therefor shall have been revoked, or annulled by the said selectmen, or expired by this act, and before the same shall have been renewed, shall be considered as an unlicensed carriage, and the owner of the same shall be subjected to the like forfeiture, as in the case of an unlicensed carriage, for every such offence.

Penalty.

Carriages not to stand in street.

SEC. 4. *Be it further enacted*, That the said Selectmen be, and they are hereby authorized and empowered to revoke and annul any license given by them as aforesaid, at any time they may think proper, for the breach of any rules and regulations by them prescribed, or for any gross misbehaviour of the driver, in driving, in abusive language, or otherwise ; complaint having been previously made to them, and they having heard the parties, or the owner after reasonable notice, making default of appearance to answer thereto.

Licenses may be revoked.

SEC. 5. *Be it further enacted*, That the person in whose name a license is taken out for a hackney carriage as aforesaid, shall for all the purposes of this act, be considered as the owner of the same, and liable for all forfeitures and penalties herein contained, unless upon the sale of his carriage, notice be given thereof, and the license delivered up to the selectmen ; and the publications of the rules and regulations of said selectmen, and of the annulling and revoking any license as aforesaid, in the newspaper printed by the printer for the Commonwealth, for the time being, shall be deemed and taken, to all intents and purposes, as sufficient notice of the same to all such owners of carriages as aforesaid.

Owners of carriages.

SEC. 6. *Be it further enacted*, That a major part of the Selectmen, be authorized and empowered to make such rules and regulations, establishing the

Rates and prices.

rates and prices to be paid for the carriage and conveyance of persons in said hackney coaches within the limits of the town of Boston, as they may from time to time judge reasonable; regard being had to the time and distance. And if any owner or driver of a hackney carriage, shall demand and extort from any person or persons a sum beyond the rates which may thus be established by the said Selectmen, the license of such carriage, upon complaint made to the Selectmen as aforesaid, after a due hearing, may be forfeited and revoked; and the owner shall be further liable to refund the sum thus received and extorted, to the party aggrieved. And all the penalties and forfeitures aforesaid, shall be recovered in an action on the case, before any Justice of the Peace of the county of Suffolk, to the use of the psoner who shall sue for the same.

Penalty for exacting unlawful rates.

See antecedent chap. for mode of prosecuting pointed out by statutes.

SEC. 7. *Be it further enacted*, That an act for regulating hackney carriages in the town of Boston, made and passed on the twenty third day of February, in the year of our Lord one thousand seven hundred and ninety-six, be and the same hereby is repealed, excepting so far as the licenses granted under the same act shall continue and be in force, but subject to the conditions and limitations of this act.

Tnere is no such act as is referred to in this section, to be found in the Volumes containing the special statutes of this Commonwealth.

[Passed Nov. 25, 1796.]

Extract from an act, entitled "an act to regulate the paving of Streets in the town of Boston, and for removing obstruction in the same."*

SEC. 5. " And if any person shall drive any horse or cart, or any wheel carriage of burthen or pleasure, or wheel any wheel barrow on the foot walk of any street in said town of Boston, such person shall forfeit and pay the sum of *one dollar* for every such offence, to be recovered by action of debt, in the

Penalty for wheeling barrows on foot walks.

*The whole of this statute is inserted in the chapter entitled "Streets."

name of the Surveyors of high ways, before any Justice of the Peace, in the county of Suffolk.

Carriages not to be left in streets.

SEC. 7. *Be it further enacted*, That if any driver, owner, or person having the ordering or care of any cart, wagon, stage or hackney coach, stage-wagon or other carriage, new or old, finished or unfinished, shall suffer the same to be and remain in any street, lane or alley of the said town, more than one hour after the same shall have first been placed there unless by the permission of the Surveyors of highways, every such owner, driver or person having the care, or ordering of such carriage as aforesaid, shall forfeit and pay the sum of *one dollar*, for each and every such offence, to be recovered as above directed : *Provided nevertheless*, that no prosecution shall be commenced against any driver of any cart or wagon coming from the country, unless by the particular direction and order of the Selectmen.

Proviso.

Disposal of fines.

SEC. 8. *And be it further enacted*, That all the forfeitures and fines which may be recovered in persuance of this act, shall go and be distributed, one moiety thereof to the poor of the town of Boston, and the other moiety to the Surveyors of high-ways.

[Passed June 22, 1799.]

An act in addition to the several acts now in force, to regulate the Paving of Streets in the town of Boston, and for removing obstructions in the same.

See title "Streets" where the whole of this statute is inserted.

SEC. 1. (This section relates altogether to the paving or repairing the pavements in the streets—for which see post title "Streets.")

SEC. 2. *Be it further enacted*, That the Selectmen of the town of Boston, shall be, and they hereby are empowered to appoint suitable place in the streets or squares of said town, in which all wagons carts, sleds or other carriages shall be directed to stand.

Carriages in streets.

SEC. 3. *Be it further enacted*, That said Selectmen shall have power, from time to time, to make and adopt such rules and orders, for the due regulation of all such carriages, in the streets of the town of Boston, as to them shall appear necessary and expedient ; which rules and orders shall be printed at least one week, in two of the news-papers published in the said town ; and any owner or driver of any carriage, who shall offend against any such rule or order, so adopted and published, shall forfeit and pay a sum not exceeding five dollars, to be recovered upon complaint of either one of the Selectmen of said town of Boston, before any one of the Justices of the Peace for the county of Suffolk ; and all such fines and forfeitures shall be paid for the use of the person prosecutiug for breach of any such rule or order.

See antecedent chapter as to the mode of recovering penalties, of By-laws.

[Passed June 19, 1809.]

An ordinance for the regulation of Horses and Carriages within the City of Boston,

SEC. 1. *Be it ordained by the Mayor, Aldermen, and Common Council of the City of Boston in City Council assembled,* That no carriage of any description, whether of burden or pleasure, shall be driven through any ·part of said city, during any time that the snow or ice shall be upon or cover the streets, squares, lanes or alleys of the said city, unless there shall be three or more bells, attached to the horse or horses or to some part of the harness, thereof ;—And whoever shall offend against any provision of this section shall forfeit and pay for each offence, a sum not less than *one dollar* nor more than *five dollars*.

Carriages in time of snow to have bells.

SEC. 2. *Be it further ordained,* That no person whatsoever shall sit or stand, in or upon any carriage, or on any beast harnessed thereto with intent to drive the same, unless he shall have strong reins, or lines fastened to the bridle of said beast, and held in his hands, sufficient to guide and restrain such beast from running, galloping, or going at immoderate rates through the streets, lanes and alleys of the city ; and

Drivers to have sufficient reins.

9

no person whatsoever, driving any such carriage, or riding upon any horse, mare, gelding, or other beast, in or through the streets, lanes or alleys aforesaid, shall suffer the said horse, mare, gelding, or other beast to go in a gallop or other immoderate gait, so as to endanger persons standing or passing in the said streets, lanes or alleys ;—And whoever shall offend against any provision of this section shall forfeit and pay for each offence a sum not less than *one dollar* nor more than *five dollars.*

Beasts not to gallop in streets.

SEC. 3. *Be it further ordained,* That every driver of any truck, cart, wagon, sled, sleigh, hackney coach, or other carriage, within the City of Boston, shall remain near to the said carriage or vehicle, whereof he is the driver, while it is unemployed, or standing in the public streets and squares of the city, unless he shall be necessarily absent therefrom, in the course of his duty and business ; and shall so keep his horse, or horses, and carriage or other vehicle, as that the same shall not obstruct the said streets, or squares or other public passages, in any other manner than is allowed by law, or the ordinances of the City Council, or orders of the Mayor and Aldermen.   And no driver of any truck, cart, wagon, sled, sleigh, hackney coach, or other carriage, while waiting for employment either at any stand which is, or may be appointed for trucks, carts, wagons, sleds, sleighs, hackney coaches, or other carriages, or in the public streets or squares of the city, shall snap or flourish his whip ;— and whoever shall offend againsty an provision of this section shall forfeit and pay, for each offence, a sum not less than *one dollar,* nor more than *three dollars.*

Driver to remain near their carriages.

To keep them so as not to obstruct any street.

Not to snap his whip.

SEC. 4. *Be it further ordained,* That the Mayor and Aldermen be, and they are hereby authorized and empowered to appoint, from time to time, as occasion may require, such and so many stands for carts, trucks, wagons, and sleds, as to them shall appear requisite.   And no owner or driver of any cart, truck, wagon, or sled, shall stand in any other place with his cart, truck, wagon, or sled, than such as has been, or shall be directed and established by the Mayor and Aldermen, in pursuance of this ordinance ;—And whoever shall offend against any pro-

Stands for carriages to be appointed.

vision of this section, shall forfeit and pay, for each offence, a sum not less than *one dollar*, nor more than *three dollars*.

SEC. 5. *Be it further ordained*, That every owner, or driver, of any cart, truck, wagon, or sled, shall place his horses and cart, truck, wagon, or sled, lengthwise, as near as possible to the post, or abutting stone of the foot or side-walk of the street in which he shall stand ; and no more than one range of carts or trucks, shall stand in streets not more than thirty feet wide, and not more than one range on each side, in streets which are of a greater width than thirty feet, and in squares and other open places, they shall be arranged by the said owners, and drivers, by order of, and conformably to, the directions of the Mayor and Aldermen, in this respect ;—And whoever shall offend against any provision of this section, shall forfeit and pay for each offence a sum not less than *one dollar* nor more than *three dollars*.

> Driver to place his carriage near to side walk.

> And in single range.

SEC. 6. *Be it further ordained*, That no owner or driver of any carriage, wagon, cart, truck, sled, or sleigh, for pleasure or burden, shall stop or place any such carriage, wagon, cart, truck, sled, or sleigh, in any such manner as to cross the street, or side-walk, or so as to prevent other carriages or foot passengers from passing in the direction of such street, except to load or unload, as is provided in the ninth section of this ordinance ; but such driver or owner, in such cases, shall, upon request of such passenger, cause the same to be removed ; and no such owner or driver, shall absent himself from his carriage, wagon, cart, truck, sled or sleigh, so as to prevent the making of such request ;—And whoever shall offend against any provision of this section, shall forfeit and pay for each offence, a sum not less than *one dollar*, nor more than *three dollars*.

> Carriages not to be placed across the street.

> Driver to remove his carriage on request.

SEC. 7. *Be it further ordained*, That every truck, cart, wagon, and sled, belonging to any inhabitant of the city, shall be marked in at least two places, with the initials of the christian, and the whole of the surname of the owner, or owners of the same, strongly and legibly, in paint, upon a plate of tin or iron, and also numbered in the same manner, which names and

> Trucks, &c. to be marked.

numbers shall be placed upon the outside of both shafts, of every truck, and upon both sides of every cart, wagon, and sled, so as to be clearly visible and

Breadth of tire. discernible to all persons passing and repassing the streets during the day time, on either side of said cart, wagon, or sled ; and the tire of the wheels of all the carts and trucks used in the city, which shall be drawn by more than one horse, shall be in breadth not less than four inches : *Provided, always,* that the above provision, relative to the breadth of the tire, shall not be held to apply to those wheels of carts or trucks which are now owned or used in the city ; and the head of the nails of the tire of all such wheels, shall be flat ;—And whoever shall offend against any provision of this section, shall forfeit and pay for each offence, a sum not less than *one dollar,* nor more than *three dollars.*

SEC. 8. *Be it further ordained,* That not more than two horses, shall be harnessed to and permitted to draw any truck, or sled, in or through any of the

Not more than three horses to be used in carts, &c. public streets, squares, lanes, or alleys of the city, and not more than three horses shall be harnessed to and permitted to draw any cart, wagon, or drag, in or through any of the public streets, squares, lanes, or alleys of the city, unless in either of the above cases, for the carriage of any one single article, exceeding one ton in weight, and which cannot be divided : *Provided,* that the Mayor and Aldermen may grant permission, upon any special application for that purpose, for more than two horses to draw

Permission in case. any truck or sled, and for more than three horses to draw any cart, wagon, or drag, when they may think it reasonable or necessary : *Provided, also,* that four horses may, without such special permission, be attached to, and permitted to draw, any wagon, employed to transport loads out of the city into the country, or from the country into the city ; said four horses being yoked in pairs, or so harnessed, that two shall travel abreast.—That the felloes of the wheels of every drag machine, (which wheels shall

Width of felloes hereafter be constructed and used in this city) for carting or removing timber, which shall exceed one ton in weight, shall not be less than six inches in widtn , that the tire of the wheels of such machine, shall be of the width of said felloes, and the heads of the nails of said tire, shall be flat. That no truck shall be used in this city, the length whereof, from the end of the shaft to the extreme end of the side, shall be greater than *twenty-four feet and six inches.* That no person hereafter shall cause to be carried on any truck or cart, any load, the weight whereof shall exceed one ton and a half; or on any wagon, any load the weight whereof shall exceed two tons; excepting the load which may consist of an article which cannot be divided : *Provided, however,* that it shall be lawful to transport from the country into the city, or from the city into the country, on any wagon, the tire of the wheels of which, shall be in breadth not less than four inches, any load, the weight whereof shall not exceed two tons and a half;—And whoever shall offend against any provision of this section, shall forfeit and pay for each offence, a sum not less than *one dollar*, nor more than *five dollars.*

Weight of loads.

SEC. 9. *Be it further ordained,* That no truck, cart, or other vehicle, shall be so placed in any street within this city, by the owner or owners, or by the driver thereof, either to load or unload, as to prevent the passing of any other truck, cart, or carriage of any description, unless it be for a reasonable time, for the loading or unloading of heavy articles the weight of which, in any several parcel or package, shall not be less than one hundred pounds; which time shall not exceed six minutes;—And whoever shall offend against any provision of this section, shall forfeit and pay, for each offence, a sum not less than *one dollar*, nor more than *five dollars.*

Trucks, &c. not to be so placed as to obstruct streets when loading.

SEC 10. *Be it further ordained,* That all trucks, owned by any inhabitant of this city, shall be registered in a book to be kept by the City Clerk for that purpose, and shall be numbered, as is provided in the seventh section of this ordinance; and after such trucks shall be so registered and numbered, if any owner thereof shall sell or otherwise dispose of his property therein, the same shall be registered anew, in the name of the person who shall become

Trucks to be registered.

the owner thereof; and such person or owner is hereby required to cause the same to be newly registered accordingly; and the numbers and names herein required to be marked, and painted upon all trucks and other carriages, shall be renewed as often as they shall become defaced or indistinct;—And whoever shall offend against any provision of this section, shall forfeit and pay, for each offence, a sum not less than *one dollar*, nor more than *three dollars*.

SEC. 11. *Be it further ordained*, That no owner or driver of any truck, cart, sled, wagon, or other carriage, intended to be used to carry for hire, shall place his cart, truck, sled, wagon, or other carriage, in any street, lane, or square, within this city, to stand there, to be employed, unless such owner shall first obtain the consent of the Mayor and Aldermen of the city, so to place the same;—And whoever shall offend against any provision of this section, shall forfeit and pay for each offence a sum not less than *one dollar*, nor more than *five dollars*.

SEC. 12. *Be it further ordained*, That all drivers and other persons, having the care, and control of any truck, cart, wagon, sled, or drag passing in or through the streets, squares or lanes of the city, shall drive their horses or beasts at a moderate foot pace, and shall not suffer or permit them to go in a gallop or trot; and such driver or other person shall hold the reins in his hands, to guide and restrain such horses, or beasts; or he shall walk by the head of the shaft or wheel horse, either holding or keeping within reach of the bridle or halter of said horse, or other beast, to enable him to guide and restrain them in manner aforesaid;—And whoever shall offend against any provision of this section, shall forfeit and pay for each offence a sum not less than *two dollars* nor more than *twenty dollars*.

SEC. 13. *Be it further ordained*, That no driver of any truck, cart, wagon, sled, or other carriage, for pleasure or burden shall stop, or place any such truck, cart, wagon, sled, or other carriage, at, or near the intersection of any street, lane or alley in this city, in such manner as to cross the foot way, or flag-stones, or prevent foot passengers from passing the street, lane, or alley, in the direction, or line of the footway, or flag-stones on the side of such street, lane or alley ; and the said drivers shall immediately, on the request of any foot passenger cause the same to be removed, and the said drivers shall not absent themselves so that such requests cannot be made ;— And whoever shall offend against any provision of this section, shall forfeit and pay for such offence, a sum not less than *one dollar* nor more than *five dollars*.

SEC. 14. *Be it further ordained*, That no person, who shall be employed in driving or conducting any cart, truck, wagon, carriage, or other vehicle whatever, which is drawn by one or more horses, shall unreasonably or cruelly beat or otherwise use or abuse any horse or horses, under his care, within the City of Boston ; and no person shall be permitted, or allowed to lead, drive, or ride, any horse, mare, or gelding to any pond, or to any part of the sea, or to any other public place, to be washed upon the Lord's Day. And no person shall turn any horse, mare, or gelding loose within the City of Boston, or voluntarily permit or suffer the same to go at large, therein ;— And whoever shall offend against any provision of this section shall forfeit and pay, for each offence, a sum not less than *one dollar* nor more than *twenty dollars*.

Drivers not to beat their beasts cruelly.

Horses not to be washed on the Lord's day.

Nor turned loose in streets.

SEC. 15. *Be it further ordained*, That all the orders and by-laws, heretofore made and passed by the Inhabitants of the town of Boston on the subjects of this ordinance, and such parts of all the orders and ordinances, heretofore made and passed by the City Council on the subjects of this ordinance, as are inconsistent with the provisions thereof, be, and the same are hereby repealed.

[Passed July 24, 1826.]

Ordinance Sept 9. 1833 - superseding —

CHAP. XI.

Chimneys and Chimney Sweepers.

An ordinance for the regulation of Chimneys, and Chimney Sweepers.

SEC. 1. *Be it ordained by the Mayor, Aldermen and Common Council of the City of Boston, in City Council assembled,* That the Mayor and Aldermen, upon complaint made to them, or upon their knowledge and view of any defective chimney, or other fire place within this city, shall, from time to time, take effectual care that the same shall be examined and inspected ; and, when in their opinion the safety of the city requires it, shall order the same to be immediately amended or repaired if the same can be properly done, otherwise, to be taken down and demolished. And if the owner or owners of such defective chimney or fire place, shall wilfully neglect or refuse to amend repair or take down the same, the said owner or owners shall forfeit and pay a sum not less than one, or more than twenty dollars : *Provided,* that such owner or owners shall have been served with an order in writing from the Mayor and Aldermen to amend, repair or take down the said defective chimney or fire place (as the case may be,) duly certified by the City Clerk ; an attested copy of which order, made and certified by the City Clerk, shall be duly served upon such owner or owners, by any person appointed for that purpose by the said Mayor and Aldermen. And the said Mayor and Aldermen for the time being, shall have full power and authority to order and direct, and they are hereby required to cause such defective chimney or fire place, to be taken down and abated as a common nuisance—and the owner or owners of such defective chimney or fire place, shall in such case bear, satisfy and pay the whole expense and charge of abating such nuisance, and of taking down and removing such defective chimney or fire place.

Marginal notes:
Chimneys to be inspected.

Proviso.

Defective Chimneys to be taken down.

SEC. 2. *Be it further ordained*, That the Mayor and Aldermen be and they are hereby authorized and directed, to appoint and license, from time to time, suitable persons to be sweepers of chimneys in this city, who, together with their apprentices, and others by them employed, shall wear such badges as the Mayor and Aldermen shall appoint and direct, and whose wages and compensation for their work and service in sweeping of chimneys, shall not exceed the rates, which are or may be fixed and appointed by the Mayor and Aldermen. And if any person who shall not be appointed and licensed as aforesaid, shall presume, either by himself or by his apprentices or others by him employed, to undertake the sweeping of any chimney in this city, excepting such as are in his own occupation, every such person shall forfeit and pay a sum not less than *one dollar*, nor more than *ten dollars*, for every offence of which he shall be duly convicted. And no inhabitant of this city shall employ any person (excepting his, or her own servant, being in his or her house,) to sweep any of his or her chimneys, within the city, other than one of the chimney sweepers appointed and licensed as aforesaid by the Mayor and Aldermen ; and if any inhabitant of this city shall employ any person, other than the chimney sweepers appointed and licensed as aforesaid, in violation of the provisions of this ordinance, he or they shall forfeit and pay a fine not less than *one dollar* nor more than *ten dollars*.

Sweepers of Chimneys to be licensed.

Penalty for sweeping without license.

SEC. 3. *Be it further ordained*, That when and so often as complaint shall be made to the Mayor and Aldermen, by any chimney sweeper appointed and licensed as aforesaid, or by any other inhabitant of the city, against any person or persons that their chimneys are unsafe by reason of foulness, the Mayor and Aldermen, or any other person by them empowered, are hereby directed to inspect and view, or order to be inspected and viewed and to them reported, every such chimney complained of as aforesaid ; and if upon such view, inspection and report, the Mayor and Aldermen shall, either from their own view, or the report of the person appointed to view as aforesaid, judge the same to be unsafe and

Chimneys to be viewed or complaint made.

10

dangerous to make and keep fire therein by reason of foulness, the said Mayor and Aldermen shall give notice thereof to the person or persons in the possession or occupancy of the house or tenement to which such chimney or chimneys belong ; and every occu-

Penalty. pier or occupiers of such house or tenement, shall forfeit and pay a sum not less than *one dollar*, nor more than *twenty dollars*, for every day in which fire shall be made and kept in such chimney or chimneys respectively, by such occupier or occupiers, after notice shall have been given them in manner aforesaid, until the same shall be properly and sufficiently swept.

SEC. 4. *Be it further ordained*, That a by-law of **By-law repealed.** the town of Boston made and passed the twenty second day of May, in the year of our Lord, one thousand eight hundred and one, entitled " a law for the regulations of Chimneys and Sweepers, be and the same is hereby repealed.

[Passed Dec. 28, 1825.]

CHAP. XII.

The Common.

An ordinance to prevent trespasses and nuisances on the Common and common lands of the City of Boston.

SEC. 1. *Be it ordained by the Mayor, Aldermen and Common Council of the City of Boston, in City Council assembled,* That no person or persons shall ride, lead or drive any horse or horses of any description, in or upon the open grounds in the city, called the Common, unless by permission or order of the Mayor and Aldermen, on pain of forfeiting a sum not less than *one dollar* nor more than ten dollars, for every such offence: *Provided however,* that on occasions of military exercise, parade or review, the introduction of any horses on the Common, which may be necessary for the purpose of such exercise, parade or review, shall not be deemed an infraction of this ordinance. *(margin: Horses not to go on the common) (margin: Proviso.)*

SEC. 2. *Be it further ordained,* That no person shall breach, dig up, or carry away, any of the sward, gravel, sand, turf, or earth, in or from any part of the Common or common lands of this city, unless by order and permission of the Mayor and Aldermen for the purpose of some public use on pain of forfeiting for every such offence a sum not less than one dollar, nor more than twenty dollars. *(margin: Sward, gravel, &c. not to be dug up.)*

SEC. 3. *Be it further ordained,* That no person except by the order or permission of the Mayor and Aldermen, shall top, peal, cut, deface, either by posting up bills of any description or otherwise injure, or destroy, any of the trees, growing, or which shall hereafter be planted and grow in the Common or either of the Malls adjoining the Common, or which now are, or may be hereafter planted and growing in the said Common or on the common lands of the city, or in any street or public place therein, on pain of *(margin: Trees not to be defaced.)*

forfeiting for every such offence a sum not less than one dollar nor more than twenty dollars.

Sec. 4. *Be it further ordained*, That no person shall lay, cart or spread, or cause to be laid, carted or spread, or otherwise carried into the said Common or common lands, of the said city, any dead carcase, ordure, filth, stones, or other offensive matter or substance whatever, on pain of forfeiting for every such offence, a sum not less than one dollar, nor more than twenty dollars.

Offensive matter not to be carried on the Common.

Sec. 5. *Be it further ordained*, That no horse, ox, steer, heifer, sheep, goat, calf, or swine, shall be allowed to go at large, or to feed upon the Common or common lands, streets, or other public places within the city, and if the owner or owners, keeper or keepers, of any such animal or animals, shall suffer and permit the same to go at large or feed upon any of the public places and common lands aforesaid, he or they shall forfeit and pay for every such offence a sum not less than one dollar, nor more than five dollars.

Animals not permitted to run at large on the Common.

Sec. 6. *Be it further ordained*, That if any person or persons, shall shake, or otherwise cleanse any carpet or carpets on the Common, within ten rods of either of the Malls, he or they shall forfeit and pay for every such offence a sum not less than one dollar nor more than three dollars.

Carpets not to be shaken.

Sec. 7. *Be it further ordained*, That the by-law of the town of Boston, made and passed on the twenty second day of May, in the year of our Lord, one thousand eight hundred and one, entitled " a law to prevent nuisances on the Common," and also an order of the City Council made and passed on the twenty fourth day of May, in the year of our Lord, one thousand eight hundred and twenty two, entitled " an order to prevent trespasses on the Common," be and the same are hereby repealed.

Laws repealed.

[Passed Dec. 26, 1825.]

An ordinance regulating the going at large of Cows, and the right of pasturage on Boston Common.

SEC. 1. *Be it ordained by the Mayor, Aldermen and Common Council of the City of Boston in City Council assembled*, That the owner of every Cow which shall be pastured on the Common, shall pay the sum of five dollars, annually, for that privilege ; the payment to be made to the City Clerk, who upon any application for such privilege, and the payment of said sum shall register such Cow, and her number and owner's name ; and shall grant the liberty of pasturage on the Common for the current year : *Provided*, that no citizen shall be entitled to pasture more than one Cow, at the same time, on the Common : *And provided, also*, that in cases of poverty, the Mayor and Aldermen, being satisfied thereof, may grant the privilege, without such payment. Cows to be registered. Proviso.

SEC. 2. *Be it further ordained*, That the Mayor and Aldermen shall cause suitable tallies with marks and numbers, to be prepared, and to be delivered by the City Clerk to the owner of such Cow, and the said City Clerk shall pay over the amount of such license, from time to time, as directed by the Mayor and Aldermen to the City Treasurer ;—And every Cow found at large in said city, not having a keeper shall be liable to be impounded by any field driver, and detained by him until the payment of *fifty cents*, together with the cost and charges of impounding and keeping said Cow : *Provided*, that any inhabitant of South Boston shall be allowed to have one Cow go at large at South Boston without a keeper. Cows to have tallies and keepers. Proviso.

SEC. 3. *Be it further ordained*, That no inhabitant of South Boston shall permit any Cow to him belonging, to go at large without a talley on her neck with the owner's name thereon, on penalty of forfeiting and paying the sum of one dollar for every offence. South Boston.

[Passed Dec. 18, 1827.]

CHAP. XIII.

Constables.

ACTS OF THE LEGISLATURE.

An act for regulating the proceedings in suits upon Constable's Bonds in the town of Boston.

See chap. 2, assessments, act of March 12, 1908, Sec. 3.

Bond broken.

Proviso.

SEC. 1. *Be it enacted by the Senate and House of Representatives in General Court assembled and by the authority of the same,* That when the condition of any bond which now is, or may hereafter be given to the treasurer of the town of Boston by any constable of said town, for the faithful performance of the duties of his office, shall be broken, to the injury of any person, such person may cause a suit to be instituted upon such bond, at his own costs, but in the name of the treasurer of the town of Boston; and the like endorsements shall be made on the writ, and the like proceedings be had thereon, to final judgment and execution, and the like writs of *scire facias,* on such judgment, as may be made and had by a creditor on administration bonds, given to any Judge of Probate : *Provided, however,* that no such suit shall be instituted by any person for his own use, until such person shall have recovered judgment against the constable, his executors or administrators, in an action brought for the malfeasance or misfeasance of the constable, or for non-payment of any moneys collected by the said constable, in that capacity, or a decree of a Judge of Probate, allowing a claim for any of the causes aforesaid, and such judgment or decree, or so much thereof as shall be unsatisfied, with the interest due thereon, shall be the proportion of the penalty for which execution shall be awarded : *Provided, however,* that this act shall not be construed to make any surety in any bond given by the constable as aforesaid, before the passing of this act, liable to any suit, which could not heretofore be legally prosecuted against him.

SEC. 2. *Be it further enacted*, That it shall be the duty of the treasurer aforesaid, to deliver an attested copy of any constable's bond to any persons applying and paying for the same, and such attested copy shall be received as evidence in any case : *Provided, nevertheless*, that if in any suit, the execution of the bond shall be disputed, the court may order the treasurer to bring the original bond into court.

Duty of Treasurer.

Proviso.

[Passed March 1, 1815.]

An act in addition to an act entitled " An act defining the general powers and duties, and regulating the office of Sheriff."

SEC. 1. *Be it enacted by the Senate and House of Representatives in General Court assembled and by the authority of the same*, That no constable shall be suffered to appear in any court, or before any Justice of the Peace, as attorney to, or in behalf of any party in a suit ; nor shall such constable be allowed to draw, make, or fill up any plaint, declaration, writ or process.

Restrictions of Constables.

SEC. 2. *Be it further enacted*, That if any constable shall be guilty of a breach of this act, he shall forfeit and pay the sum of *fifty dollars*, to be recovered by action of debt, in any court proper to try the same, to be for the use of the person who may sue or prosecute therefor.

Penalties.

SEC. 3. *Be it further enacted*, That this act shall take effect, and be in force from and after the first day of July next.

[Passed June 15, 1822.]

CHAP. XIV.

Common Criers.

An ordinance to regulate Common Criers.

Sec. 1. *Be it ordained by the Mayor, Aldermen, and Common Council of the City of Boston, in City Council assembled,* That no person whatever shall presume to become a Common Crier within the City of Boston, or to cry any sort of goods, wares or merchandize, lost or found, stolen goods, strays, or public sales, in any of the streets, squares, lanes, or market places within the city, unless the person so presuming to be a common crier, shall be licensed therefor by the Mayor and Aldermen ; and every person so licensed, shall keep a true and perfect list of all the matters and things by him so cried, and the names of the persons by whom he was employed, and ordered to cry the same ; which list shall be open, and subject to the inspection of the Mayor and Aldermen, whenever they shall demand the same ; and no common crier shall publish or cry any abusive, libellous, profane, or obscene matter or thing whatsoever. And if any common crier shall be guilty of a breach of this ordinance, or any part thereof, he shall forfeit and pay, for each offence, a sum not less than one dollar, nor more than twenty dollars.

Sec. 2. *Be it further ordained,* That the Mayor and Aldermen of said city, for the time being, may from time to time grant licenses to such person or persons, as shall produce to them satisfactory evidence of his or their good character, to be common criers in this city, and such license shall continue in force until the first day of May, after the date thereof, unless sooner revoked by the Mayor and Aldermen, (which they have authority to do,) and no longer.

[Passed Oct. 9, 1826.]

Criers to be licensed.

Penalty.

Licenses may be revoked

CHAP. XV.
Courts.

ACTS OF THE LEGISLATURE.

An act to establish a Municipal Court in the town of Boston.

WHEREAS, from the peculiar situation and circumstances of the town of Boston, as a metropolis and great seaport, the usual mode of enforcing the laws, and administering justice in criminal cases, is attended with great delays and burthensome expenses; *Preamble.*

SEC. 1. *Be it therefore enacted by the Senate and House of Representatives, in General Court assembled, and by the authority of the same,* That there shall be holden, within and for the town of Boston, on the first Monday of every month, by such learned, able, and discreet person as the Governor shall appoint and commission, pursuant to the constitution, a court of justice, by the name of the Municipal Court for the town of Boston; that the same court shall have power to adjourn from day to day, and shall have cognizance of all crimes and offences committed within the town of Boston, which are now cognizable in the Court of General Sessions of the peace, and cognizance of all offences against the By-laws of the said town; of frauds, deceits, monopolies, forestalling, regrating, thefts, and nuisances. And the said court shall have power to impose and administer all oaths necessary to the legal conviction and punishment of offenders; and to punish, at the reasonable discretion of the court, and in like manner as other courts may lawfully do, all contempts committed against the authority of the same. And the same court shall have power to appoint and remove its own clerks, who, when appointed, shall take such oaths, as are by law provided to be taken by the clerks of other courts. And if it shall so happen that the judge of

To be held monthly.

[" Municipal Court of the City of Boston:" 1822: ch. 13.]

[All crimes in the County of Suffolk, not capital: 1812, 183.]

Power of the court.

11

said Court shall be unable to attend, from sickness

Clerk authorized to adjourn in certain cases.

Or to a earlier time, see p. 86.

or any other cause, on any day upon which said court shall be by law to be held, or to which said court shall stand adjourned, it shall and may be lawful for the clerk of said court to adjourn the same to the next stated term, by proclamation.

Sec. 2. *Be it further enacted*, That the grand jurors, annually chosen for the town of Boston, to

Grand Jurors.

serve in the Court of General Sessions of the peace, shall be increased to fifteen within said town, and

Altered.

shall be summoned to attend said Municipal Court, with all the powers and authority vested in grand jurors by the constitution and laws of this Common-wealth, and within the jurisdiction of said Municipal Court; and that the petit jurors who shall hereafter

Petit Jurors.

be appointed in the town of Boston, and returned to

Altered.

serve in the Court of General Sessions of the peace, shall not be less than fifteen in number, whose duty it shall be to attend the said Municipal Court, and to serve in all cases where by law, trial by jury is re-quired, and until another petit jury is appointed for the Court of Sessions; and the said petit jurors shall be summoned accordingly. And the said grand jurors and petit jurors, shall receive for their services in said Municipal Court, the like compensation and in like manner, as they by law are entitled to at the Court of Sessions.

Sec. 3. *Be it further enacted*, That the judge of

Judge's salary.

said Municipal Court, shall receive in full compen-sation for the discharge of the duties of his office, a stated annual salary, which shall be paid by said town of Boston, and which shall be voted and estab-

And an additional sum from the State treasury.

lished, at any meeting of the inhabitants legally as-sembled for that purpose, and which shall not be diminished, during his continuance in office. And all fees taxed in said court, for the clerk, wit-nesses, and officers thereof, and for all processes is-suing from said court, and other court charges, shall

Court fees.

be the same as by law are allowed in the Court of General Sessions of the peace in similar cases. And the precepts of the said Municipal Court shall be directed to, and served by, the sheriff of the County of Suffolk, by his deputies residing within the town of Boston, and by the constables thereof respectively ; and all prisoners who shall be arrested and ordered to be committed, by any sentence or judgment of said Municipal Court, or who shall be ordered to be committed, either by the judge of said court, or by any justice of the peace, upon any complaint, to take trial at the said court, shall and may be committed to the gaol of the said County of Suffolk, and there held until discharged by order of said court, or by order of the Supreme Judicial Court of this Commonwealth ; and the keeper of the gaol for the said County of Suffolk, is hereby directed and required to take the custody of the said prisoners accordingly.

Prisoners to be confined in Suffolk gaol.

Sec. 4. *Be it further enacted,* That the said town shall be allowed to choose, annually, some person learned in the law, to appear as an advocate in the same court, and to conduct the prosecutions therein ; and the said town may allow him such compensation as to them shall appear reasonable ; and the said judge shall tax such fees, for said advocate, in the cases that shall be tried by said court, as the attorney general for the Commonwealth, or the attorney for the county, is or shall be allowed in the Court of General Sessions of the peace ; the said fees, when received by the advocate of said court, shall be accounted for to the town of Boston ; *Provided, nevertheless,* that all criminal prosecutions in the said court, shall be under the management of the attorney or solicitor general, when either of them shall be present, the appointment of such advocate by the town notwithstanding.

Advocate

How appointed by Governor and Council.

Salary established and fees paid to county treasurer, see St : 1821. c. 104, laws of Mass.

Sec. 5. *Be it further enacted,* That all costs which may arise in any criminal prosecution in said Municipal Court, the judge of said court is hereby authorized and empowered to examine and tax, not exceeding in any case, the fees stated by law, and such costs so taxed shall be paid out of the treasury of the County of Suffolk. And the clerk of said Municipal Court shall attest and deliver to the county treasurer, copies of all bills of costs allowed by the court, and certificates of all fines and forfeitures imposed and accruing to the county aforesaid, or to the Common-

Cost of criminal prosecution.

wealth, either before the rising of said Court, or as soon after as may be. And the clerk of said Municipal Court, and all sheriffs, deputy sheriffs, coroners, and constables, who may hereafter receive any fines, forfeitures, or bills of cost, in pursuance of the judgment or sentence of said court, which shall accrue either to the county aforesaid, or the Commonwealth, shall forthwith pay the same to the treasurer of said county; and upon the neglect thereof for the space of ten days after such receipt, he shall forfeit and pay double the amount of such fine, forfeiture, or bill of cost, to such county treasurer, who is hereby empowered and directed to sue for the same; to be recovered, with costs, by action of debt, in the Court of Common Pleas in the same county; one third of said penalty to the use of said treasurer, and the other two thirds to the use of said County of Suffolk.

Penalty for with holding fines.

SEC. 6. *Be it further enacted,* That this act shall take effect, from and after the first day of May next; and the first Municipal Court, shall be held on the first Monday of June next ensuing.

SEC. 7. *Be it further enacted,* That an appeal shall be had from all sentences and judgments of the said Municipal Court, to the Supreme Judicial Court, in the same manner that appeals are had from the Court of General Sessions of the peace.

Appeal allowed.

[Passed March 4, 1800.]

An act for relieving the County of Suffolk, in the choice and service of Jurors, and for further regulating the administration of justice therein.

WHEREAS the number of grand jurors now by law to be chosen by the towns in the County of Suffolk is unnecessarily inconvenient and burthensome;

Preamble.

Sec. 1. *Be it enacted by the Senate and House of Representatives in General Court assembled, and by the authority of the same,* That from and after the passing of this act, the several towns in the said county be, and they are hereby exempted from appointing annual Grand Jurors to serve in the Court of General Sessions of the peace to be held therein, or at the Municipal Court of the town of Boston, and from appointing petit Jurors to serve at the said Court of Sessions, as heretofore by law required; and such Jurors as may have been before appointed, and shall then be liable to serve as aforesaid, shall be discharged from the said services, from and after the last day of April next.

Towns exempted from appointing certain grand Jurors.

Sec. 2. *Be it further enacted,* That such Jurors as are now appointed, or may hereafter be appointed by the town of Boston to serve on the Grand Jury, at the Supreme Judicial Court, within and for the said county of Suffolk, shall be summoned and shall attend the Municipal Court for the town of Boston, by law to be holden within and for the said town, and after the said last day of April next, until other Grand Jurors are appointed, and returned to serve at the Supreme Judicial Court in the county aforesaid, and are hereby vested with all the powers given by the constitution and laws of this Commonwealth to Grand Jurors, touching all matters within the Jurisdiction of the said Municipal Court. [And that the petit Jurors who are or shall be hereafter appointed in the town of Boston, to serve in the Court of Common Pleas in said County, and who shall not be less than fifteen in number, shall also be appointed for and returned to said Municipal Court. And it shall be their duty to attend the said Municipal Court, and to serve in all causes where by law trial by jury may be required, and until another petit jury be appointed for the said Court of Common Pleas; and the said petit Jurors shall be summoned accordingly.] And the said grand Jurors and petit Jurors shall receive for their services in said Municipal Court, the like compensation and in like manner, as such Jurors are now by law entitled to, at the Court of Sessions.

Grand Jurors of Supreme Court to attend.

Repealed by statute 1822. chap.13.

Sec. 3. *Be it further enacted,* [That the Supreme Judicial Court to be by law holden within and for the said County of Suffolk, shall have cognizance and Jurisdiction of all crimes and other matters heretofore cognizable by the said

Repealed 1812. ch. 183. 1821, ch. 109.

Court of Sessions, and triable by a Jury, the causes of which may arise in any other part of the County of Suffolk than the town of Boston.]　And that all appeals from the judgments of Justices of the Peace in criminal matters happening within the said town of Boston, and which might heretofore have been made the said Court of general Sessions of the peace, shall be made to, and be cognizable by the said Municipal Court.

SEC. 4. *Be it further enacted*, That the precepts of the said Municipal Court may be directed to all such officers, and run into any Counties within this Commonwealth, that precepts from the said Court of General Sessions of the peace might by law, and that the grand and petit Jurors, appointed and summoned to attend at the said Municipal Court, shall be subject to the same penalties for non attendance, as such Jurors are now respectively subject to by law, for not attending at the Court of General Sessions of the peace.

Courts to issue precepts to other Counties.

SEC. 5. [*And be it further enacted*, That the terms now by law established for holding the said Municipal Court on the first Mondays of March and September, annually, be and hereby are abolished.]

Repealed, 1808. ch. 21. 1813. ch. 179.

[Passed Feb. 17, 1801.]

An act to enlarge the Jurisdiction of the Municipal Court in the town of Boston.

Be it enacted by the Senate and House of Representatives in General Court assembled, and by the authority of the same, That the Municipal Court in the town of Boston, shall have original Jurisdiction, concurrent with the Supreme Judicial Court, of all crimes and offences arising or happening within the County of Suffolk, not capital ; and the said Municipal Court shall and may exercise such Jurisdiction, any law, usage, or custom to the contrary notwithstanding, saving, to any party the right to appeal to the said Supreme Judicial Court, as is now provided by law in other cases.

[Passed Feb. 27, 1813.]

An act to increase the number of terms of the Municipal Court of the town of Boston, and to compensate the Judge thereof.

Be it enacted by the Senate and House of Representatives in General Court assembled, and by the authority of the same, That in future, the said Municipal Court shall be holden on the first Monday of every month, with power to adjourn as originally provided for, in the act of March the fourth, in the year of our Lord one thousand eight hundred, which established said Court : and that in addition to the salary allowed the Judge of said Court by the town of Boston, there shall be paid to him out of the Treasury of this Commonwealth, every quarter of a year, the sum of one hundred and eighty seven dollars and fifty cents, the first quarter to be considered as having commenced the first day of January last ; and said additional allowance to be continued, so long as the act of the twenty seventh of February, in the year of our Lord one thousand eight hundred and thirteen, enlarging the Jurisdiction of said Court, shall remain unrepealed, and the said Judge shall be obliged by law to perform the duties therein required.

[Passed Feb. 26, 1814.]

An act respecting the Municipal Court in the city of
Boston, and regulating the selections, the empan-
nelling and services of Grand, Traverse and Petit
Jurors.

SEC. 1. *Be it enacted by the Senate and House of
Representatives, in General Court assembled and by
the authority of the same,* That the Court of Criminal
Jurisdiction established by an act passed on the fourth
day of March in the year of our Lord one thonsand
eight hundred, and stiled the Municipal Court for the
town of Boston, the jurisdiction of which was afterwards extended to the County of Suffolk, shall hereafter be known and stiled " The Municipal Court of
the City of Boston," with all the jurisdiction, power
and authority vested in the said Court.

Title.

SEC. 2. *Be it further enacted,* That if it shall so
happen, that the Judge of said court shall be unable
to attend from sickness, or any other cause, on any
day upon which said court shall be by law to be held,
or to which said court shall stand adjourned, it shall
and may be lawful for the clerk of the said court to
adjourn the same, either to the next stated term, or
to such earlier time, and to such place, as the public
convenience may, in his judgment, require, and it
shall be the duty of the Sheriff in attendance, or his
deputies, to give notice of such adjournment by proclamation, and by posting or publishing notice thereof,
or in such manner as the said court may, by any order or rule thereof direct or appoint.

*Powers of
Clerk.*

SEC. 3. *Be it further enacted,* That the said Court
shall have power and authority to issue writs of *ve-
nire facias,* for the return of traverse Jurors from
the City of Boston, conformable to law ; whose duty
it shall be to attend the said Municipal Court, and to
serve in all cases where by law, trial by Jury is required therein ; and the said traverse Jurors, who
may be drawn and returned for the respective terms
of said Courts held in January, April, July and October, in each year, shall be held and required to
serve as such, at the said terms respectively, and

*General powers
of Court.*

also at the two terms next succeeding the said respective terms.

SEC. 4. *Be it further enacted*, That so much of the laws heretofore made, as required the traverse Jurors drawn and returned to the Court of Common Pleas for the County of Suffolk, to serve at any term of the said Municipal Court be, and the same are hereby repealed. **Repeal of laws.**

SEC. 5. *Be it further enacted*, That all the duties required of and powers given to towns by the several laws " regulating the selections, the empanelling, and the services of the Grand, Traverse, and petit Jurors," shall be exercised by the Mayor and Aldermen of the City of Boston. **Powers respecting Jurors.**

[Passed June 15, 1822.]

An Act to regulate the Administration of Justice within the County of Suffolk, and for other purposes.

SEC. 1. *Be it enacted by the Senate and House of Representatives, in General Court assembled, and by the authority of the same*, That the town of Chelsea shall continue to be a part of the County of Suffolk, for all purposes relating to the administration of justice, as though this act had not been passed ; excepting that the town of Chelsea shall not be liable to taxation for any county purposes, until the Legislature shall otherwise order ; and excepting also, as herein after provided, concerning the jurisdiction of Justices of the Peace. That the Court of Common Pleas in the County of Suffolk, shall have jurisdiction in all matters and things, which, in relation to the town of Chelsea, or the inhabitants thereof, were cognizable by the Court of Sessions, in the County of Suffolk, before the passing of this act. **Judicial connexion.**

SEC. 2. *Be it further enacted*, That there shall be, and hereby is established within and for the City of Boston, a Police Court, to consist of three learned, able and discreet persons, to be appointed and com- **Police Court.**

missioned by the Governor, pursuant to the constitution, and the senior justice shall preside in said court ; and a court shall be held daily, at nine o'clock in the forenoon, and at three o'clock in the afternoon, by some one or more of said justices, and at any other times when necessary, to take cognizance of all crimes, offences, and misdemeanors, whereof Justices of the Peace may take cognizance by law, and of all offences which may be cognizable by one or more of said Justices, according to the by-laws, rules, and regulations which may be established by the proper authority of the City of Boston. And the Court hereby constituted, shall hear and determine all suits, complaints, and prosecutions, in like manner as is by law provided for the exercise of the powers and authority which are, or may be vested in Justices of the Peace, and do all such acts necessary to, or consistent with, such powers and authority, reserving to any party aggrieved an appeal, in like manner as appeals may be claimed in all other cases ; *Provided, always,* that no one of said Justices shall be of counsel, or attorney, to any party, in any matter or thing whatsoever, which may be pending before said Justices, or either of them.

SEC. 3. *Be it further enacted,* That all warrants issued by said Justices, or either of them, or by any Justice of the Peace within the City of Boston, shall be made returnable, and be returned, before the said Police Court : *Provided, always,* that no process returnable before a Justice of the Peace residing in the said Town of Chelsea, except for causes of complaint arising in Chelsea, shall be served within the City of Boston. And if any warrant shall be issued by any Justice of the Peace, who is not one of the Justices of the said Police Court, the lawful fees payable therefor shall not be paid nor allowed, unless, on the examination or hearing before said Police Court, it shall appear to said Court, that there was just and reasonable cause for issuing said warrant ; in which case, such fees, costs, and charges, shall be allowed and taxed, in like manner, as though said warrant had been issued by a Justice of the Peace, according to the law now in force.

Marginal notes:

Recognizances

Powers of the Court.

Appeals.

Returns of warrants.

Costs, &c.

SEC. 4. *Be it further enacted*, That the said Justices of said Court shall severally receive, in full compensation for all services herein before assigned to them, such salary, annually, payable out of the Treasury of the City of Boston, as the City Council shall fix and determine, payable quarter yearly; —the said annual salary shall include, and be payment in full, not only for the services rendered by the said Justices, in all prosecutions, suits, and complaints, but also in full for all other services required of them by this act, excepting when acting as members of the Board of Accounts, as herein after provided for. *Salaries.*

SEC. 5. *Be it further enacted*, That there shall be a Clerk of said Police Court, to be appointed and commissioned by the Governor, with the advice of Council, and removable by the same authority, whose duty it shall be to attend every Court held by the said Justices of the said Police Court, or either of them, and to record all proceedings therein had, and to make out all warrants and processes, which the said Justices, or either of them may order; to tax all bills of cost, and receive fines, penalties, and costs; and to exhibit, quarter yearly, to the Board of Accounts, herein after established, a particular account of all sums of money by him received as such Clerk, and shall pay over all sums by him so received, to the City Treasurer, immediately after his accounts shall have been examined and certified by said Board of Accounts; and the accounts so exhibited, from time to time, shall be recorded by the City Treasurer, in a book to be by him kept for that purpose, when the same, with the certificate of allowance thereof, by said board, shall be exhibited to him by said Clerk, and the said accounts shall be filed and safely kept by said Treasurer. That the said clerk shall be sworn to the faithful performance of his duty; and shall give bond, with one or more surety or sureties, to the acceptance of the said City Treasurer, for the faithful performance of the duties of his office, in such penalty as the City Council shall determine; and the said clerk shall receive from the city Treasury such annual compensation, payable quarter yearly, as the City Council shall fix and determine, and no other compensation whatever. That the said clerk *Clerk of Police.*

Account of fees.

Clerk's bonds.

shall not advise with, nor be of counsel, nor attorney, to any party in any suit, complaint or process whatsoever, pending, or to be brought before said Court; and shall be removable for any act by him done in contravention of this provision. The said clerk is hereby authorized and empowered, with the consent and approbation of the Justices of said Court, to employ, if it be found necessary so to do, one or more assistant clerks; but the said clerk shall be responsible for all persons by him so employed; and the said City Council may allow to such assistant clerk or clerks a reasonable and just compensation, payable out of the City Treasury, on the certificate of the said Board of Accounts, that such assistant clerk or clerks were necessarily employed : *Provided, always*, that the said clerk of said Police Court shall take all lawful fees, for copies which he may make out and certify, at the request of any party or person, and shall endorse thereon the amount of said fees, and account for all fees by him so received, to the City Treasurer.

Assistant Clerks.

Proviso.

SEC. 6. *Be it further enacted*, That a Court shall be held by one or more of said Justices on two several days in each week, and as much oftener as may be necessary, to be called and styled the Justices' Court for the County of Suffolk; which Court shall have original, exclusive jurisdiction and cognizance of all civil suits and actions, which before, and until the passing of this act, might by law be heard, tried and determined before any Justice of the Peace, within and for the County of Suffolk; and an appeal shall be allowed from all judgments in said Justices' Court, in like manner as appeals are now allowed by law, from judgments of Justices of the Peace in civil actions in the said County of Suffolk. All writs, and summons, and processes, may be tested by either of the Justices of said Court; and it shall be the duty of said Justices to keep a true and faithful account of all fees by them respectively received in civil suits and actions, and to render a just and true account thereof, on oath, quarter yearly, to the Board of Accounts; and all sums of money, by them so received, shall be accounted for, and paid

Justices' Court.

Board of Accounts.

into the City Treasury : and it shall be the duty of such Justice, to make a true and faithful record, according to law, of his proceedings in every trial and process of a civil nature, which may be had before him. That all the Justices of the said Court shall, from time to time, assemble, to establish all necessary rules for the orderly and uniform conducting of the business of said Court, both of civil and criminal jurisdiction, and to agree upon the manner and course, in which they shall respectively perform the duties by this act assigned to them, so as to insure a constant, prompt and punctual performance thereof, and to equalize the same, as near as may be, among themselves. And the said Justices, when assembled, shall have power to discharge from prison any person or persons, who may be there held, for no other cause than the non-payment of fine and costs, if it shall appear to said Justices that such person or persons are poor and unable to pay the same : *Provided, always,* that when such person or persons are held under sentence of the Municipal Court, that the assent of the Judge of that Court, that such person or persons shall be discharged, shall be first given.

Uniform Rules.

Discharges from Prison.

SEC. 7. *Be it further enacted,* That all suits, actions and prosecutions, which shall be instituted, and which shall be pending before any Justice of the Peace, within the County of Suffolk, at the time when the said Police Court, and the said Court of the Justices of the County of Suffolk, shall have been organized, and shall have been duly qualified to perform the duties hereby assigned to said Courts, shall be heard and determined as though this act had not been passed.

Pending suits.

SEC. 8. *Be it further enacted,* That the Court of Common Pleas, holden within and for the County of Suffolk, shall have, exercise, and perform, all the powers and duties, which, before the passing of this act, were by law had, exercised, and performed, by the Court of Sessions in said county, with regard to streets and ways, and with regard to all other suits, processes, and proceedings whatsoever, in which a trial by jury may be had or required ;—and such trial shall be had at the bar of said Court of Common

Common Pleas.

Pleas, in the same manner as other civil causes are there tried, by the Jurors there returned and empannelled ; and the Jury, to whom such cause may be committed, shall be taken to view the place in question, if either party shall request it. And all suits and processes, pending in said Court of Sessions, at the passing of this act, whereof cognizance and jurisdiction is hereby given to the said Court of Common Pleas, shall be transferred to and heard and determined in the said Court of Common Pleas, as though the same had been originated or instituted in said court, in pursuance of this act.

Jury trials.

Transfer of Suits.

SEC. 9. *Be it further enacted,* That the Judge of Probate for the County of Suffolk, and the Judge of the Municipal Court of the Town or City of Boston, and the said Justices of the Police Court, shall be, and they hereby are constituted a Board of Accounts ; and the said board shall assemble quarter yearly, and as much oftener as may be found necessary ; and when so assembled, shall have power, and it shall be their duty, to adjust, liquidate, examine, and allow, all bills of costs, accounts and charges, which may be made, or which may arise in the course of proceedings in the said Police Court and in the Municipal Court, and in the maintenance and keeping of the prisoners in the gaol of the County of Suffolk, and of all other charges and expenses in keeping said goal, and of all other places of confinement and punishment, within the City of Boston ; and the said Board of Accounts shall certify, that said accounts, charges, and expenses, have been examined and allowed by them—and the certificate of such examination and allowance shall be endorsed on the accounts exhibited to said board, and shall be addressed to the public officer by whom such charges, fees, and expenses, may be payable by law.

Board of Accounts.

General powers.

SEC. 10. *Be it further enacted,* That the said Judges and Justices are empowered, and it is hereby made their duty, to assemble quarter yearly, and proceed to inspect the gaol in the County of Suffolk, and all other places of confinement and punishment for crimes, offences, or non-payment of fines or debts, and to make report of their proceedings to the Mayor and

Inspection of Prison.

Aldermen of the City of Boston; and therein to state all grievances, mismanagement, and negligence, which they may find to exist; and therein to suggest such changes and improvements, as to them may seem wise and expedient. Any three or more of said Justices and Judges shall constitute a quorum for the performance of the duties hereby assigned to them. And the said Judges and Justices shall be entitled to have and receive, out of the City Treasury, the sum of three dollars respectively, for each and every day which may be by them devoted to the performance of the duties hereby assigned to them. *Pay of Justices.*

SEC. 11. *Be it further enacted,* That the Court of Sessions, within and for the County of Suffolk, be, and the same is hereby abolished : And the Mayor and Aldermen of the City of Boston, for the time being, shall have all the powers, and perform all the duties, which before and until the passing of this act, were had and performed by the Court of Sessions, excepting as otherwise provided for by this act, or any other act relating to the transfer of the powers heretofore vested in said Court of Sessions. *Court of Sessions abolished.*

SEC. 12. *Be it further enacted,* That the Treasurer of the City of Boston shall be, *ex officio,* Treasurer of the County of Suffolk ; and shall keep all such books as may be proper and necessary, as Treasurer of the City of Boston and as Treasurer of the County. *Treasurer.*

SEC. 13. *Be it further enacted,* That all taxes which may be assessed for city or county purposes, within the City of Boston, may be assessed separately, as county taxes and as city taxes, or under the denomination of city taxes only, as the city government may see fit, from time to time, to order and direct. *Assessment of Taxes.*

SEC. 14. *Be it further enacted,* That the City Government of the City of Boston shall have power and authority to provide for the appointment and compensation of one or more Auditors, and of one or more clerks in the Treasury Department, as said government may find to be necessary or convenient. *Auditors.*

SEC. 15. *Be it further enacted,* That it shall be the duty of the Mayor and Aldermen of the City of Boston, to provide convenient and proper places for the holding of the courts by this act established.

SEC. 16. *Be it further enacted,* That this act shall go into operation on and after the first day of June next ; and that all acts and parts of acts, which are repugnant to the provisions of this act, be, and the same are hereby repealed.

SEC. 17. *Be it further enacted,* That this act shall be of no force or effect, unless a certain act, passed at the present session, entitled " an act establishing the City of Boston," shall be accepted by the inhabitants of the Town of Boston, pursuant to the provision therein made. And in case said act shall be so accepted, and that fact certified to His Excellency the Governor by the Selectmen of the Town of Boston, His Excellency is hereby authorized to announce the same by proclamation ; whereupon this act shall be in full force, and go into operation at the time herein before limited.

[Passed Feb. 23, 1822.]

An act in addition to an act entitled " An act to regulate the administration of Justice within the County of Suffolk, and for other purposes."

SEC. 1. *Be it enacted by the Senate and House of Representatives in General Court assembled, and by the authority of the same,* That the Clerk of the Police Court within and for the City of Boston, shall also be Clerk of the Justices' Court of the County of Suffolk. All writs, summons and processes issuing from said last mentioned court, may be tested by either of the Justices thereof, not a party thereto, and shall be signed by the clerk. And said clerk, or his assistant, shall attend all sessions of said Justices' Court, and record all proceedings therein had

And said clerk shall make out all writs and processes which the said Justices, or either of them, may order, and tax all bills of costs.   And said clerk shall receive and keep a true and faithful account of all fees taxable by law, and payable for blanks, fees of court, and copies in civil suits and actions, and render a true and just account thereof, quarter yearly, to the board of accounts; and all sums of money by him so received, shall be accounted for and paid into the City Treasury.   And it shall be the duty of said clerk to make a true and faithful record, according to law, of the proceedings in every trial and process of a civil nature, which may be had before said Justices' Court.   And said quarterly account of said clerk shall be filed and recorded by the City Treasurer, as is provided in the fifth section of the act, providing for the administration of Justice within the County of Suffolk and for other purposes, to which this act is in addition.   And said clerk shall be sworn, give bond, and receive a compensation, as is provided in the fifth section of the act aforesaid.

SEC. 2. *Be it further enacted,* That so much of the act aforesaid, as is inconsistent herewith, be, and the same hereby is repealed.

[Passed June 15, 1822.]

An act to provide a Salary for the County Attorney for the County of Suffolk.

SEC. 1. *Be it enacted by the Senate and House of Representatives in General Court assembled, and by the authority of the same,* That from and after the first day of April next, there shall be allowed and paid out of the Treasury of the County of Suffolk, annually, the sum of one thousand dollars, to the County Attorney for said county, in full compensation for his services, and in lieu of all fees and charges heretofore received by him.

SEC. 2. *Be it further enacted*, That all fees, in all indictments, informations or other prosecutions, or **Fees to be accounted for.** suits, criminal or civil, which shall, from and after the said first day of April next, be taxed or received by the County Attorney for said County of Suffolk, shall be paid over to the Treasurer of said County of Suffolk, and the County Attorney for said county shall, from and after the said first day of April, render a quarterly account to the said Treasurer, of all fees received by him, and also a further account of all fees taxable by law, for services performed by him, and which have not been received by him.

[Passed Feb. 23, 1822.]

An act in addition to an act, to provide a Salary for the County Attorney for the County of Suffolk.

SEC. 1. *Be it enacted by the Senate and House of Representatives in General Court assembled, and by the authority of the same,* That the sum of twelve **Salary.** hundred dollars, be established as the annual salary of the Attorney of the Commonwealth, within and for the County of Suffolk, to be paid out of the Treasury of said county, in quarterly payments ; and to be in full compensation for his services, and in lieu of all fees and charges heretofore received by him, and also for services for administering oaths to witnesses, as commissioner, or otherwise, inclusive.

SEC. 2. *Be it further enacted,* That said Attorney shall account to the treasurer of said county for **Fees to be accounted for.** all fees received by him ; and the amount shall be deducted from his salary ; or if they exceed the amount thereof, the balance shall be paid by him into the County Treasury ; and in the settlement of the accounts for expenses in criminal proceedings between the Commonwealth and said county, there shall no more be charged to the Commonwealth, for the services of said Attorney, than his salary as aforesaid.

[Passed Feb. 8, 1823.]

Police Ct June 5. 1830

ORDINANCES OF THE CITY.

An ordinance prescribing the penalty of the Bond
to be given by the Clerk of the Police Court, and
Justices' Court.

SEC. 1. *Be it ordained by the Mayor, Aldermen,
and Common Council of the City of Boston in City
Council assembled,* That the penalty of the bond to Penalty.
be given by the Clerk of the Police Court, and Justices' Court, shall be *five thousand dollars ;* that the
form be prescribed by the Mayor, with the approbation of the board of Aldermen ; that the City Treasurer have the custody of said bond, and be accountable therefor.

SEC. 2. *Be it further ordained,* That the bond,
which is to be taken as aforesaid, shall be in force
for one year from the date thereof, and until a new
bond shall be given, and that the bond of said Clerk Bond to be re-
shall be renewed annually, in manner as aforesaid. newed annually.

[Passed June 17, 1822.]

CHAP. XVI.

Deeds and Leases.

An ordinance authorizing the Mayor of the City of Boston to sign and execute all Deeds and Leases of Lands sold or leased by order of the City Council.

Sec. 1. *Be it ordained by the Mayor, Aldermen, and Common Council of the City of Boston, in City Council assembled,* That the Mayor of the city be, and he is hereby authorized and empowered to affix the Common Seal of the city unto, and sign, seal, execute, and deliver on behalf of the city, all deeds and leases of lands, sold or leased, and all deeds, agreements, indentures, or assurances made and entered into by order of the City Council. And that so much of a By-law of the town of Boston, passed May 22, 1801, as relates to the leasing of the town lands and buildings, be, and the same is hereby repealed.

[Passed Dec. 18, 1826.]

Nov. 18. 1833. Superseding

CHAP. XVII.

Drains and Common Sewers.

ACT OF THE LEGISLATURE.

An act for regulating Drains and Common Sewers.

SEC. 1. *Be it enacted by the Senate and House of Representatives in General Court assembled, and by the authority of the same,* That if any person shall dig or break up the ground in any highway, street, or lane in any town, for the laying, altering, repairing, or amending of any drain or common sewer, without the consent of the selectmen of the town, signified in writing under the hand of the town clerk, such person shall forfeit and pay *four dollars* for each offence, to the use of the poor of the town, to be recovered, with costs of suit, in an action of debt, by the treasurer thereof, before any disinterested Justice of the Peace in the County.

SEC 2. *Be it further enacted,* That all drains and common sewers for the draining of cellars, which shall hereafter be made or repaired in any streets or highways, shall be substantially done with brick or stone, or with such other materials as the selectmen of the town shall permit, and in such manner as the said selectmen shall direct. And when any one or more of the inhabitants of any town shall, by the consent, and under the direction aforesaid, at his or their own charge, make and lay any common sewer or main drain, for the benefit of themselves and others who may think fit to join therein, every person who shall afterwards enter his or her particular drain into the same, or by any more remote means, shall receive any benefit thereby, for the draining of their cellars or lands, shall be held to pay the owner or owners of such common sewer or main drain, a proportionable part of the charge of making or repairing the

Marginal notes:
6 Anne, ch. 2.
3 Geo. III.
Streets not to be dug up without permit.

Drains how to be made.

Persons benefitted to share in the expense of making or repairing.

same, to be ascertained and determined, by the selectmen of the town or a major part of them, and certified under their hands ; saving always to the party aggrieved at any such determination, a right of appeal to the Court of the General Sessions of the peace.

Sec. 3. *Be it further enacted*, That when any common sewer or main drain shall be stopped or gone to decay, so that it shall be necessary to open the same in order to repair it or remove such stoppage, all the persons who shall be benefited by such repairs or removal of obstructions, shall be held to pay their proportionable parts of the expenses thereof, as well those who do not, as those who do cause such repairs to be made, or obstruction removed ; to be ascertained and determined by the selectmen as aforesaid, saving an appeal as aforesaid. And each person so held to pay his or her part, shall have notice thereof, of the sum, and to whom to be paid ; and if such person shall not pay the same within ten days after such notice, to the person appointed by the selectmen to receive it, he or she shall be held to pay the person so appointed, double the sum mentioned in such certificate, with all cost arising upon such neglect ; and such person is hereby empowered to bring an action or actions for the same accordingly: *Provided, always,* that the person or persons who shall have occasion to open any common sewer or main drain in order to clear and repair the same, shall, seven days at least before they begin to open the same, notify all persons interested therein, by advertising in such manner as the selectmen may direct, that they may, (if they think proper,) object thereto, and lay their objections in person or writing before the selectmen ; and if the selectmen or the major part of them shall judge the objections reasonable,then the person or persons, making the same, shall not be held to pay any part of such expenses ; but if they do not make their objections as aforesaid to the selectmen, within three days after being so notified, or if they shall deem the objections not to be sufficient, then they shall, under their hands, give liberty to the persons applying to proceed to open such common

To share in expenses of repairs, &c.

To pay double in cases of refusal.

Proviso for a hearing of objections.

sewer or main drain, and clean and repair the same ;
and all interested therein shall pay their proportions,
as is provided in this act : *Provided, also,* that no- Further proviso.
thing in this act shall be understood or construed to
affect or make void, any covenants or agreements
already made, or that may hereafter be made among
the proprietors of such drains or common sewers.

SEC. 4. *Be it further enacted,* That this act shall
take effect and be in force on and after the first
day of July next ; and that an act passed Anno Former acts re-
Domini one thousand seven hundred and nine, for pealed, 8 Anne
regulating drains and common sewers, and another ch. 2. 3 Geo. III.
act passed Anno Domini one thousand seven hundred
and sixty three, in addition thereto, and continued in
force to the first day of November next, be repealed
on and after the first day of July, except as to the
enforcing payment of such forfeitures, as may before
that time accrue by virtue thereof.

[Passed Feb. 20, 1797.]

ORDINANCES OF THE CITY.

An ordinance relative to Drains and Common Sewers.

SEC. 1. *Be it ordained by the Mayor, Aldermen
and Common Council of the City of Boston, in City
Council assembled,* That all common sewers, which
shall hereafter be considered necessary by the Mayor Common Sewers
and Aldermen, in any street or high way, in which in streets.
there is at present no common sewer, shall be made
and laid, and forever afterward shall be kept in repair, at the expense of the city and under the direction of the Mayor and Aldermen, or of some person
or persons by them appointed.

SEC. 2. *Be it further ordained,* That every person
who shall enter his or her particular drain into such
common sewer, or shall otherwise be benefited there-

by, shall be held to pay the city such sum of money as the Mayor and Aldermen shall deem just and reasonable, having reference always to the valuation of each estate connected with said drains in the Assessors books ; and in case of any subsequent repair of such common sewer, the Mayor and Aldermen shall assess the amount of such repair on those whose particular drains connect therewith, or are otherwise benefited thereby, in such amount as they may deem just and reasonable.

Sec. 3. *Be it further ordained,* That all common sewers shall be laid as nearly as possible, in the centre of the street or high way, and shall be built of brick or stone, or such other materials and of such dimensions as the Mayor and Aldermen shall direct. And where it is practicable, it shall always be of sufficient size to be entered and cleared without disturbing the pavement above. And before the commencement of any common sewer, it shall be the duty of the Mayor and Aldermen to cause the level of the street to be taken, in order to determine the proper depth, capacity and dimensions of the common sewer proposed to be laid in such street or high way. And all those particulars together with a plan of the same, shall be recorded in a book to be kept for that purpose ; in which shall also be recorded the size and direction of the particular drains which shall from time to time be permitted to be entered into such common sewers.

Sec. 4. *Be it further ordained,* That all particular drains which shall hereafter enter into such common sewer shall be built of brick or stone or such materials as the Mayor and Aldermen shall direct ; and shall be laid under the superintendence of the Mayor and Aldermen, or of some person or persons by them appointed ; and they shall be laid in such direction, of such size, and with such descent, and (where required) with such strainers as the Mayor and Aldermen, or the person or persons appointed by them, shall require ; and shall, if practicable, be of a size sufficient to be cleared from the common sewer without disturbing the pavement above.

[margin notes:] Manner of instruction.

Size of sewers.

SEC. 5. *Be it further ordained,* That the Mayor and Aldermen shall have power in all cases where there is any common sewer in any street or highway, to cause every owner of land adjoining such street or highway, his agent or tenant, to make a sufficient drain from his house, yard, or lot, whenever in their opinion, the same shall be necessary, and shall thereupon give such owner, agent or tenant, notice in writing, specifying the time within which such drain shall be completed : *Provided, however,* in case the said owner, agent or tenant, shall neglect to complete the same within the time so specified, the Mayor and Aldermen shall cause the same to be done ; and shall recover the whole amount of the expense thereof, together with *ten per cent.* damages, by an action of the case, to be brought by the Mayor and Aldermen, in the name and behalf of the City of Boston, before any court proper to try the same :— *Provided, however,* that in no case shall ten *per cent.* claimed by way of damage, exceed the sum of *twenty dollars.*

Drains from houses to be made.

Proviso.

Additional proviso.

SEC. 6. *Be it further ordained,* That every person entering his or her particular drain into any common sewer without a permit in writing from the Mayor and Aldermen, first had and obtained, shall forfeit and pay the sum of twenty dollars ; and shall also be liable to pay all such damages by way of indemnification, to the city, or to the proprietors of the common sewer, as the Mayor and Aldermen shall deem just and reasonable.

Drains not to be entered without a permit.

SEC. 7. *Be it further ordained,* That whenever any common sewer shall go to decay, and the Mayor and Aldermen shall deem it necessary to rebuild or repair the same, they shall have power to cause the same to be done under their direction ; and to assess the amount of such rebuilding or repairs, upon the owner, agent or tenant, as is in the foregoing ordinance provided, for the case of streets in which there is no common sewer.

Persons entering may be assessed.

[Passed July 7, 1823.

14

CHAP. XVIII.

Dogs.

ACT OF THE LEGISLATURE.

An act authorizing the City of Boston, and Towns in this Commonwealth to make By-laws restraining Dogs going at large.

SEC. 1. *Be it enacted by the Senate and House of Representatives in General Court assembled and by the authority of the same,* That the City Council of the City of Boston, and the inhabitants of any town in this Commonwealth, at any legal meeting thereof, be, and they are hereby authorized and empowered, to make any such by-laws and regulations concerning the licensing, regulating, and restraining of dogs going at large, as they may deem proper and expedient ; with power to affix any penalty for the breach thereof, not exceeding ten dollars ; to be recovered by complaint before the Police Court of the City of Boston, or any Justice of the Peace in the county where such town shall be situated ; and to be paid into the city or town treasury for the use of said city, or such town, as shall pass any such by-law.

Power to make by-laws, &c.

Penalty.

SEC. 2. *Be it further enacted,* That no person shall be obliged to pay more than two dollars annually, for a license for his or her dog to go at large, subject to any by-law as aforesaid, and no by-law of said city, shall extend to any dog owned or kept in any town, and no by-law of any town shall extend to any dog owned or kept in any city or other town ; and all money received for licenses as aforesaid, shall be paid into the Treasury of the city or town where such license is given, for the use of such city, or town, any laws of this Commonwealth to the contrary of this act notwithstading.

[Passed Feb. 26, 1825.]

An ordinance restraining the going at large of Dogs within the City of Boston.

SEC. 1. *Be it ordained by the Mayor, Aldermen and Common Council of the City of Boston, in City Council assembled,* That from and after the thirty-first day of January next, no dog shall be allowed to go at large or loose, in any street, lane, alley, or court, nor in any uninclosed or public place in this city, until the owner or keeper of such dog, or the head of the family or the keeper of the house where such dog is kept or harboured, shall have paid to the City Clerk, two dollars for a license for such dog to go at large, nor unless he shall also cause a collar to be constantly worn by such dog, having the christian and surname of the owner thereof, legibly written, stamped, or engraved thereon. And it shall be the duty of said clerk, to grant a license to any citizen for his or her dog to run at large upon payment of such sum, and he shall keep a record of the names of all persons to whom such licenses shall be by him granted.

No dog to go at large without license and a collar.

SEC. 2. *Be it further ordained,* That the licenses which have been or shall be issued as aforesaid, shall endure and be in force until the first day of February, next after the time of issuing the same and no longer ; but they may and shall be at that time renewed, and thereafter annually, on payment to the City Clerk, the like sum of two dollars, for each renewal ; and in case any dog shall be found loose, or going at large as aforesaid, contrary to the provisions of this ordinance, the owner or keeper thereof, or the head of the family, or keeper of the house where such dog is kept or harboured, shall forfeit and pay a sum not exceeding ten dollars.

Licenses how long to endure.

SEC. 3. *Be it further ordained,* That on complaint being made to the Mayor, of any dog within this city which shall, by barking, biting, howling, or in any other way or manner disturb the quiet of any person or persons whomsoever, the Mayor on such

Dogs disturbing the quiet of the city to be sent out of it.

complaint shall issue notice thereof to the person keeping, or permitting such dog to be kept, or to the owner thereof; and in case such person or owner shall, for the space of three days after such notice, neglect to cause such dog to be removed and kept beyond the limits of the city, or to be destroyed, he shall forfeit and pay a sum not exceeding one dollar for every day which shall elapse until such dog be removed or destroyed as aforesaid : *Provided*, that the Justice before whom such complaint shall be heard and tried, shall be satisfied that such dog had in manner aforesaid disturbed the quiet of any person or persons in the said city.

City Marshal to destroy dogs.

SEC. 4. *Be it further ordained*, That if any person, after being convicted under the provision of the third section of this ordinance, shall still neglect or refuse to destroy his dog, on being ordered so to do, or if any dog of which no owner or keeper shall be discovered, or whose owner or keeper shall refuse or neglect to take out a license for him, shall be found going at large contrary to the provisions of this ordinance, it shall be the duty of the City Marshal to cause such dog or dogs to be destroyed.

Dogs owned out of the city.

SEC. 5. *Be it further ordained*, That nothing in this ordinance contained shall be applied to any dog owned and usually kept out of the city ; excepting however, it shall be the duty of the City Marshal at all times hereafter to cause every dog to be destroyed wheresoever owned or kept going at large within the city not having a collar upon his neck according to the provisions of a law of this Commonwealth, passed February 27, 1813, and laws to which that is in addition.

Former order repealed.

SEC. 6. *Be it further ordained*, That the order entitled " an order respecting the going at large of dogs," passed the seventh day of July in the year of our Lord one thousand eight hundred and twenty three, be, and the same is hereby repealed.

[Passed Dec. 26, 1825.]

CHAP. XIX.

Enacting Style.

An ordinance relative to the acts of the City Council, and the Enacting Style.

Be it ordained by the Mayor, Aldermen and Common Council, of the City of Boston, in City Council assembled, That hereinafter all acts of the City Council, shall be denominated *Ordinances,* and that the enacting style shall be, " Be it ordained by the Mayor, Aldermen, and Common Council of the City of Boston, in City Council assembled," and that an order respecting City Ordinances passed September 1, 1823, be, and the same is hereby repealed.

[Passed Dec. 12, 1825.]

CHAP. XX.

Election.

An ordinance relative to the election of certain City
Officers.

*Be it ordained by the Mayor, Aldermen,
and Common Council of the City of Boston, in City
Council assembled,* That the mode of electing the
following officers to wit : Fence Viewers, Surveyors
of the High Ways,* Surveyors of Lumber, Cullers
of Hoops and Staves, Hogreeves, Haywards and
Field Drivers, Pound Keepers, Inspectors of Lime,
Surveyors of Hemp, Surveyors of Wheat, Assay
Masters, and Cullers of Fish, shall be as follows to
wit : they shall first be elected by the Mayor and Aldermen, and sent down to the Common Council for
its concurrence, rejection or amendment.

[Passed May 9, 1822.]

* Mayor and Aldermen may be Surveyors of High Ways, statute 1822,
Chap. 2, post. See also City Charter, Sec. 3, 8, 16.

CHAP. XXI.

Engine and Enginemen.

ACTS OF THE LEGISLATURE.

An Act empowering the Selectmen of such town where there may be Fire Engines, to appoint Enginemen ; and repealing the laws heretofore made for that purpose.

WHEREAS it is of importance that provision should be made to render the use of Engines, for extinguishing fires, as beneficial as possible :

SEC. 1. *Be it enacted by the Senate and House of Representatives, in General Court assembled, and by the authority of the same*, That the Selectmen of such towns in this Commonwealth, as are or may be provided with a fire engine or engines, be, and they are hereby empowered, if they judge it expedient; as soon as may be after the passing of this act, to nominate and appoint a number of suitable persons, (not exceeding fifteen* to one engine,) for enginemen ; who shall continue in said office, during the pleasure of such selectmen ; which enginemen shall be, and they are hereby authorized and empowered to meet together some time in the month of May annually, at which meeting they shall have authority to choose a master or director, and clerk of said engine ; and establish such rules and regulations, respecting their duty as enginemen, as shall be approved of by the selectmen, and to annex penalties to the same ; which may be recovered by the clerk of said enginemen, before any Justice of the Peace in the same County : *Provided*, no penalty shall exceed forty shillings, and

Selectmen of towns provided with engines are empowered to appoint enginemen.

Proviso

* Twenty-one, 1806, ch. 82, post.

that such rules and regulations, shall not be repugnant to the laws of this Commonwealth.

SEC. 2. *Be it further enacted*, That the respective companies of enginemen, who may be nominated and appointed in pursuance of this act, shall be held and obliged to meet together once a month, and oftener if necessary, for the purpose of examining the state of the engine to which they belong, and the appendages belonging to the same, and seeing that the said engine is in good repair, and ready to proceed on any emergency, to the relief of any part of the community that may be invaded by the calamity of fire ; and the said enginemen appointed as aforesaid shall be held and obliged to go forward, either by night or by day, under the direction of the Firewards in the same town, and to use their best endeavors to extinguish any fire that may happen in the same town or the vicinity thereof, and shall come to their knowledge without delay.

AND WHEREAS, in some towns there may be an engine or engines the property of individuals, who would incline the same might be employed for the benefit of the said town, subject to the like regulations and privileges, as though the said engine or engines appertained to the said town.

SEC. 3. *Be it further enacted*, That whenever the proprietor or proprietors of any engine or engines, shall apply to the selectmen of any town in which the said engine or engines may be, setting forth that they have such engine or engines, which they are desirous should be employed for the benefit of the said town, the selectmen of such town, upon application as aforesaid, may appoint enginemen in the same manner, with the same privileges, and subject to the same regulations, as though the said engine or engines were the property of the said town.

SEC. 4. *Be it further enacted*, That the persons who may be appointed enginemen in pursuance of this act, shall be, and they are hereby exempted from common and ordinary Military duty, and from serv-

Marginal notes:

Enginemen to meet together once a month.

Enginemen may be appointed for engines belonging to individuals

Exempted from military duty, &c

ing as Jurors, or in the office of constable, during the time they may be employed in the service aforesaid.

SEC. 5. *Be it further enacted*, That if any person, being appointed in manner herein before directed, shall, in the opinion of the said selectmen, be negligent and remiss in the duties required of him, as an engine-man, by this act, it shall be the duty of the selectmen in the same town, upon sufficient evidence thereof, to discharge him from said company, and proceed to appoint another engine-man in his room, in the manner herein before directed.

Persons negligent or remiss in duty to be discharged.

SEC. 6. *Be it further enacted*, That all the acts heretofore made, providing for the appointment of engine-men, be, and they are hereby repealed.

[Passed Feb. 7, 1786.]

An act more effectually to secure Fire Engines from being injured.

WHEREAS it has sometimes happened, that some people from a wanton, and others from a malicious disposition, have injured the public fireengines, provided for the extinguishment of fires, which may unfortunately happen in the habitations and other buildings of the inhabitants ; for prevention whereof in future,

Preamble.

Be it enacted by the Senate and House of Representatives in General Court assembled, and by the authority of the same, That if any person shall wantonly or maliciously spoil, break, injure, damage, or render useless, any engine, or any of the apparatus thereto belonging, prepared by any town, society, person or persons, for the extinguishment of fire, and shall be convicted thereof before the Supreme Judicial Court, he shall be punished by a fine not exceeding five hundred dollars, or by imprisonment not exceeding two years, at the discretion of the court, and be further ordered to recognize with

Penalty for damaging an engine.

15

sufficient surety or sureties, for his good behaviour, for such term as the court shall order.

[Passed Feb. 8, 1802.]

An act in addition to an act entitled "An act empowering the Selectmen of such towns where there may be Fire Engines, to appoint Engine-men, and repealing the laws heretofore made for that purpose.

SEC. 1. *Be it enacted by the Senate and House of Representatives in General Court assembled and by the authority of the same,* That the Selectmen of the several towns in this Commonwealth, be and they hereby are respectively authorized and empowered, if they shall judge it expedient, to nominate and appoint, from time to time, from and after the passing of this act, any number, not exceeding six men to each engine, in addition to the number of fifteen men, now authorized by the act to which this is an addition, amounting to twenty one men for each engine.

Selectmen authorized to increase the number of Engine-men.

SEC. 2. *Be it further enacted,* That the Selectmen of the several towns in this Commonwealth be, and they hereby are, respectively authorized and empowered, if they shall judge it expedient, to nominate and appoint from time to time, from and after the passing of this act, any number not exceeding four men to each engine, in addition to the said number of twenty one men : *Provided, however,* that such addition be made with the consent of the commanding officers of the respective military companies from which such additional number may be taken : *And provided, also,* that no military company be thereby reduced under the number prescribed by law ; and all engine-men appointed in pursuance of this act, shall continue in office during the pleasure of the Selectmen of the several towns, whereto they may

A further increase allowed in case.

belong, and shall enjoy all the privileges and exemptions to which other engine-men are or may hereafter be by law entitled.

SEC. 3. *Be it further enacted*, That the said Selectmen may, in their discretion select from the engine-men aforesaid, any number for each engine, in their respective towns, whose duty it shall be, under the direction of the fire wards, to attend fires therein, with axes, fire hooks, fire sails and ladders, and who shall do such further duty as the said Selectmen shall from time to time prescribe, and shall be entitled to all the exemptions and privileges aforesaid

Select engine men, and their duty.

[Passed March 8, 1806.]

An act to empower the several towns in this Commonwealth to excuse such of their Inhabitants, as are engine-men, from serving as Jurors in any Court within this Commonwealth.

Be it enacted by the Senate and House of Representatives in General Court assembled, and by the authority of the same, That all persons legally attached to any engine within this Commonwealth, be and they hereby are excused from being chosen or drawn to serve as Jurors in any court within this Commonwealth, in all cases where the town, to which such engine-men belong, shall at a legal meeting of its inhabitants, by vote, declare the expediency of excusing such persons from serving as Jurors.

[Passed Nov. 17, 1808.]

An act to authorize the Mayor and Aldermen of the City of Boston, to increase the number of Engine-men, in certain cases.

Be it enacted by the Senate and House of Representatives, in General Court assembled, and by the authority of the same, That whenever the firewards of the City of Boston, shall represent in writing to the Mayor and Aldermen of said city that an increase of the number of men, now by law authorized to be appointed to any particular engine within said city, may be required, in consequence of suction hose, or any increased power of such engine, or the additional apparatus thereto, for the more speedy and effectual extinguishment of fire, within said city, it shall be lawful for the said Mayor and Aldermen to nominate and appoint such additional number of men not exceeding ten in any one case, to the number now by law authorized to be appointed; who shall be held to perform all the duties, and enjoy the privileges and exemptions, other engine-men are entitled to by the several laws now in force.

[Passed Jan. 30 1823.]

CHAP. XXII.

Fires.

ACTS OF THE LEGISLATURE.

An act to secure the town of Boston from damage by fire. See title "Buildings," Chap. VIll, in which this act is inserted.

An act for the Extinguishment of Fire, and to direct the proceedings thereat.

Sec. 1. *Be it enacted by the Senate and House of Representatives in General Court assembled, and by the authority of the same,* That each town in this Commonwealth, in their March or April meeting annually, wherein the qualified voters shall think it expedient to choose firewards, shall hereafter have power to elect such number of suitable persons to be firewards therein, as shall be deemed necessary; and each person so elected shall be notified thereof within three days, and shall within three days after being so notified, enter his acceptance or refusal of the said office with the town Clerk. And if any person being so elected and notified, shall neglect to enter his acceptance or refusal as aforesaid, he shall forfeit and pay *ten dollars*, unless excused by the town; and the town shall have power to elect another in his place, in case of such neglect or refusal. And when any fire shall break out in any town, wherein firewards shall be appointed, they shall immediately attend thereat, and carry with them a suitable staff or badge of their office

Sec. 2. *Be it further enacted*, That when any fire shall break out in any town, the firewards thereof,

10 Anne ch. 2.
26 Geo. 2. ch. 2.

Firewards to be chosen in town meetings.

See chap. VIII. the act to secure the town &c. against fire—ante. p. 43.

Penalty for not serving.

who shall be present at the place in immediate
danger, or any three of them ; and where no firewards shall be appointed, a major part of the Selectmen present ; or in their absence, two or three of the
civil officers present ; or in their absence, two or three
of the chief military officers of said town present,
shall have power to direct the pulling down or demolishing any such house or building as they shal
judge necessary to be pulled down or demolished in
order to prevent the further spreading of the fire ;
and during the continuance of any fire, the said firewards or officers, as the case may be, shall have
power to require assistance for extinguishing the
same, and for removing any furniture, goods or
merchandize from any building on fire or in any danger thereof, and to appoint guards to secure the same ;
and also assistance for pulling down or demolishing
any house or building, as the case may require ; and
further to suppress all tumults and disorders. And
the said firewards, selectmen or officers, as the case
may be, shall have authority to direct and appoint
the stations, and operations of the engine-men, and
their engines, and of all other persons, for the purpose of extinguishing the fire and preventing its increase ; and if any person shall refuse or neglect to
obey any order given by said firewards or officers in
the premises, the person so offending shall forfeit and
pay for each offence ten dollars.

SEC. 3. *Be it further enacted*, That if the pulling
down or demolishing of any house or building, by
the directions aforesaid, shall be the means of stop-
ing the said fire ; or if the fire stop before it come to
the same, then every owner of such house or building shall receive a reasonable compensation and be
paid for the same by the inhabitants of the town in
which the fire shall happen : And it shall be the
duty of the qualified voters in such town, to grant
such sum or sums of money as shall be thought necessary and proper by the Selectmen of the same
town ; and of the assessors to assess the same : *Provided always*, that when it shall be adjudged fit that
the house or building where the fire shall first begin
and break out, should be pulled down or demolished,

Marginal notes:

Power of fire-
wards to order
the pulling down
of buildings.

To require assis-
tance.

To direct engine-
men.

Penalty for not
obeying fire
wards.

Persons whose
houses are pulled
down to be de-
molished by the
town.

to prevent the further spreading and increase of the same fire, then the owner of such house or building shall receive no compensation for the same : *Provided also*, that if any person shall find him or herself aggrieved by the doings of the town, Selectmen or Assessors thereof, in estimating, voting or assessing such sum or sums, he or she shall have a right to appeal and complain to the next court of General Sessions of the peace to be holden in the county ; and the said court thereon shall have power, on a consideration of all the circumstances of the case, to confirm said doings of said town, selectmen or assessors, or to alter the same in such manner as the said court shall · judge proper ; and in either case to award legal costs, as the justice of the case may require ; and the collectors, to whom the said assessments shall be committed to collect, shall have the same powers, and be subject to the same duties, as in the collection of other town taxes, as well in collecting an assessment so confirmed or altered, as in cases wherein there shall be no appeal.

Except it be a a house where fire begins.

Estimate of damage to be revised by court of sessions.

Stat. 1785. c. 70.

SEC. 4. *Be it further enacted*, That if any person shall, in such case of fire, plunder, purloin, embezzle, convey away or conceal any furniture, goods, or chattles, rights or credits, merchandize or effects, of the inhabitants whose houses or buildings shall be on fire, or endangered thereby, and said inhabitants shall be put upon removing the same, and shall not restore or give notice thereof to the owner (if known) or to one of the firewards of the town, or bring them into such public place as shall be assigned by the selectmen of the town within two days after public notice shall be posted in some public place in the town by the Selectmen thereof for that purpose ; the person or persons so offending and being thereof convicted, shall be deemed guilty of larceny, and punished accordingly.

Sequestering property at fires to be larceny. Stat. 1804. c. 143.

SEC. 5. *Be it further enacted*, That if any person shall occupy or improve any tenement or building whatever, in any part of any maritime town in this Commonwealth, for the business or employment of a sailmaker, or rigger, or keeper of a livery stable,*

Penalty for erecting riging lofts or livery stables.

*See stables, post.

except only in such parts of the town as the Selectmen* thereof, or a major part of them, shall direct
and determine, such sailmaker or rigger, so offending, shall forfeit and pay for each offence, *ten dollars*:
and such keeper of a livery stable shall forfeit and
pay for each offence *fifty dollars* for every month so
occupying the same, and so in proportion for a longer
or shorter time.

Except at select-men direct.

SEC. 6. *Be it further enacted*, That the several
fines and forfeitures aforesaid, shall be two third
parts thereof to the use of the poor of the town,
where the offence shall be committed, and the other
third part thereof to him or them who shall inform
and sue for the same, and shall be recoverable with
costs of suit, in any court proper to try the same.

Appropriation of fines.

[Passed March 10, 1797.]

An act authorizing the appointment of Firemen in the town of Boston.

SEC. 1. *Be it enacted by the Senate and House of
Representatives, in General Court assembled and by
the authority of the same*, That the Selectmen† of the
town of Boston, for the time being, be, and they are
hereby authorized and empowered, if they judge it
expedient, as soon as may be after the passing of this
act, to nominate and appoint a number of suitable
persons, not exceeding thirty, who shall continue in
office during the pleasure of the selectmen of said
town, whose duty it shall be, under the direction of
the firewards of said town, to attend fires therein, and
the vicinity, with axes, ladders, fire-hooks, and such
implements and apparatus for the extinguishment of
fires, and the preservation of persons and property,

Number limited.

*The 7th section of this act relates to the setting fire to woods, and is not
applicable to this city, and the other and last section repeals the several pro
vincial statutes, enacted before the revolution, and are not here inserted.

† Mayor and Aldermen. See City Charter, p. 11.

as may be provided for that purpose, and placed under their care ; and to perform such further duty, as such selectmen shall from time to time prescribe.

SEC. 2. *Be it further enacted*, That the fire-men so appointed shall and may be organized into one or more distinct companies, under the direction of such selectmen. And each of said companies is hereby authorized to meet together some time in the month of May annually ; at which meeting they shall have authority to choose a master or director, and clerk of such company, and establish such rules and regulations respecting their duty as fire-men, as may be approved by such selectmen, and to annex penalties for the violation of the same, which may be recovered by the clerk of such company, before any Justice of the Peace* of the County of Suffolk : *Provided*, that no such penalty shall exceed the sum of six dollars and sixty seven cents, and that such rules and regulations shall not be repugnant to the laws of this Commonwealth.

Organization of Companies.

SEC. 3. *Be it further enacted*, That the respective companies of fire-men, who may be nominated and appointed in pursuance of this act, shall be held and obliged to meet together, once a month, and oftener if necessary, for the purpose of inspecting and examining the fire-hooks, ladders and other implements and apparatus which may be placed under their care, management and superintendence, and the appendages belonging to the same, and seeing that the same are in good repair, and ready to proceed on any emergency to the relief of any part of the community which may be invaded by the calamity of fire. And the firemen appointed as aforesaid, shall be held and obliged to go forward, under the direction of the firewards of said town, and to use their best endeavours to extinguish and prevent the spreading of any fire, which may happen in said town, or in the vicinity thereof, and which shall come to their knowledge, without delay ; and also to use their best exertions for the preservation of all persons and property which may be exposed to danger thereby.

Monthly meetings.

* See Police Court.

16

SEC. 4. *Be it further enacted*, That the persons who may be appointed firemen in pursuance of this, act, shall be, and they are hereby exempted from common and ordinary military duty, and from serving as Jurors, or in the office of constable, during the time they may be employed in the service aforesaid.

Exemption.

SEC. 5. *Be it further enacted*, That if any one who may be appointed pursuant to the provisions of this act, shall, in the opinion of such selectmen, be negligent or remiss in the duties required of him, as a fireman, by this act, or by any rules and regulations which may be prescribed and made in pursuance thereof, it shall be the duty of such selectmen, upon sufficient evidence thereof, to discharge him from such company, and from his office and duty as a fireman ; and thereupon to proceed and appoint another person in his room, in the manner herein before directed.

Discharge for neglect of duty.

[Passed Feb. 7, 1820.]

An Act to prevent damage from firing Crackers, Squibs, Serpents, and Rockets.

SEC. 1. *Be it enacted by the Senate and House of Representatives, in General Court assembled, and by the authority of the same*, That from and after the first day of July next, if any person shall have in his possession any cracker, squib, serpent or rocket, within this Commonwealth, with intent to sell, or with intent to set fire to the same, or if any person shall offer for sale, sell or give any cracker, squib, serpent, or rocket, or if any person shall set fire to any cracker, squib, serpent, or rocket, or shall throw any lighted cracker, squib, serpent, or rocket, within the same, without the license of the Mayor and Aldermen of the City of Boston, or of the Selectmen of the several towns in this Commonwealth respectively, first obtained therefor, he shall forfeit for every such offence the sum of five dollars, one moiety to the use of the poor of the city, or town in which the offence shall be committed, and the other moiety to the use of the prosecutor, to be recovered by action of debt, or by information, before the Justices of the Police Court of the City of Boston, or before any Justice of the Peace of the county, in which the offence may be committed, with costs of suit.

How recovered.

SEC. 2. *Be it further enacted*, That an act passed the fourth day of March, one thousand eight hundred and six, entitled, " An act to prevent damage from firing crackers, squibs, serpents and rockets, within this Commonwealth," be and the same is hereby repealed, from and after the time when this act shall take effect.

Repeal.

[Passed June 20, 1826.]

ORDINANCES OF THE CITY.

An ordinance forbidding the firing of Guns, prohibiting Fire-Works in certain cases, and to prevent damages by fire.

SEC. 1. *Be it ordained by the Mayor, Aldermen and Common Council of the City of Boston, in City Council assembled*, That no person shall fire or discharge any gun, fowling piece, or fire arms within the limits of the city, which shall be loaded with balls or shot, or with powder only, under a penalty for every such offence, of a sum not less than *one dollar* nor more than *twenty dollars : Provided, however,* that the provisions of this section shall not extend to the firing of any gun or other fire arm, in the lawful defence of the person, family, or property of any citizen ; nor to the firing of any such gun or fire arm at any military exercise or reviews.

Act to secure the town, &c. against fire, Sect. 9, 10 11, 12, 13.

See streets, post p.

SEC. 2. *Be it further ordained*, That no person or persons shall discharge or set off, any squibs, ser-

See streets, post p.

pents, rockets, or other fire works, or make any bon-fire, or other fire, in any of the streets, squares, commons, lanes, or alleys, or upon or from any house or other building, or on any wharf, within the city, without leave first had and obtained therefor from the Mayor and Aldermen, under a penalty for every such offence, of a sum not less than *one dollar*, nor more than *twenty dollars*.

SEC. 3. *Be it further ordained*, That no person henceforth, shall erect make or fire, or cause to be erected, made or fired, within any part of this city, (excepting that part thereof called South Boston,) any brick kiln or lime kiln, or any furnace for the melting of Iron, or other metals, unless it be in such places as the Mayor and Aldermen, shall by their license, in writing allow and approve of for such purpose, under penalty of a sum not less than *one dollar*, nor more than *twenty dollars*, and a like sum for every week he shall continue such kiln or furnace after notice to remove the same.

[Passed Dec. 18, 1826.]

CHAP. XXIII.

Fire Department.

ACT OF THE LEGISLATURE.

An act establishing a Fire Department in the City of Boston.

S**EC**. 1. *Be it enacted by the Senate and House of Representatives, in General Court assembled, and by the authority of the same,* That the Fire Department of the City of Boston, shall hereafter consist of one Chief Engineer, and as many other Engineers, Fire Wardens, Firemen, Hosemen, and Hook and Ladder men, as shall or may, from time to time, be elected and appointed by the Mayor and Aldermen, such election of the chief and other Engineers to be concurred in by the Common Council of said city. Officers and members.

SEC. 2. *Be it further enacted,* That the Mayor and Aldermen of said city be, and hereby are, authorized so to elect and appoint all, or as many of the said officers, to cause certificates to be issued of such election and appointment, and to fix a compensation for the services of the Chief Engineer, annually ; said compensation to be concurred in by the Common Council. Authority to elect and appoint.

SEC. 3. *Be it further enacted,* That it shall be the duty of the City Council of said city, to fix and ordain, from time to time, the powers and duties of those officers respectively, in relation to fire Engines, and all other fire apparatus belonging to, or used in the said city, and also to the care and management thereof, and to the conduct of said officers, and of the citizens present at fires, and to annex penalties for the breach of any rules, or regulations they may so fix and ordain, not exceeding twenty dollars. Duty of City Council.

SEC. 4. *Be it further enacted,* That the Chief Engineer, Engineers, and Fire Wardens, so elected and appointed, shall have the same powers and authorities relative to the pulling down or demolishing any house or other building to prevent the spreading of fires, and also relative to all other matters and things affecting the extinguishment or prevention of fires or the commanding assistance at them, as Fire Wardens now by law have, subject always to such modification as the City Council, or the Legislature of this Commonwealth may ordain and establish. And the said City of Boston shall be liable to pay all such reasonable compensation for damage done by, or consequent upon, the acts or directions of said Chief Engineer, Engineers, and Fire Wardens, as other towns in this Commonwealth are liable to pay in like cases, for like acts and directions, done or given by their Fire Wardens; and all fines and forfeitures arising within the said City of Boston, under the laws of this Commonwealth, relative to the extinguishment of, or proceeding at fires, shall be distributed in such way and manner, and applied to such use as the said City Council shall from time to time ordain and determine, any thing in said laws to the contrary notwithstanding, subject always to repeal or alteration by the Legislature of this Commonwealth.

SEC. 5. *Be it further enacted*, That every member of said Fire Department shall be exempt from
militia services so long as he shall continue to serve in said department; and it shall be the duty of the person so exempted, to produce to the commanding officer of the militia company within whose bounds he may reside, on or before the first Tuesday of May, in each year, a certificate signed by the Mayor of the city, stating that he is a member of said Fire Department.

SEC. 6. *Be it further enacted*, That from and
after the organization of a Fire Department under this Act, and notice thereof given in one or more newspapers published in said city, by the Mayor thereof, all laws of this Commonwealth relating to the election and appointment of Fire Wards, so far as they affect the election or appointment of Fire Wards within the said city, be and the same are hereby repealed.

SEC. 7. *Be it further enacted*, That the provisions of this Act shall not take effect until the same shall have been accepted by the ballots of the citizens of Boston, at a general meeting called for that purpose.

[Passed June 18 1825.]

This Act was accepted by ballot, at a general meeting of the citizens, held at Faneuil Hall, July 7th, 1825, according to the provisions of the same.

Attest,   S. F. M'CLEARY, *City Clerk.*

ORDINANCE OF THE CITY.

An ordinance for the preventing and extinguishing of Fires, and establishing a Fire Department.

SEC. 1. *Be it ordained by the Mayor, Aldermen and Common Council of the City of Boston, in City Council assembled,* That the Fire Department of the city shall consist of one Chief Engineer, twenty other Engineers, one of whom shall reside in each Ward, and as many Fire men, Engine men, Hose men, and Hook and Ladder men, to be divided into companies, as the number of engines and the number and quantity of the other fire apparatus belonging to the city, shall, from time to time, require or make expedient ; and the election and appointment of the said Engineers shall take place according to law, in the month of January annually : *Provided,* that vacancies may be filled in any month.

SEC. 2. *Be it further ordained,* That the Chief Engineer shall, in all cases of fire, have the sole and absolute control and command over all the engineers and all other persons of the Fire Department. And it shall be the duty of the said Chief Engineer to direct the other engineers to take proper measures that the several engines be arranged in the most advantageous situations and be duly worked for the effectual extinguishment of fires. And it shall, more-

Chief Engineer's duties.

over, be the duty of the said Chief Engineer to examine once at least, in every month, and within five
days at least, after every fire, into the condition and
number of the engines, buckets attached thereto, and
other fire apparatus, and engine houses belonging to
the city, and report the same at least once a year to
the Mayor and Aldermen, and as much oftener as
they may direct, together with the names of all the
members of the Fire Department, and the respective companies to which they belong ; which shall be
published in the month of March, in every year, by
the City Clerk, in the manner the Mayor and Aldermen shall direct.   And whenever any of the said
engines, and fire apparatus, shall require to be repaired, the Chief Engineer, under the direction of
a committee of the board of Aldermen, on the Fire
Department, shall cause the same to be well and
sufficiently done.—And it shall, moreover, be the
duty of the Chief Engineer, to report in writing, all
accidents by fire that may happen in this city, with
the causes thereof, as well as they can be ascertained, and the number and description of the buildings
destroyed or injured, together with the names of the
owners or occupants, to the City Clerk, who shall
keep a faithful register of the same ; and in the case
of the absence of the Chief Engineer, the engineer
next in rank, who may be present, shall execute his
office, with full powers ; and the respective rank of
the other engineers shall be determined by the Mayor
and Aldermen.

SEC. 3. *Be it further ordained,* That in each ward
of the city, the Mayor and Aldermen shall be authorized to form a company of firemen, each of whom,
upon his appointment by the Mayor and Aldermen,
shall receive a printed certificate or warrant in the
words following, viz :

Firemen.

This certifies that A. B. is a member of the Company of Firemen in Ward No.   appointed by the
Mayor and Aldermen of the City of Boston, and is
entitled to all the immunities belonging to the said
office.   Given under my hand, this   day of
A. D. 18

E. F. *City Clerk.*   C. D. *Mayor.*

And each of said companies shall choose a Foreman, Assistant or Assistants, and Clerk, at such times and may make such rules and regulations for the internal government of the said company, as they may deem expedient. And it shall be the duty of the members of the said companies, whenever a fire shall break out in the city, by night or by day, to repair forthwith to, or near the place where the fire may be, and in conformity with the directions of the chief or other engineer, to exert themselves with all their skill and power in supplying water for the engines, in protecting the engine-men and other persons of the Fire Department from being interrupted in the performance of their duty by the bystanders, in saving and protecting furniture, merchandize and other property, and in performing any other duties or services that they may be called upon to do, by any engineer: *Provided*, that in the absence of all the engineers, such directions may be given by the respective foremen. And each of the members of said companies shall be furnished [at the expense of the city] with a pair of Leather Fire Buckets, which it shall be his duty on all occasions to carry to any place where fire shall break out and the same to secure and carry home again on his return, or as soon afterwards as may be. And once in every three months, the foreman or assistant of each company shall examine the said buckets, to see that they are kept in good order, and the clerk shall make report, in writing to the Chief Engineer, within ten days after each quarterly examination, of the names of all the members of the said company, and of the state and condition of their buckets, and at the expiration of the term of service of any member of said companies, the said buckets shall be returned to the Mayor and Aldermen, unless lost or destroyed by unavoidable accident.

Sec. 4. *Be it further ordained*, That there shall be as many companies of Engine men, and each company shall consist of as many members, as the Mayor and Aldermen, from time to time, shall think expedient, each of whom, upon his appointment by the Mayor and Aldermen, shall receive a certificate

Officers to be chosen.

Duties.

Chief Engineer to report.

Enginemen.

17

or warrant similar to that provided for firemen, and each of said companies shall choose a Foreman, Assistant and Clerk, at such times, and may make such rules and regulations for the internal government of said company as they may deem expedient; and it shall be the duty of the members of said companies, whenever a fire shall break out in the city, by night or by day, to repair forthwith to their respective engines, and to convey them to or near the place where the fire may be, and in conformity with the directions of the chief or other engineer, to exert themselves with all their skill and power in working and managing the said engines, and the same shall return to their respective places of deposit, upon permission of the chief or other engineer: *Provided*, That in the absence of all the engineers, such directions and such permission may be given by their respective foremen; and on return of the said engines, they shall, by the said companies respectively, be well washed and cleansed, and securely housed; and once in every month the said company shall meet. and oftener, if necessary, for the purpose of examining the state of their respective engines, and seeing that the same are in good order, and fit for service, and once in each of the months of May, June, July, August, September, October, and November, shall draw out their respective engines, to wash and cleanse them, and to exercise the members, and the same engines carefully shall return.

Sec. 5. *Be it further ordained*, That there shall be as many companies of Hose men, and each company shall consist of as many members, as the Mayor and Aldermen, from time to time, shall think expedient, each of whom, upon his appointment by the Mayor and Aldermen, shall receive a certificate or warrant similar to that provided for firemen; and each of said companies shall choose a Foreman, Assistant and Clerk, at such times, and may make such rules and regulations for the internal government of said company as they may deem expedient; and it shall be the duty of the members of said companies, whenever a fire shall break out in the city, by night or by day, to repair forthwith to their respective hose

[Margin notes:]
Officers to be chosen.

Duties.

Monthly examination.

Hose companies.

Officers to be chosen.

wagóns, and to convey them, with their hose, to or near the place where the fire may be, and in conformity with the directions of the chief or other engineer, to exert themselves with all their skill and power in working and managing the said hose in obtaining and conveying water, and the same shall return to their respective places of deposit upon permission of the chief or other engineer : *Provided*, That in the absence of all the engineers, such directions, and such permission may be given by their respective foremen, and on return of the said hose, they shall, by the said companies respectively, be well washed, cleansed, and securely housed ; and once in every month the said companies shall meet, and oftener, if necessary, for the purpose of examining the state of their respective hose and wagons, and seeing that the same are well oiled, in good order, and fit for service.

Duties.

SEC. 6. *Be it further ordained,* That there shall be as many companies of Hook and Ladder men, and each company shall consist of as many members, as the Mayor and Aldermen from time to time, shall think expedient, each of whom, upon his appointment by the Mayor and Aldermen, shall receive a certificate or warrant similar to that provided for firemen ; and each of said companies shall choose a Foreman, Assistant and Clerk at such times, and may make such rules and regulations for the internal government of said company, as they may deem expedient ; and it shall be the duty of the members of said companies, whenever a fire shall break out in the city, by night or by day, to repair forthwith to their respective hooks and ladders, and to convey them to or near the place where the fire may be, and in conformity with the directions of the chief or other engineer, to exert themselves with all their skill and power in working and managing the said hooks and ladders, and the same shall return to their respective places of deposit upon permission of the chief or other engineer : *Provided,* That in the absence of all the engineers, such directions and such permission may be given by their respective foremen ; and on return of the said hooks and ladders, they shall

Hook and Ladder companies.

Officers to be chosen.

Duties.

be, by their respective companies, securely housed; and once in every month the said companies shall meet, and oftener, if necessary, for the purpose of examining their respective Hooks and Ladders and seeing that the same are in good order and fit for service.

SEC. 7. *Be it further ordained,* That it shall be the duty of the Marshal and Constables of the city, under the general direction of the Mayor, to repair with their staves of office, on the alarm of fire, immediately to the place where such fire may be, and then and there to report themselves to the Mayor, or in his absence, to the Marshal or head Constable, and to conform to such orders as may be given to them respectively, for the preservation of the public peace, and the prevention of theft and dilapidation of property, and the removal of all suspected persons, for which service the Constables shall receive such compensation only as shall be in each case ordered by the Mayor and Aldermen.

SEC. 8. *Be it further ordained,* That the engineers, and members of the several companies shall wear such caps, badges, or insignia, as the Mayor and Aldermen may direct, to be furnished at the expense of the city.

SEC. 9. *Be it further ordained,* That the names and places of abode of the Mayor, Engineers, Firemen, Enginemen, Hose and Hook and Ladder men, of the respective companies shall annually, as soon as may be, after the organization of the fire department, be printed and set up in the several watch and engine houses of the city, by the City Marshal.— And immediately on the alarm of fire, it shall be the duty of the respective watchmen to give notice to the Mayor, Engineers, Firemen, and other members of the said department, within their respective districts; and it shall be the duty of every watchman, upon the breaking out of any fire, to alarm the citizens by crying "*fire*", and mentioning the street where it may be, so that the firemen and citizens may thereby be generally directed where to repair, and if any watchman shall neglect so to do, he shall forfeit and pay one dollar; and if it shall happen that a chim-

Marshal and Constables to repair to fires.

Engineers 'and Members to wear insignia.

Names and abodes of Members, to be printed.

Duty of Watchmen.

ney only shall be on fire, either by day or night, the Bells not to be rung for chimneys only. bells shall not be rung, but only on occasions when a building shall be proclaimed to be on fire.

SEC. 10. *Be it further ordained,* That if any chimney, stove pipe, or flue, within the city, shall take fire, the occupant of the house, to which such Penalty for fire in chimney &c. chimney, stove pipe or flue appertains, shall forfeit and pay the sum of two dollars : *Provided,* that it shall be lawful for any person to set fire to and burn When lawful to set chimney on fire. his chimney, stove pipe, or flue, between sunrising and noon, provided, the buildings contiguous are wet with rain or covered with snow. And it shall be the Chief Engineer to report. duty of the Chief Engineer to report to the Mayor and Aldermen, the name of every person liable to the penalty in this section, provided : and also the name of every member of either of the several companies neglecting or refusing to comply with the duties by this ordinance enjoined.

SEC. 11. *Be it further ordained,* That at the end Annual compensation to companies. of each year, from the organization of the several companies of Engine men, Hose men, and Hook and Ladder men, there shall be paid from the City Treasury, in lieu of all premiums or other compensation, on warrant of the Mayor and Aldermen, to the foremen of the respective companies for the encouragement of the said companies, as follows :—to the largest engine company, the sum of seventy-five dollars, and to each of the other engine companies a sum in proportion to the number of members attached by the Mayor and Aldermen to said company, compared with the largest company, and a proportionate sum to each of the Hose companies, and to each of the Hook and Ladder companies.

SEC. 12. *Be it further ordained,* That whenever it shall be necessary at any fire to pull down or other- Buildings to be pulled down. wise demolish any building, the same shall be done only by the joint orders of the chief and one other engineer ; or, in case of the absence of the Chief Engineer, by the joint orders of three other engineers of whom the next in rank to the chief, who may be present, shall be one.

SEC. 13. *Be it further ordained,* That the power Powers and duties of Engineer. and duty of making and establishing rules and regulations for the transportation and keeping of gunpowder, within the City of Boston, and of granting licenses for the keeping and sale thereof in the city, according to the provisions of an act entitled, " An act further regulating the storage, safe keeping, and transportation of gunpowder in the town of Boston," and of any other act or acts on the same subject matter, shall be exercised and performed by the chief and other engineers ; and the power and duty of seizing any gunpowder kept, or being within the said city or the harbour thereof, contrary to the provisions of the said act or acts, shall be exercised and performed by the said engineers or any of them ; and in case of any seizure being made by any engineer, other than the Chief Engineer, he shall forthwith report the same to the Chief Engineer, who shall cause the said gunpowder to be libelled and prosecuted in the manner prescribed in the said first mentioned statute ; and all the other powers and duties granted or enjoined in and oy the said acts or statutes, shall be performed by the said chief or one of the other engineers.

Powers and duties of fire wards transferred to engineers. SEC 14. *Be it further ordained*, That the powers and duties given to the Fire Wards of the town of Boston in and by virtue of an act entitled, " An act to secure the town of Boston from damage by fire," or in and by virtue of any other act, shall be henceforth exercised and performed by the chief and other engineers, by this ordinance established ; and that it shall be the duty of the Chief Engineer to make all inquiries, returns, complaints, notices, permissions, and to do all other acts required by the statutes of this Commonwealth from Fire Wards of the town or city of Boston. And it shall be the duty of the chief and other engineers to inquire for, and examine into, all shops and other places where shavings or other such combustible materials may be collected and deposited, and from time to time, and at all times, to be vigilant in taking care for the removal of the same whenever in the opinion of any two of them, the same may be dangerous to the security of the city from fires, and to direct the tenant or occupant of said shops or other places to remove the same, or

Shavings to be removed.

pay the expense of such removal, under the directions of said engineers.

SEC. 15. *Be it further ordained*, That if any member of either of the several companies shall, at any fire, wilfully neglect or refuse to perform his duty, he shall, for each such default, forfeit and pay a fine of three dollars ; and all persons, not members of either of the said companies, are hereby enjoined to obey the directions of any engineer, given at any fire, and to render their services, if required by said engineer, under a penalty of not less than two, nor more than twenty dollars, for each offence.

Penalty on members neglecting or refusing duty.

SEC. 16. *Be it further ordained*, That all moneys received for licenses to keep and sell gunpowder, for fines, forfeitures and penalties, arising under this ordinance and the laws of the Commonwealth, regulating the storage and the transportation of gunpowder, the erection of buildings within the town of Boston, and the prevention and extinguishment of fire, shall be paid into the treasury of the city, to constitute a fund for the benefit of the members of the fire department, the income of which shall be applied in such way and manner as the City Council shall hereafter determine.

Penalties and forfeitures to constitute a fund.

SEC. 17. *Be it further ordained*, That the Mayor and Aldermen shall proceed to organize a fire department under this ordinance, as soon as circumstances will permit ; and that, whenever such organization shall be effected, it shall be the duty of the Mayor to issue notice thereof, conformably to the provisions of the sixth section of an act of the Legislature of this Commonwealth, entitled, " An act establishing a Fire Department in the City of Boston." And that the City Council may, by a concurrent vote, at any time, remove the Chief Engineer, or any of the other engineers, and that the Mayor and Aldermen may, at any time, remove any member of either of the said companies.

Organization of Fire Department.

[Passed Dec. 5, 1825.]

An act in addition to an act, entitled " An act establishing a Fire Department, in the City of Boston.

Certificates to be annually produced to officers of the militia.

SEC. 1. *Be it enacted by the Senate and House of Representatives in General Court assembled, and by the authority of the same*, That every member of the fire department of the City of Boston, established by the act to which this is in addition, shall be holden to produce, within thirty days after he shall have become a member of said department, and annually, in the month of May thereafter, to the Commanding Officer of the Militia Company, within whose bounds he may reside, a certificate from the Mayor of said city, stating that he is a member of said fire department.

Engineers to have same power as firewards relative to gunpowder.

SEC. 2. *Be it further enacted*, That the Chief Engineer and Engineers of said city, shall have the same powers and authorities heretofore granted to and invested in the firewards of the town of Boston, by the act, entitled " An act regulating the storage, safe keeping, and transportation of Gunpowder, in the town of Boston," or by any other act heretofore enacted on that subject.

[Passed March 2, 1827.]

act passed Mar 3, 1829 —
Ordinance passed July 15. 1833 —

CHAP. XXIV.

Gunpowder.

ACTS OF THE LEGISLATURE.

An act in addition to the several acts already made for the prudent storage of Gun powder within the town of Boston.

WHEREAS the depositing of loaded arms in the houses of the town of Boston, is dangerous to the lives of those who are disposed to exert themselves when a fire happens to break out in said town. Preamble

SEC. 1. *Be it enacted by the Senate and House of Representatives in General Court assembled, and by the authority of the same,* That if any person shall take into any dwelling house, stable, barn, out house, ware house, store, shop or other building within the town of Boston, any cannon, swivel, mortar, howitzer, cohorn, or fire arm, loaded with or having gunpowder in the same, or shall receive into any dwelling house, stable, barn, out house, store, ware house, shop, or other building within said town, any bomb, grenade, or other iron shell, charged with, or having gun powder in the same, such person shall forfeit and pay the sum of *ten pounds,* to be recovered at the suit of the Firewards of the said town, in an action of debt before any court proper to try the same; one moiety thereof, to the use of said Firewards, and the other moiety to the support of the poor of said town of Boston. Taking loaded arms into houses prohibited. Penalty

SEC. 2. *Be it further enacted,* That all cannons, swivels, mortars, howitzers, cohorns, fire arms, bombs, grenades and iron shells of any kind, that shall be found in any dwelling house, out house, stable, barn, store, ware house, shop or other building, charged with or having in them any gunpowder, shall be Loaded arms in houses to be seized.

liable to be seized by either of the Firewards of the said town ; and upon complaint made by the said Fire-wards to the Court of Common Pleas, of such cannon, swivels, mortars, or howitzers, being so found, the Court shall proceed to try the merits of such complaint by a jury; and if the jury shall find such complaint supported, such cannon, swivel, mortar; or howitzer, shall be adjudged forfeit, and sold at public auction ; and one half of the proceeds thereof shall be disposed of to the Firewards, and the other half to the use of the poor of the town of Boston.   And when any fire arms, or any bomb, grenade or other shell, shall be found in any house, out-house, barn, stable, store, ware-house, shop or other building, so charged, or having gun powder in the same, the same shall be liable to be seized in manner aforesaid ; and on complaint thereof, made and supported before a Justice of the Peace, shall be sold and disposed of, as is above provided for cannon.

How disposed of in cases of forfeiture.

Sec. 3. *Be it further enacted*, That appeals shall be allowed in prosecutions upon this act, as is usual in other cases.

Appeals allowed

[Passed March 1, 1783.]

[An act in addition to the several acts now in force, which respect the carting and transporting Gunpowder through the streets of the town of Boston, and the storage thereof in the same town.] (Repealed by the provisions of the act of 3d February, 1821, see post and 5 vol. special laws, 401.

An act to provide for the storing and safe keeping of Gunpowder in the town of Boston, and to prevent damage from the same. Passed June 19, 1801. Repealed by the provisions of the act of 3d February, 1821, see post (and 5 vol. special laws 401.

An act in addition to the several acts now in force, which respect the transporting, storing and safe keeping of Gunpowder in the town of Boston. Passed March 7th, 1804— and repealed by the provisions of the act of 3d February 1821, see post and 5 vol special laws, 401.

An act in further addition to " an act in addition to acts regulating the storage, safe keeping and transportation of Gunpowder within the town of Boston.

SEC. 1. *Be it enacted by the Senate and House of Representatives in General Court assembled and by the authority of the same*, That from and after the first day of April next, no commissary, or any other officer or officers, or any person or persons, in the service of the United States, or acting in the department of Commissary or Quarter Master General of this Commonwealth, shall be permited to have, keep, or possess within the town of Boston, a greater quantity of Gunpowder than four hundred pounds ; and that the powder so had and possessed within the said town, shall be kept in a place approved of by the Firewards of the said town, either under ground in a vault, or in a stone or brick building secured against explosion by fire.

Powder where kept.

SEC. 2. *Be it further enacted*, That any Gun Powder which shall be found in the possession of, or which may be had or kept within the town of Boston, by any officer or officers, or any person or persons whatsoever, acting in the behalf or under the authority of the United States, or by any agent or servant of any such officer or persons ; and all Gunpowder possessed, had or kept, by any officer of the Commissary or Quarter Master General's Department of the State of Massachusetts, or persons acting under the authority of these departments, contrary to the provisions of this act, may be seized by any two or more of the Firewards of the town of Boston, and the same may be libelled and condemned and sold, and the proceeds thereof distributed as is by law provided for the forfeiture of Gunpowder in other cases within said town.

See Fire Department, ante.p 345.

[Passed Feb. 22, 1814.]

NOTE.—This act is to be found in 4 vol. Special Laws, 584—at the conclusion of which is quoted a statute of 1816, ch 26 ; but no such statute is to be found among the statutes of that year published. either in the Special Laws, or the late edition of the General Laws of the Commonwealth. It is however, inserted among the printed By-laws of the town of Boston p. 184—but as all the provisions of it appear to be re-enacted in the late and last law upon this subject, (which immediately follows,) it has not been inserted.

An act further regulating the storage, safe keeping and transportation of Gunpowder in the town of Boston.

SEC. 1. *Be it enacted by the Senate and House of Representatives in General Court assembled, and by the authority of the same,* That no person, except on military duty in the public service of the United States, or of this Commonwealth, shall keep, have or possess, in any house, warehouse, shop or other building, nor in any street, lane, alley, passage way, yard or cellar, nor in any wagon, cart or other carraige, nor on any wharf, nor on board of any ship or other vessel, within two hundred yards of any wharf, or of any part of the shore or the main land, nor in any place within the town of Boston, gunpowder in any quantity exceeding five pounds, in any way or manner, other than by this act, and by the rules and regulations hereinafter mentioned, may be permited and allowed. And all gunpowder, had, kept or possessed, contrary to the provisions of this act, and of such rules and regulations, shall be forfeited, **Liability to seizure.** and liable to be seized and proceeded against in the manner hereinafter provided.

SEC. 2. *Be it further enacted,* That it shall not be lawful for any person or persons to sell any gunpowder, which may at the time be within the Town of Boston, in any quantity, by wholesale or retail, without first having obtained from the Firewards of said town, a license to sell gunpowder ; and every such license shall be written or printed, and duly signed by said Firewards, or by their Secretary, authorized for that purpose, on a paper, upon which shall be written or printed, a copy of the rules and regulations by them established relative to keeping, selling, and transporting gunpowder within the said town ; and every such license shall be in force for one year from the date thereof, unless annulled by the Firewards, and no longer ; but such license may, prior to the expiration of that term, be renewed by endorsement thereon by the said Firewards, or by their Secretary, for a further term of one year, and so from year to year : *Provided, always,* that the said Firewards may annul and rescind any such license,if,in their opinion, the person or persons licensed, have forfeited the right of using the same,by disobeying the law, or infringing any rules or regulations established by said Firewards. And every person who shall receive a license to sell gunpowder as aforesaid, shall pay for the same the sum of five dollars ; and every person, on having a license renewed, shall pay therefor the sum of one dollar, which sum shall be paid to the Secretary of the Firewards, for their use, for the purpose of defraying the expenses of carrying this act into execution. Fees for licenses.

SEC. 3. *Be it further enacted,* That the Firewards of the town of Boston be, and they are hereby authorized and empowered to make and establish rules and regulations, from time to time, relative to the times and places at which gunpowder may be brought to, or carried from said town, by land or by water, the times when, and manner in which the same may be transported through said town ; to direct and regulate the kind of carriages, boats and other vehicles in which the same may be so brought to, carried from and transported through said town ; to direct the manner in which gunpowder may be kept by licensed dealers and other persons ; and to direct and require all such precautions as may appear to them needful and salutary, to guard against danger in the keeping of gunpowder, and in the transportation thereof to, from and through the town of Boston. Manner of keeping powder.

SEC. 4. *Be it further enacted,* That any person or persons who shall keep, have, or possess any gunpowder within the Town of Boston, contrary to the provisions of this act, and to the rules and regulations made as aforesaid, or who shall sell any gunpowder therein, without having a license therefor then in force, or contrary to the conditions of the said license, or the rules and regulations made as aforesaid, shall forfeit and pay a fine of not less than one hundred dollars, and not exceeding five hundred dollars, for each and every offence ; and if any gunpowder, kept contrary to the provisions of this act, Penalties.

shall explode in any shop, store, dwelling house, ware house, or other building, or in any place in said town, the occupant, tenant or owner of which has not then a license in force to keep and sell gunpowder therein, or which gunpowder shall have been kept in any manner contrary to the terms and conditions of such license, or to the rules and regulations established as aforesaid, such occupant, tenant or owner, shall forfeit and pay a fine of not less than five hundred dollars, and not exceeding one thousand dollars ; one moiety of the sums which may be so forfeited shall accrue to the use of the poor of the town of Boston, and the other moiety to the use of any person or persons who shall prosecute and sue for the same ; which forfeitures may be recovered by action of the case, in any court proper to try the same.

SEC. 5. *Be it further enacted,* That all gunpowder, which shall be kept, had or possessed, within the town of Boston, or brought into, or transported through the same, contrary to the provisions of this act, and to the rules and regulations made as aforesaid, may

Seizures

be seized and taken into custody, by any one or more of the Firewards of said town, and the same shall, within twenty days next after the seizure thereof, be libelled, by filing in the office of the Clerk of the Municipal Court of the town of Boston, a libel, stating the time, place and cause of such seizure ; a copy of which libel, or the substance thereof, together with a summons or notice, which such Clerk is hereby authorized to issue, shall be served on the person or persons, from whose custody or possession, or in whose tenement such gunpowder shall have been seized, if such person be an inhabitant of this Commonwealth, by delivering a copy thereof to such per-

Trial of offences

son or persons, or leaving such copy at his, her, or their usual place of abode, fourteen days at least, before the sitting of the court, at which the same is to be heard ; that such person or persons may appear and shew cause why the gunpowder so seized and taken should not be adjudged forfeit. And if the gunpowder so seized shall be adjudged forfeit, the person or persons, in whose custody or possession the same was seized, or the occupant or tenant of the place wherein the same was so seized, shall pay all costs of prosecution, and execution shall be issued therefor ; *Provided*, it appear to the court, that such Proviso. person or persons had notice of such prosecution by service as aforesaid ; and in case the person or persons in whose custody or possession, or in whose tenement such gunpowder may be seized, shall be unknown to the Fireward or Firewards making such seizure, or in case such gunpowder, at the time of seizure, may not be in the custody or possession of any person, or if it shall appear by the return of the officer, that such person cannot be found, or has no place of abode in this Commonwealth, then the said court shall, and may proceed to adjudication thereon. And such libel or summons, and also such writ of execution for costs, shall, and may be served and executed in any county in this Commonwealth, and by any officer competent to execute civil process in like cases.

Sec. 6. *Be it further enacted*, That any person or persons, who shall rescue or attempt to rescue any gunpowder seized as aforesaid, or who shall aid or assist therein, or who shall counsel or advise, or procure the same to be done, or who shall molest, hinder, or Fines. obstruct any Fireward in such seizure, or in carrying gunpowder so seized to a place of safety, shall forfeit and pay a fine, for each offence, of not less than one hundred dollars, and not exceeding five hundred dollars ; to be sued for, and recovered by action of the case, by any person or persons who shall sue for the same, in any court proper to try the same ; and it is hereby made the duty of all magistrates, civil officers, and of all good citizens of said town, in their respective stations, and as far as they may be required, to aid and assist such Fireward or Firewards in executing the duties hereby required.

Sec. 7. *Be it further enacted*, That the said Firewards, or any of them, may enter the store or place of any person or persons, licensed to sell gunpowder, to examine and ascertain whether the laws, rules and regulations relating thereto, are strictly observed, and also whenever there shall be an alarm of fire ; and in such last case may cause the powder there deposited to be removed to a place of safety, or to be destroyed by wetting or otherwise, as the exigency of the case may require; and it shall be lawful for any one or more of the Firewards of said town, to enter any dwelling house, store, building, or other place, in the town of Boston, to search for gunpowder, which they may have reason to suspect to be concealed, or unlawfully kept therein, first having obtained from some Justice of the Peace for the County of Suffolk, a search warrant therefor, which warrant the Justices of the Peace for said county are hereby respectively authorized to issue upon the complaint of such Fireward 'or Firewards, supported by his or their oath.

SEC. 8. *Be it further enacted,* That any person who shall suffer injury by the explosion of any gunpowder, had, kept or transported, within the town of Boston, contrary to the provisions of this act, and of the rules and regulations established as aforesaid, may have an action of the case in any court proper to try the same, against the owner or owners of such gunpowder, or against any other person or persons who may have had the possession or custody of such gunpowder, at the time of the explosion thereof, to recover reasonable damages for the injury thus sustained.

SEC. 9. *Be it further enacted,* That it shall be the duty of the Firewards of the town of Boston, to cause all such rules and regulations, as they may make and establish by virtue of the authority given by this act, to be published in two or more newspapers printed in the town of Boston, and to cause such publication to be continued three weeks successively, for the information and government of all persons concerned.

SEC. 10. *Be it further enacted,* That all fines, penalties and forfeitures which may arise and accrue under the provisions of this act, shall, and may be prosecuted for, and recovered, either in the manner herein before specially provided, or by indictment, complaint or information, in any court proper to try the same. And this act shall be taken and deemed to be a public act, of which, all courts, magistrates and citizens are bound to take notice as such; and in any libel, action, indictment, information or complaint upon this act, it shall not be necessary to set forth any more of the same, than so much thereof as relates to, and may be necessary truly and substantially to describe the offence alleged to have been committed.

SEC. 11. *Be it further enacted*, That all fines, penalties and forfeitures which shall be recovered by force of this act, and which are not otherwise appropriated, shall accrue and enure, one half to the poor of the town of Boston, to be paid over to the Overseers Distribution of fines. of the Poor thereof, and one half to the Firewards of said town : *Provided, however*, that whenever on the trial of any prosecution, under this act, any one or more of the said Firewards shall be sworn and examined as a witness or as witnesses therein, record shall be made in court ; and in that case, the whole of such fine, penalty and forfeiture, shall accrue and enure to the poor of the town of Boston, and be paid over as aforesaid.

SEC. 12. *Be it further enacted*, That this act shall take effect and be in force from and after the passing thereof, and that all acts and parts of acts heretofore passed, which come within the purview of this act, and which are inconsistent with, or repugnant to the provisions of this act, be, and the same Repeal of former law. are hereby repealed : *Provided, however*, that the same shall continue in force for the purpose of pros- Proviso. ecuting all offences which may have been committed prior to the passing of this act, in the same manner, to all intents and purposes, as if the same had not been repealed : *And provided, further*, that all rules Proviso. and regulations made and established by the Firewards of Boston, under and by virtue of the provisions of such.former acts, shall continue to have the same force and effect, until altered or annulled by said Firewards,* as if this act had not been passed.

[Passed Feb. 9, 1821.]

*The power of Firewards relative to the transportation of gunpowder transferred to the engineers of the city.

act passed Mar. 25, 1833

CHAP. XXV.

Hay.

An act to regulate Hay Scales.

SEC. 1. *Be it enacted by the Senate and House of Representatives in General Court assembled and by the authority of the same,* That the Selectmen for the time being, of every town, or the City Council of any city, in this Commonwealth, be, and they are hereby authorized from time to time, as they may think expedient, to appoint for a term not exceeding one year, one or more person or persons, to have the superintendence of the Hay Scales, belonging to such town or city, whose duty it shall be to weigh hay offered for sale in such town or city, and any other article offered to be weighed ; and the person or persons so appointed shall conform to all such rules and regulations as shall from time to time be made and established by the selectmen or City Council, concerning the said Hay Scales, and the use of the same, and the compensation or fees for weighing hay and other articles ; and the said selectmen or City Council, for the time being, are hereby authorized to remove any weigher, and to fill any vacancy that may occur from death or otherwise, and if any person not authorized as aforesaid shall set up any Hay Scales, in any town or city, for the purpose of weighing hay, or other articles, he shall forfeit and pay for such offence, the sum of twenty dollars a month, so long as the same shall be continued, to be recovered by an action of debt in any court proper to try the same, to be appropriated to the use of said town or city : *Provided, however,* that this act shall apply to such towns only, as may adopt the same at their annual meeting, in March or April, and shall cease to operate in such towns, whenever, at any meeting, the said town shall so determine : *And provided, also,* that the same

Authorized to remove, &c.

Penalty.

Proviso.

Proviso.

shall apply to such cities only as may adopt the same, and shall cease to operate in such city, whenever the city government shall so direct.

[Passed Feb. 24, 1825.]

In the Board of Aldermen, Dec. 1, 1825. *Resolved*, That the City Council of the City of Boston do hereby adopt an act, entitled " An act to regulate Hay Scales," passed the twenty-fourth day of February, in the year of our Lord, eighteen hundred and twenty-five.

Read and passed. Sent down for concurrence.

JOSIAH QUINCY, *Mayor.*

In Common Council, Dec. 5, 1825. Read and concurred.

FRANCIS J. OLIVER, *President.*

ORDINANCE OF THE CITY.

An ordinance for regulating the Weighing of Hay, and for assigning the stands for the sale of that article.

SEC. 1. *Be it ordained by the Mayor, Aldermen, and Common Council of the City of Boston, in City Council assembled,* That hereafter there shall be two public scales, established under the authority of the city, for the weighing of Hay, Straw, and Merchandize ; one at the south end of Charles-street, and the other on the land denominated the Market, adjoining Merrimack and Canal-streets ; and it shall be the duty of the Mayor and Aldermen to cause the same to be erected and provided, and furnished with decimal weights, which only shall be used in all cases, on and after the first day of January next. Two Scales,

SEC. 2. *Be it further ordained,* That hereafter there shall be two stands for the sale of hay and straw within the city, and no more ; one on that side of Charles-street on which the scales shall be placed, Two Stands.

extending from the said scales towards Beacon-street, the other on Canal or Merrimack-street.

SEC. 3. *Be it further ordained,* That the owner or driver of any wagon, cart, sled, or other carriage containing hay or straw for sale, who shall before or after the weighing thereof, stand for sale of such hay or straw in any other street, or place than one of those above specified, or who shall sell and *proceed to deliver* such hay or straw within the city without having had the same previously weighed and certified according to the provisions of this ordinance, shall forfeit and pay for the use of the city the sum of five dollars, to be recovered by complaint before the Justices of the Police Court.

SEC. 4. *Be it further ordained,* That the City Council shall annually in the month of January appoint by concurrent vote two suitable and discreet persons to be weighers of hay, straw, and merchandize within the city, who shall hold the said offices during the pleasure of the City Council, and until other persons shall be appointed in their places respectively; and they shall be entitled to receive one cent and a half for every hundred pounds of hay, straw, or merchandize weighed by them; the cart or vehicle containing the same and other tare, to be weighed without any charge; and no fees shall be taken for any weighing done on account of the city.

SEC. 5. *Be it further ordained,* That it shall be the duty of the person, so appointed, to attend personally at the scales, which may be assigned to them respectively, every day through the year, Sundays, public fasts, thanksgivings, and the anniversary of American Independence excepted, from sunrise to sunset, (with liberty to close their respective offices from seven to eight o'clock in the forenoon during the months of April, May, June, July, August, and September, and from eight to nine o'clock during the other six months, and from one to two o'clock through the whole year,) to deliver to the driver of every load of hay or straw weighed, a certificate in such form as is herein after provided; to keep an account of all hay or straw and other articles which shall be weighed at said scales, in books to be fur-

Hay &c. to be weighed before sale.

Weighers to be annually appointed.

Days and hours of attendance.

Accounts.

nished by the Mayor and Aldermen, which shall be always open to their inspection, and when filled, shall be deposited in their office ; and the persons so appointed shall settle their accounts quarterly with the Mayor and Aldermen, and after paying over to the city, fifteen per cent of the amount of all fees received for weighing, shall divide the residue with each other ; and each of said persons, after his appointment and before entering upon the duties of his said office, shall be duly sworn to the faithful discharge of the same before the Mayor, or City Clerk.

Weighers to be sworn.

SEC. 6. *Be it further ordained,* That the accounts kept by said weighers, and the certificates given to the drivers of hay or straw, shall specify the name of the owner or driver, the town from which driven, the weight and tare, the amount of fees received, and the date of the certificate.

Manner of keeping accounts.

SEC. 7. *Be it further ordained,* That it shall be the duty of the Mayor and Aldermen to furnish each of the persons so appointed with duplicate copies of all laws in force relating to the weighing of hay, straw, or merchandize, and of all ordinances of the city of Boston relative thereto ; one of which copies shall be posted up in some conspicuous place in the office of each of said weighers, and to give public notice in one or more of the newspapers printed in this city, of the persons appointed annually ; and if either of the persons so appointed shall be guilty of any negligence, fraud, or other misbehaviour, the said City Council on any proof thereof, shall remove the person so offending, and appoint another in his place.

Laws &c. to be furnished.

SEC. 8. *Be it further ordained,* That all by-laws and ordinances, or parts of by-laws and ordinances, relative to the weighing of hay, straw, or merchandize, heretofore passed, be and the same are hereby repealed.

Repealed

[Passed Dec. 5, 1825.]

ordinance passed July 15. 1833 superseding

CHAP. XXVI.

Health.

ACTS OF THE LEGISLATURE.

Extracts from the " Act establishing the City of Boston."

Sec. 17. *Be it further enacted,* That all the power and authority, now by law vested in the Board of Health for the town of Boston relative to the quarantine of vessels, and relative to every other subject whatsoever, shall be, and the same is hereby transfered to, and vested in the City Council, to be carried into execution by the appointment of Health Commissioners, or in such other manner as the health, cleanliness, comfort and order of the said city, may in their judgment require ; subject to such alterations as the legislature may from time to time adopt.

Vested in City Council.

Sec. 28. *Be it further enacted,* That so much of the act heretofore passed relative to the establishment of a Board of Health for the town of Boston as provides for the choice of members of the said board ; also, all such acts, and parts of acts, as come within the purview of this act, and which are inconsistent with, or repugnant to the provisions of this act, shall be, and the same are hereby repealed.

Repeal. See an te. P. 14.

Extract from the " act to establish the Boston and Roxbury Mill Corporation."

Sec. 5. *Be it further enacted,* That the Board of Health of the town of Boston, be, and hereby is authorized and empowered to cause the flats on the

Transferred to the City Council 1821, sect. 17.

Westerly side of Boston within said empty bason (between the dam and Boston neck,) or any portion thereof, to be kept constantly covered with water, if in the opinion of said board, it shall be necessary to the health of the inhabitants of said town ; and for that purpose to cause a dam of a suitable height, at their discretion, to be placed and kept at the sluice gate or gates in the principal dam of said empty bason, in order to retain the water therein, at the sole expense of said Corporation.

[Passed June 14, 1814.]

An act to prevent the spreading of Contagious Sickness.

SEC. 1. *Be it enacted by the Senate and House of Representatives in General Court assembled, and by the authority of the same,* That for the better preventing the spreading of infection, when it shall happen that any person or persons coming from abroad, or belonging to any town or place within this State, shall be visited, or shall lately before have been visited with the plague, small pox, pestilential or malignant fever, or other contagious sickness, the infection whereof may probably be communicated to others, the selectmen of the town where such person or persons may arrive, or be, are hereby empowered to take care and make effectual provision, in the best way they can, for the preservation of the inhabitants by removing such sick or infected person or persons, and placing him or them in a seperate house or houses, and by providing nurses, attendance, and other assistance and necessaries for them ; which nurse, attendance, and other assistance and necessaries, shall be at the charge of the parties themselves, their parents or masters (if able) or otherwise at the charge of the town or place whereto they belong ; and in case such person or persons are not inhabi-

Selectmen to remove and accommodate persons sick with contagious distempers.

tants of any town or place within this State, then at the charge of the Commonwealth.

SEC. 2. *Be it further enacted*, That any person or persons coming from any place out of this State, where the small pox or other malignant distemper is prevailing, into any town within this State, shall, when thereto required by the selectmen of such town, within the space of two hours from the time they shall be first informed of their duty by law in this particular, give notice to one or more of the selectmen, or the clerk of such town, of their coming there, and of the place from whence they came, upon pain of forfeiting, in case of neglect, the sum of *one hundred dollars*. And such person or persons, if not disabled by sickness, shall, within the space of two hours after warning given to him or them by the selectmen of such town for that purpose, depart from this State, in such manner and by such road, as the said selectmen shall direct ; and in case of refusal, it shall be lawful for any Justice of the Peace in the county where such town may lie, by warrant directed to a constable or other proper officer, or other person whom the Justice shall judge proper, to cause such person or persons to be removed into the State from whence he or they may come ; and any person removed by warrant as aforesaid, who, during the prevalence of such distemper, shall presume to return into any town of this State, without liberty first obtained from such Justice, shall forfeit and pay the sum of *four hundred dollars* :— And any inhabitant of this State, who shall entertain in his house any person warned to depart as aforesaid, for the space of two hours after notice given him of such warning, by one or more of the selectmen aforesaid, shall forfeit and pay the sum of *two hundred dollars*.

Persons arriving from places infected to inform selectmen.

Such persons shall depart, if so directed by the selectmen.

Penalty for returning without previous permission.

Penalty for retaining persons warned to depart

SEC. 3. Provides that selectmen may appoint persons to attend at ferries, to examine suspected persons.

SEC. 4. *Be it further enacted*, That if need be, any two Justices of the Peace may make out a warrant directed to the sheriff of the county, or his deputy, or constables of the town, or place where any such sick person or persons may be, requiring

Sheriffs, &c may be required to remove infected persons or take up houses, &c.

them or any of them, in the name of the Commonwealth, with the advice and direction of the selectmen of the same, to remove such infected person or
persons, or to impress and take up convenient houses,
lodging, nurses, attendance and other necessaries,
for the accomodation, safety and relief of the sick.
And such sheriff, his deputy and constable, are hereby authorized and required to execute such warrant
accordingly.

SEC. 5. *Be it further enacted*, That whenever there shall be brought into any town within this
State, either from any other town therein, or from
parts without the State, any baggage, clothing or
goods of any kind whatsoever, and it shall be made
to appear by the selectmen of the town to which such
baggage, clothing, or other goods shall be brought,
or by the major part of such selectmen, to the satisfaction of any Justice of the Peace, that there is
just cause to suspect such baggage, clothing, or other
goods, to be infected with the plague, small pox, pestilential fever, or other malignant contagious distemper, it shall be lawful for such Justice of the Peace,
and he is hereby required, in such case, by warrant
under his hand and seal, directed to the sheriff or
his deputy, or any constable of the town in which
such baggage, clothing, or other goods shall be, requiring him to impress so many men as said Justice
shall judge necessary to secure such baggage, clothing or other goods, and said men to post as a guard
and watch over the house or other place or places
where such baggage, clothing, or other goods shall
be lodged; which guard and watch are hereby required to take effectual care to prevent such baggage,
clothing or other goods, being removed or intermed-
dled with, by any persons whatsoever, until due inquiry be made into the circumstances thereof; requiring likewise the said sheriff, his deputy, or the
constable aforesaid, if it shall appear necessary, with
the advice and direction of said selectmen, to impress and take up convenient houses or stores, for
the receiving, lodging and safe keeping of such baggage, clothing, or other goods, until the same shall
be sufficiently cleansed from infection: And in case

20

Marginal notes:
Baggage goods, &c. to be secured if infected.

To be guarded.

If necessary, to be stored till free from infection.

it shall appear highly probable to the said Justice, that such baggage, clothing, or other goods, are infected as aforesaid, he is hereby empowered and directed to issue his warrant in manner as aforesaid, requiring said sheriff, his deputy, or any constable, or other person therein specially named, to remove said

Or may be removed at a distance.

baggage, clothing, or other goods, to some convenient place, where there shall be the least danger of the infection spreading; there to remain, until the same shall be sufficiently aired and freed from in-

Ware houses &c. may be broken in search of infected baggage, &c.

fection in the opinion of said selectmen : And the said sheriff, deputy sheriff, or constable, in the execution of said warrants, are empowered and directed, if need be, to break up any house, ware-house, shop or other place, particularly mentioned in said warrant, where such baggage, clothing, or other goods shall be ; and in case of opposition, to require such aid as shall be necessary to effect the execution of said warrants, and repel such opposition ; and all persons

Citizens are to afford assistance, if called upon.

are hereby required, at the commandment of either of the said officers, having either of the warrants aforesaid, under penalty of *ten dollars*, to be recovered before any Justice of the Peace in the county where such opposition may happen, to assist such officer in the execution of the same warrant, against any opposition as aforesaid ; and the charges of se-

Expenses of removal, &c. to be defrayed by the owners.

curing such baggage, clothing, or other goods, and of airing and transporting the same, shall be borne and paid by the owners thereof, at such rates and prices as shall be set and appointed by the selectmen of the town, where such baggage, clothing or other goods shall be, to be recovered by action of debt, by any person or persons who may have been employed in the business aforesaid, in any Court of Record proper to try the same.

Inquiry to be made of vessels passing the Castle.

SEC. 6. *Be it further enacted,* That inquiry shall be made by the officer or other person on duty at the Castle in the harbour of Boston, of every vessel coming from sea, and passing by the said Castle, whether any infectious sickness be on board, or has been on board, since such vessel left the port from whence she last came ; and if any such vessel has any sickness on board, or has had any on board, since her leaving such port, in such case, orders shall be given by said officer, or other person on duty, to the master or commander of such vessel, immediately to anchor, and to remain at anchor until a certificate shall be obtained from the major part of the selectmen of the town of Boston, that they are of opinion such vessel may come up to the town without danger to the inhabitants, or until the said master or commander shall receive orders from the said selectmen to anchor his vessel near the Hospital on Rainsford Island, in the harbour of Boston. And in case any master or commander of a vessel shall, by himself, or the people on board, make false answer, when inquired of as aforesaid, by the officer or other person on duty as aforesaid, or after orders are given as aforesaid, shall neglect or refuse to anchor near the Castle as aforesaid, or come on shore, or suffer any passenger or other person belonging to the vessel to come on shore, or any goods to be taken out before the vessel shall have anchored, or without liberty from the selectmen as aforesaid ; or in case any master or commander of a vessel ordered to anchor near the hospital aforesaid, shall neglect or refuse so to do ; in every such case, every master or commander so offending, shall forfeit and pay for each offence the sum of *four hundred dollars*, or suffer six months imprisonment.

Vessels to be detained, if conceived infectious.

Castle island ceded to the U. States, 1798—ch. 13, and powers of selectmen transferred to the Board of Health.

Penalty for falsely answering at the Castle

SEC. 7. *Be it further enacted*, That upon application made to the selectmen of the town of Boston, by any master or commander of any vessel at anchor near the Hospital as aforesaid, the said selectmen are hereby empowered to permit such passengers, goods, or lading, as they shall judge free from infection, to come on shore, or to be taken out and disposed of as the owners shall see fit ; and such passengers and goods as shall not be permitted as aforesaid, shall remain on board, or be landed on said Island : and if any master or commander of any such vessel, for the time being, shall come on shore, or suffer any of his people or passengers to come on shore, or any boat to come on board, or suffer any goods to be taken out of his vessel, unless permitted as aforesaid, or shall come up to said town with his vessel, until by

Goods supposed free from infection may be permitted to be landed.

Persons landing, or holding communication with persons on shore, forbidden till legally permitted.

a certificate under the hands of said selectmen, or the major part of them, it shall appear that said vessel, company and goods are clear of infection, and the orders for stopping the same be removed or taken off, he shall, for every such offence, forfeit the sum of *two hundred dollars;* and in case he be not able to pay that sum, he shall suffer three months imprisonment ; and if any sailors or passengers, coming in said vessel, shall, without the knowledge or consent of the master or commander, presume to come on shore, or up above the Castle aforesaid, or if any person shall knowingly presume to go on board from shore, or go to the aforesaid House or Island in time of infection there, without leave as aforesaid ; or if any person put sick into the said house, or sent there on suspicion of being infected, shall presume to go off the said Island without leave as aforesaid ; any person offending in any of the particulars above mentioned, shall forfeit the sum of *two hundred dollars ;* and in case such person be not able to pay said forfeiture, he shall suffer two months imprisonment.   All prosecutions for offences contrary to this and the preceeding section, shall be by indictment or information in the Supreme Judicial Court, or Court of General Sessions of the Peace ; and one moiety of all fines mentioned in said sections, shall be to the use of the town of Boston, and the other moiety to the use of the selectmen of said town for the time being, whose particular duty it is hereby made to prosecute therefor.

Stat. 1828, ch. 154, § 3.

Vessels may be ordered to Hospital Island. SEC. 8. *Be it further enacted,* That whenever any ship or vessel, wherein any infection or infectious sickness hath lately been, shall come to any harbour within this State ; or whenever any person or persons belonging to, or that may, either by sea or land, come into any town or place near the public Hospital aforesaid, shall be visited, or shall lately before have been visited with any infectious sickness, two of the Justices of the Peace, or selectmen of such place, be, and hereby are empowered immediately to order the said vessel and sick persons to the said Hospital, there to be taken care of, according to the directions of this act : and where any such ship, vessel, or persons cannot, without great inconvenience and damage, be ordered to the aforesaid Hospital, in any such case, the rules and directions are to be observed, which are provided in the first enacting clause of this act; and in case the master or mariners of any vessel ordered to the Hospital as aforesaid, shall refuse or delay, for the space of six hours after such order being given to said master, or either of the owners of said vessel, or of the factors, or either of said owners of the goods, to come to sail, if wind and weather permit, in order to proceed to said Hospital, such master so refusing, shall forfeit and pay the sum of *four hundred dollars;* and each mariner so refusing, the sum of *one hundred dollars;* and in case they be not able to pay said sums, they shall suffer six months imprisonment; one half of said fine to be to the informer, and the other half to the poor of the town or district, to which such port or harbour belongs, and to be recovered in any Court of Record proper to try the same, by indictment or information.

Penalty for refusal to go to the Hospital.

SEC. 9. *Be it further enacted,* That if any master, seaman, or passenger, belonging to any vessel, on board which any infection is, or may have lately been, or suspected to have been, or which may have come from any port where any infectious mortal distemper prevails, shall refuse to make answer on oath to such questions as may be asked him or them, relating to such infection, by the selectmen of the town to which such vessel may come, (which oath the said selectmen are hereby empowered to administer,) such master, seaman, or passenger, so refusing, shall forfeit the sum of *two hundred dollars;* and in case he be not able to pay said sum, he shall suffer six months imprisonment; said penalty to be adjudged on prosecution by indictment or information in any court proper to try the same; one moiety of said fine to the use of the town where the offence may be committed, and the other moiety to the use of the selectmen thereof, whose particular duty it is hereby made to prosecute therefor. And the selectmen of Boston are hereby authorized and directed to provide nurses, assistance, and other necessaries, for the comfort and relief of such sick persons as may be sent to said

Penalty for refusing to answer properly, when questioned by the selectmen.

Nurses, &c. to be provided.

Hospital as aforesaid : the charge thereof to be borne by the said persons themselves, if able ; or if poor, and unable, by the towns to which they respectively belong ; or if not inhabitants of any particular town, or other place within this State, then by the Commonwealth.

Sec. 10. Provides that courts may adjourn from infectious towns.

Sec. 11. Provides that a Health Committee or officer may be appointed by towns at their annual meetings.

Sec. 12. Provides the manner of disposing of infectious vessels. at other towns than Boston.

Sec. 13. Provides that previous laws be repealed.

[Passed June 22, 1797.]

An act to empower the Town of Boston to choose a Board of Health, and to prescribe their power and duty.

Sec. 1. Irrellevant since the organization of the City Government as it provides for the choice and organization of the Board of Health.

Powers.

Sec. 2. *Be it further enacted,* That said Board of Health shall have power, and it hereby is made their duty, to examine into all causes of sickness, nuisances, and sources of filth that may be injurious to the health of the inhabitants of the town of Boston, which do, or may exist within the limits of the town of Boston, or on any island, or in any vessel within the harbour of Boston, or within the limits thereof, and the same to destroy, remove or prevent, as the case may require ; and whenever said board shall think it necessary for the preservation of the lives or health of the inhabitants of Boston, to enter forcibly any building, or vessel, having been refused such entry by the owner. or occupier thereof, within the limits of the said town of Boston or the harbour thereof, for the purpose of examining into, destroying, removing or preventing any nuisance, source of filth, or cause of sickness aforesaid, which said board have reason to believe is contained in such building or vessel—any member of said board, by order of said board, may apply to any Justice of the Peace, within and for the County of Suffolk, and on oath complain and state, on behalf of said board, the facts as far as said board have reason to believe the same relative to such nuisance, source of filth or cause of sickness aforesaid ; and such Justice shall thereupon issue his warrant, directed to the sheriff of the County of Suffolk, or either of his deputies, or any constable of the town of Boston, therein requiring them or either of them, taking with them sufficient aid and assistance, and also in company with said Board of Health, or some two members of the same, between the hours of sun rise and sun set, to repair to the place where such nuisance, source of filth or cause of sickness complained of as existing as aforesaid ; and there, if found, the same to destroy, remove or prevent, under the directions and agreeable to the order of said Board of Health, or such members of the same, as may attend and accompany such officer for such purpose : *Provided, however*,that no sheriff or deputy sheriff shall execute any civil process, either by arresting the body or attaching the goods and chattels of any person or persons under colour of any entry made for the purposes aforesaid, unless such service could by law have been made without such entry ; and all services so made, under colour of such entry, shall be utterly void,and the officer making such service shall be considered as a trespasser to all intents *ab initio*. And in all cases where such nuisance, source of filth, or cause of sickness shall be removed, destroyed or prevented in manner aforesaid, the cost of so removing, destroying, or preventing the same, together with all costs attending the proceedings relative thereto, shall be paid by the person or persons who caused or permitted the same nuisance, source of filth, or cause of sickness to exist, or in whose possession the same may be found. And in all cases where any contagious and malignant disorder exists, within the limits of the town of Boston, or on board of any vessel, or on any island within the harbour of Boston, and it appearing to said Board of Health, after the same has been examined into by the Physician of said board, or some other

Proviso.

respectable Physician of the town of Boston, that the public safety requires that any person or persons affected with any contagious, malignant disorder, should be removed to the Hospital on Rainsford Island, or to any other place within the limits of said town of Boston, on any island in the harbour of Boston, or should be confined or remain in the place where such person or persons thus affected then are; in every such case the said Board of Health shall pass an order relative to the same, which order, all persons, dwelling in or occupying such place, builing or vessel, notified thereof by said board, or called on by said board, shall be obliged to obey; and any person refusing to obey such order, or resisting any officer or person acting under the authority of said board, or any member of said board, in any of the duties or requirements in this section of this act, shall severally forfeit and pay for such offence a sum not less than five, and not exceeding five hundred dollars, according to the 'nature and aggravation of the offence.

Sec. 3. *Be it further enacted*, That the said Board of Health shall have power to make such rules, orders and regulations, from time to time, for the preventing, removing, or destroying of all nuisances, sources of filth and causes of sickness within the limits of the town of Boston, or on board any vessel, or on any island in the harbour of Boston, which they may think necessary; which rules, orders and regulations, from and after the same have been published in two newspapers, printed in the said town of Boston, shall continue in force and be obeyed by all persons, until changed, altered or repealed by the same board who made them, or by some succeeding Board of Health. And any person or persons who disobey or violate any such rules, orders or regulations, so as aforesaid made by such board, shall severally forfeit and pay for such offence, a sum not less than one, and not more than fifty dollars, according to the nature and aggravation of such offence.

Sec. 4. *Be it further enacted*, That the said Board of Health shall have power to seize, take and des-

Rules and orders.

troy, or to remove to any safe place without the limits of the town of Boston, or cause the same to be done, any unwholesome and putrid or tainted meat, fish, bread, vegetable or other articles of the provision kind, or liquor, which in their opinion, first consulting the Physician of said board, or some other reputable Physician of the town of Boston, shall not be fit for food and nourishment, and injurious to the health of those who might use the same : and the cost of such seizing, taking, destroying or removing shall be paid for by the person or persons in whose possession the same unwholesome, putrid, or tainted articles shall or may be found.

May seize and destroy provisions.

SEC. 5. *Be it further enacted*, That the said Board of Health shall have power, from time to time, to make and establish all such rules, orders and regulations relating to clothing or any article capable of containing or conveying any infectious disease, or creating any sickness, which may be brought into, or conveyed from, the town of Boston, or into or from any vessel, or on or from any island in the harbour of Boston, as they shall think proper for public safety, or to prevent the spreading of any dangerous or contagious disease.   And all such rules, orders and regulations, so as aforesaid by said board made and established, shall be obeyed by all persons, from and after the same have been published in two of the newspapers, printed in the town of Boston, and shall continue to be in full force until altered or repealed by the board who made and established the same, or some other succeeding board ; and every person who shall disobey or violate any of such rules, orders and regulations, shall forfeit and pay a sum not less than one dollar, and not more than one hundred dollars, according to the nature and aggravation of such offence.

May make rules concerning Clothing.

Fines

SEC. 6. *Be it further enacted*, That the said Board of Health shall have power to establish and regulate the Quarantine to be performed by all vessels arriving within the harbour of the town of Boston ; and for that purpose shall have power, from time to time, to establish, make and ordain all such orders, rules and regulations relating to said quaran-

May regulate Quarantine.

21

tine, as said board shall think necessary for the safety of the public and the security of the health of the inhabitants of the said town of Boston ; which said rules, orders and regulations, so as aforesaid established, made and ordained, shall be obeyed by all persons, and shall continue to be in force from and after the same shall have been published in two newspapers, printed in the town of Boston, until the same are altered or repealed by the said board establishing, making and ordaining the same, or by some succeeding Board of Health. And said rules, orders and regulations may extend as well to all persons arriving in such vessels, and to their property and effects aboard such vessels, and to all such persons as may visit, or go on board such vessels, after their arrival in said harbour of Boston, and to the cargo of all such vessels, as to the vessels themselves ; as also to every matter and thing relating to, or connected with such vessel, or the cargo of the same, or to any person or persons going on board or returning from the same ; and every person who shall knowingly or wilfully violate or disobey any of such rules, orders and regulations, so as aforesaid made, established or ordained by said Board of Health, shall severally forfeit and pay a sum not exceeding five hundred dollars, according to the nature

Fines.

and aggravation of such offence. And the Board of Health shall have power at all times, to cause any vessel arriving in the harbour of Boston, which is foul and infected, or whose cargo is foul and affected

May remove vessels to Quarantine Ground.

with any malignant and contagious disease, to be removed and placed on quarantine ground, and the same to be thoroughly cleansed and purified at the expense and charge of the owners, consignees or possessors of the same ; and also all persons arriving in or going on board such infected vessel, or handling such infected cargo, to be removed to Hospital or Rainsford Island, under the care of said board, and to the Hospital on the same, there to remain under the orders and regulations of said board. All expenses incurred on account of any person under the quarantine rules, orders and regulations of said Board of Health, shall be paid by such persons.

SEC. 7. *Be it further enacted,* That said Board
of Health shall have power, and it shall be their duty to elect and appoint a principal Physician to said
board, who shall reside in Boston, and an assistant
Physician, who shall, during the time of quarantine,
reside on Hospital Island, also an Island-Keeper, to
reside on said Hospital Island, boatmen and such
other officers and servants as will be necessary to
carry into effect the rules, orders and regulations of
said Board of Health, as it respects the quarantine ;
and shall prescribe to them their duty, and establish
their salary and fees, and displace or remove them
at pleasure, and elect and appoint others in their places ; also said board shall, from time to time, establish and regulate the fees or expenses attending the
said quarantine regulations, shall have the care of
said Rainsford or Hospital Island, and of the Hospital on the same, and of all property on said Island
and belonging to or connected with the Hospital on
the same ; and shall annually in the month of January in each year, file in the Secretary's Office of
this Commonwealth, an exact and true account of the
state of the property in and connected with the Hospital establishment on said Island, and of the property belonging to the Commonwealth on said Island,
and of all money expended thereon.

Officers appointed for Hospital Island.

SEC. 8. *Be it further enacted,* That said Board
of Health shall have power to elect and appoint
scavengers, superintendents of burying grounds, funeral porters or undertakers, and such other officers
and servants, as shall be necessary to carry into effect all the powers and duties in this act given to, or
required of, the said Board of Health, and to fix and
establish their fees of office or compensation ; and
all officers elected or appointed by said board, shall
be removeable from their said offices, at the pleasure
of said board, and others substituted, elected or appointed in their place. And a majority of said board
shall be competent to transact any business which the
whole board, were they all present, might or could
transact.

Scavengers and funeral porters.

SEC. 9. *Be it further enacted,* That all the powers
and duties which are given to, or required of the se-

lectmen of the town of Boston, by a law of this
Commonwealth, passed the twenty second day of
June, in the year of our Lord one thousand seven
hundred and ninety seven, entitled, " An act to prevent the Spreadiug of Contagious Sickness," and by
the several acts in addition thereto, shall be and they
Transfer of pow- hereby are transferred to and made the duty of the
ers. Board of Health of the town of Boston, any thing in
said laws to the contrary notwithstanding.

Residue irrelevant since the organization of the city government, as it provides for examination of accounts, and filling
vacancies in the old Board of Health.

SEC. 10. *Be it further enacted*, That whenever any
prisoner confined in the gaol in Boston, or within the
limits of said prison, shall be attacked with any contagious, malignant disorder, which, in the opinion of
said Board of Health, first having consulted with the
Physician of said board or some other respectable
Physician of the town of Boston, endangers the safety and health of the other prisoners in said goal, or
the inhabitants of said town, and that the suffering
such prisoners, so attacked as aforesaid, longer to remain in said gaol, or within the limits of said prison, is
May remove sick not consistent with the public safety, or the health of
prisoners. the inhabitants of said town, or the prisoners in said
gaol ; in every such case, the said Board of Health
shall make application in writing to any two Justices
of the Peace, *quorum unus*, therein stating the facts
relative to such case ; and the said Justices to whom
such application shall be made, shall examine into
such case, and if satisfied that the facts stated are
true, shall issue their warrant to said Board of Health,
authorizing and directing them to remove said prisoner so attacked with such contagious and malignant
disorder, to the Hospital on Rainsford Island, or to
some other place of safety, there to remain under
the directions of said board, until such prisoner
either recovers or dies ; and in case of recovery,
then to be returned by said board to the place from
which he was taken ; and such warrant so executed
by said board or any member thereof, shall be by
them returned, with their doings thereon, into the

Clerk's office of the court, from which the process for committing such prisoner to gaol, shall have issued ; and the place to which such prisoner shall be removed by virtue of such order, shall be considered as the gaol of the County of Suffolk ; and every prisoner removed as aforesaid, for the causes aforesaid, shall not thereby be considered as having committed any escape, so as to prejudice either himself, his bondsmen, or the persons who had the custody of him in his confinement aforesaid.

SEC. 11. *Be it further enacted*, That the said Board of Health of the town of ·Boston are hereby authorized and empowered, from time to time, to make and establish rules, orders and regulations for the interment of the dead in said town, to establish the police of the burying grounds, appoint and locate *Burying grounds.* the places where the dead may be buried in said town, and cause the places for the deposit of the dead in said town, and the burying grounds, to be repaired and properly enclosed. Also, to make regulations for *Funerals.* funerals and funeral processions, and appoint all necessary officers and persons to carry the same into effect, and to appoint to them their duties and fees ; and shall also have the power to establish such penalties for the violation of any such rules, orders and regulations, as they may think proper : *Provided*, no one penalty for any one violation, shall exceed the *Proviso for penalties.* sum of fifty dollars. And all such rules, orders or regulations, so as aforesaid made and established by said board, shall be obeyed by every person, from and after the same have been published in two of the newspapers printed in Boston, and shall continue in . full force, until the same are altered or repealed by the said board, who made and established them, or by some succeeding board.

SEC. 12. *Be it further enacted*, That the said Board of Health shall have power to grant permits for the removal of any nuisance, infected article, or *Permits.* sick person, within the town of Boston, when they think it safe and proper so to do ; and said board, whenever they think justice requires it, may stop, discontinue, discharge or compromise any suit, complaint or information, originating under this act.   And all fines, forfeitures, penalties, sums to be paid or recovered, arising under any of the provisions of this act, shall be prosecuted for, by and in the name of " The Board of Health of the town of Boston," by complaint or information by said board, to be made in writing to some Justice of the Peace within and for the County of Suffolk ; which said Justice, upon said complaint or information being made to him as aforesaid, shall receive the same, and thereupon issue his warrant, therein reciting the said complaint or information, directed · to the sheriff of the County of Suffolk or either of his deputies, or any constable of the town of Boston, commanding them or either of them, to summon the party informed against or complained of, to appear before him at a time and place to be named in said warrant, to shew cause, if any they have, why they should not pay the sum demanded of them in such complaint or information : which said warrant, shall by the officer who · receives the same, be served on the party informed or complained against as aforesaid, at least seven days before the day in said warrant stated, as the said day of trial, by giving such party in hand, a copy of such warrant, reading the same to him, or leaving the copy thereof at the last and usual place of the abode of such party ; and if such party shall not appear at the time and place appointed, or appearing shall not show sufficient cause as aforesaid, the said Justice shall proceed to render judgment in every such case, that the said Board of Health shall recover such sum in damages or as fine, as the case may be, as according to the provisions of this act, they ought by law to recover, with costs, and shall proceed to issue his execution therefor, in the same manner as executions issue from Justices of the Peace in civil cases triable before them ; and such executions shall be served and made returnable in the same manner as executions in civil actions are by law served, and made returnable, which issue on judgments rendered in the Supreme Judicial Court of this Commonwealth :— *Provided, however,* that in all such prosecutions as aforesaid, if the said Board of Health shall discon-

May prosecute.

Forms of process.

Proviso.

tinue such prosecution or become nonsuit, or the same on the merits should be decided by such Justice trying such prosecution against them, in every such case, the said party informed against and complained of, shall recover his legal costs against said board, which costs shall be paid by the Treasurer of the town of Boston. And in every prosecution under this act, before any Justice of the Peace as aforesaid, the party complained against in such prosecution, being dissatisfied with the judgment in the same, given by such Justice, may appeal therefrom to the Boston Court of Common Pleas, next to be holden at Boston, within and for the County of Suffolk, after such judgment is so as aforesaid given, or rendered by such Justice : *Provided*, such appeal be entered within twenty-four hours after such judgment is given as aforesaid ; and the same proceedings in all respects relating to such appeal, shall be had as by law required on appeals from judgments rendered in civil causes by the Justices of the Peace in this Commonwealth ; and on the entry of such appeal in said court, the said court shall have cognizance and jurisdiction of the same, and shall proceed to hear and determine the same in the same manner, and award execution in the same way and manner as they have cognizance and jurisdiction, proceed to hear and determine and award execution in civil causes, on appeals to them from judgments given by Justices of the Peace in this Commonwealth. And in all cases of such appeals on prosecutions under this act, the party prevailing in the said court shall recover his costs, to be paid in the manner prescribed in this section of this act: *Provided, however,* that no appeal shall be allowed or granted to said court in any prosecution under the provisions of this act, where the amount of the judgment rendered and had before, and by any Justice of the Peace, shall not amount to more than five dollars exclusive of costs. And all fines and forfeitures recovered by said Board of Health, under the provisions of this act, shall enure to the use of the inhabitants of the town of Boston, and be accounted for by said Board of Health, to and with the town Treasurer of said

[margin note:] Appeals.

[margin note:] Costs.

Proviso.

town of Boston : *And provided, also*, that in consequence of said appropriation of said fines and forfeitures, or the appropriation of any other moneys by virtue of this act, no inhabitant of the said town of Boston shall be disqualified as a Justice of the Peace, a witness or juror in any prosecution under this act, nor shall the said Board of Health or any member of the same, or any officer of the same, be rendered thereby incompetent witnesses in any prosecution under this act ; and the members of said Board of Health, while they continue in such office, shall be

Exemptions.

exempted from all militia duty and every other duty and service, which by law the selectmen of towns in this Commonwealth are exempted from : and all laws heretofore made relating to a Board of Health in the town of Boston, so far as they are inconsistent with or contrary to the provisions of this act,

Acts repealed.

shall be, and the same are hereby repealed : *Provided, however*, that the election of the present Board of Health for the said town of Boston, and all their doings under the said laws are hereby confirmed, and they shall have and exercise all the powers and duties required or permitted by this present act : *And provided, also*, that all prosecutions now pending, shall be proceeded in, in the same way and manner as though this act had never been passed. And in all prosecutions under this act, the persons prosecuted, may plead the general issue, and give any special

May plead the general issue.

matter in evidence under the same ; and the complaint, information, pleadings or proceedings in any prosecutions under this act, may by leave of court, before whom the same is, or may be pending, be amended in any state of such prosecution, without the payment of costs by either party.

[Passed June 20, 1816.]

NOTE. This act was intended to embody and re-enact all the former laws upon the same subject. And although these laws are not expressly repealed, but only such of them as are "inconsistent with or contrary to the provisions of this act," it is not perceived that any parts of them of importance to be continued in force, are omitted. The statutes referred to and which are by this act repealed, are "An act to empower the town of Boston to choose a Board of Health, and for removing and preventing nuisances, passed June 20, 1799, 2 vol. spe. laws 307. An act in addition thereto, passed June 18, 1803. 3 vol. spe. laws 211. An act to repeal a part of the first mentioned act, passed March 7, 1804, 3 vol. spe. laws 385. And an act relative to the official duties of the Board of Health, passed Feb. 3, 1806, 4 vol. spe. laws p. 1.

An act to incorporate the Boston Gas Light Company. Stat. 1822, C. 41, Sec. 3, in which it is " provided, that the Mayor and Aldermen for the time being, shall, at all times have the power to regulate, restrict, and control the acts and doings of said corporation, which may, in any manner, affect the health, safety, or convenience of the inhabitants of said city."

[Passed Jan. 22, 1823.]

An act concerning the regulation of the House of Correction in the City of Boston, and concerning the form of actions commenced under the By-laws of said city and for filling vacancies in the Board of Aldermen.

SEC. 4. *Be it further enacted,* That all fines, penalties and forfeitures, accruing under a statute of this Commonwealth, passed the twentieth day of June, in the year of our Lord, one thousand eight hundred and sixteen, entitled " An act to empower the town of Boston, to choose a Board of Health, and to prescribe their power and duty," or accruing under any rules, regulations, by-laws, or ordinances, which have been, or hereafter shall be passed by the City Council of the City of Boston, in relation to the health of the said city, or of the inhabitants thereof, shall be sued for, prosecuted and recovered by complaint or information, before the Justices of the Justices Court for the County of Suffolk, in the name of the City of Boston, by any officer or person authorized to institute the same, and in the manner prescribed in the statute above mentioned, and such fines, penalties, and forfeitures, shall enure, and be recovered for the use of the said city ; and no person shall be disqualified from acting as a magistrate, juror, or witness, in any such suit or prosecution by reason of any interest

Fines, penalties, &c. how to accrue, and be recovered.

22

which he may have as an inhabitant of the said city, in the sum or sums of money to be recovered thereby.

Prosecutions by complaint, how set forth.

SEC. 5. *Be it further enacted,* That in all prosecutions by complaint; before the Police Court for the City of Boston, founded on the special acts of the Legislature, the by-laws of the town of Boston, or the ordinances or by-laws of the City of Boston, it shall be sufficient, to set forth in such complaint, the offence, fully and plainly, substantially and formally, and in such complaint, it shall not be necessary to set forth such special act, by-law, ordinance, or any part thereof.

[Passed June 12, 1824.]

act passed Feb. 24. 1831. Dead bodies

ORDINANCES OF THE CITY.

An ordinance relative to the Police of the City of Boston.

Police.

SEC. 1. *Be it ordained by the Mayor, Aldermen, and Common Council of the City of Boston in City Council assembled,* That the Police of the City of Boston, so far as it regards its execution, be vested in three departments, to wit : that of Internal Police ; that of External Police ; and that for the Interment of the dead.

Internal Police.

SEC. 2. *Be it further ordained,* That the department of internal police be placed under the superintendence of the City Marshal ; whose duty it shall be, and he shall have power, to carry into execution, all the ordinances, rules, and laws made by the City Council, relative to causes of sickness, nuisances, and sources of filth that may be injurious to the health, or may affect the comfort of the inhabitants of the city, which do, or may exist within the limits thereof; subject always to the direction, authority, and control of the Mayor and Aldermen ; and it shall be the duty of the City Marshal, to cause all such nuisances, sources of filth, and causes of sickness to be prevented, removed, or destroyed, as the case may require, conformably to the ordinances of the City Council, as aforesaid, and the laws of the Commonwealth; and to this department shall belong, the care of the streets, the care of the common sewers, and the care of the vaults, and whatever else affects the health, security, and comfort of the city, from causes or means arising or existing within the limits thereof.

Streets, Sewers, Vaults.

Sec. 3. *Be it further ordained,* That the department of external police, shall be placed under the superintendence of an officer, to be denominated the Commissioner of Health, whose duty it shall be, and he shall have power to carry into execution, all the ordinances, rules and laws, power and authority, made by, and vested in the City Council, relative to causes of sickness, nuisances, and sources of filth, that may be injurious to the health of the inhabitants of the city, which do, or may exist within the limits of the harbour of said city; or on any island, or in any vessel within the said harbour, or the limits thereof; subject always to the direction, authority, and controul of the Mayor and Aldermen; and it shall be the duty of the said Commissioner of Health to cause all such nuisances, sources of filth, and causes of sickness, so existing as aforesaid, to be prevented, removed, or destroyed, as the case may require, conformably to the ordinances of the City Council, and the laws of the Commonwealth; and to this department shall belong the execution of all ordinances, orders, rules and regulations, relative to the quarantine of vessels, and to the police and preservation of the health of the inhabitants of the islands, or on board any vessel within the harbour of said city.

External Police.

Nuisances.

Sec. 4. *Be it further ordained,* That the department relative to the interment of the dead, shall be placed under the control of one superintendent, whose duty it shall be, and he shall have power, to carry into execution all the power and authority vested in the City Council, relative to the interment of the dead, the establishment and police of the cemeteries, and burying grounds, and the regulation of funerals, and funeral processions; subject always to the direction, authority, and control of the Mayor and Aldermen: And it shall be the duty of said Superintendent, to

Interment of dead.

Funeral processions.

carry into effect all the ordinances of the City Council and the laws of the Commonwealth relative thereto.

Sec. 5. *Be it further ordained,* That it shall be the duty of the Mayor and Aldermen, and they shall have power, whenever they shall deem it expedient, to direct either of the officers above mentioned, to execute the duties of the other, or to aid such other officer, in the execution of his said duties; and during the period, or for the purposes to which the said direction of the Mayor and Aldermen may relate, such officer, so directed, shall have like power and authority, in or over such subject matter, as the officer to whom such department may belong; and it shall also be the duty of the Mayor and Aldermen, and they shall have power from time to time, to appoint such assistants or clerks to either department, as from experience may be found expedient, or any particular exigency may make necessary.

Assistants and Clerks may be appointed.

Sec. 6. *Be it further ordained,* That the said Commissioner of Health, and said Superintendent, shall be chosen by concurrent vote of the City Council, in the month of May or June annually, to be always first acted upon by the Mayor and Aldermen; and the said Commissioner of Health and said Superintendent, shall respectively hold their offices, until the next annual election, unless previously removed, by the said City Council, by vote, and thereupon, or in case of death or resignation of either, the said City Council shall proceed to appoint a successor, for the residue of the year; and each of said officers, their assistants or clerks, shall respectively be compensated as the City Council shall deem just and reasonable, and shall be sworn to the faithful execution of his office.

Superintendent of burial grounds

[Passed May 31, 1824.]

An ordinance prescribing rules and regulations, relative to nuisances, sources of filth, and causes of sickness within the City of Boston.

SEC. 1. *Be it ordained by the Mayor, Aldermen and Common Council of the City of Boston in City Council assembled,* That all house offal, whether consisting of animal or vegetable substance, shall be deposited in such vessels as will not contain liquids ; and be kept in some convenient place to be taken away by the city scavengers ; which shall be done not less than twice in each week, during the months of June, July, August, and September. And no person or persons shall throw or deposite, or cause to be thrown or deposited in any street, court, square, lane, alley, public place, or vacant lot, or into any pond, any sawdust, soot, ashes, cinders, shavings, hair, shreds, manure, oyster or lobster shells, or any animal or vegetable matter or substance whatever ; nor shall any person or persons throw or cast any dead animal, or any foul or offensive ballast, in any dock or place, between the channel and the shore ; nor shall land any such foul or offensive animal or vegetable substance, within the city ; nor shall cast any dead animal into the channel, without securing thereto a sufficient weight to prevent it from floating.

SEC. 2. *Be it further ordained,* That if any of the substances in the preceeding section mentioned, shall be thrown or carried from any house, ware-house, shop, cellar, yard, or other place, into any street, lane, alley, court, square, public place, or vacant lot, as well the owner of such house, or other place, whence the same shall have been thrown, or carried, as the occupant thereof, and the person who actually threw and carried the same, shall severally be held liable for such violation of this ordinance ; and all such substances shall be removed from any street, lane, alley, court, square, public place, or vacant lot, by and at the expense of the owner or occupant of the house, or other place whence the same were thrown

Marginal notes: House offal. — Dead animals. — Filth not to be thrown into the streets.

or carried, within two hours after personal notice in writing to that effect, given by the Mayor, any Alderman, the City Marshal, or Commissioner of Health.

SEC. 3. *Be it further ordained,* That all dirt, sawdust, soot, ashes, cinders, shavings, hair, shreds, manure, oyster or lobster shells, or any animal or vegetable substance, or filth of any kind, in any house, warehouse, cellar, yard, or other place, which the Mayor and Aldermen, or City Marshal shall deem it necessary for the health of the city to be removed, shall be carried away therefrom, by and at the expense of the owner or occupant of such house, or other place where the same shall be found, and be removed to such place as he shall be directed, within four hours after notice in writing to that effect, given by the Mayor, any Alderman, the City Marshal, or Commissioner of Health.

Dirt, &c. to be removed.

SEC. 4. *Be it further ordained,* That all waste water shall be conveyed through drains under ground to the common sewer, if there be any in the street, lane, alley, or court adjoining; and if there be no such common sewer, then to such reservoir, sunk under ground as shall be approved by the City Marshal.

Waste water.

SEC. 5. *Be it further ordained,* That no vault of a necessary or privy, shall be dug or placed within two feet of the line of any lot of land, street, lane, alley, court, square, or public place or passage-way, nor shall there be any communication between any vault or privy and the common sewer. Every vault or privy shall be boxed, or made tight, so that the contents thereof shall not escape therefrom; and the said contents shall never be permitted to rise within two feet of the surface of the earth. Whenever any vault or privy shall become offensive to any inhabitants, the same shall be cleansed; and the owner, or his agent, or the occupant of the land, in which any vault or privy may be situated, the state and condition of which shall be in violation of the provisions of this ordinance, shall remove, cleanse, alter, amend, or repair the same within a reasonable time after notice in writing to that effect, given by the Mayor, any Alderman, the City Marshal, or the Commissioner of

Vaults.

Notice to be given.

Health. And in case of neglect or refusal, the same shall be performed by the orders of the Mayor and Aldermen, at the expense of the owner, agent, or occupant aforesaid.

SEC. 6. *Be it further ordained,* That no vault or privy shall be emptied, without a permit from the City Marshal, or his deputy ; nor in any other mode, or at any other time, than he shall direct and appoint, conformable to such regulations as the Mayor and Aldermen, from time to time shall make on the subject. And no vault shall be opened, (except the present year,) in the months of June, July, August, or September, unless, on inspection caused to be made, the Mayor and Aldermen shall be satisfied that the same is absolutely necessary for the health or comfort of the inhabitants. And in such case, no more of such contents shall be taken away, than shall be deemed absolutely necessary for present safety and relief, and with such precautions relative to the preventing of any offensive effluvia, as the Mayor and Aldermen shall direct ; all the expenses of which shall be borne by such owner, agent, or occupant, and which shall never be less than double the amount charged during any other months in the year.

Vaults not to be emptied without permit.

See Stat. 1824, ch. 28, Sec. 4.

SEC. 7. *Be it further ordained,* That the City Marshal, or his deputy, or any person authorized by the Mayor for that purpose, shall and may at any time between sun-rise and sun-set, enter into any building within the city, for the purpose of examining into, destroying, removing, or preventing any nuisance, source of filth, or cause of sickness therein ; or in any cellar belonging thereto. And if any person shall refuse to admit such officer, or other person so authorized, into said building, the City Marshal shall, on oath, complain to the Justices of the Police Court, and shall apply for their warrant, according to the statute in such case made and provided, and shall thereupon proceed, under the authority of the said Court, to examine such building or other place, and to destroy, remove, or prevent any nuisance, source of filth, or cause of sickness, that may be found there, in such manner as the Mayor and Aldermen shall direct. And the said City Marshal, or his deputy, or

City Marshal may enter houses, &c.

any person authorized as aforesaid, shall and may, at any time between sun-rise and sun-set, enter into any yard, or lot of ground, or into any out-house, and examine any alley, sink, cist-pool, privy, vault, public or private dock, or slip, drain, or sewer, and shall report to the Mayor and Aldermen all such as the health or security of the city may require to be cleansed, altered, or amended.

Every house to have a vault.

SEC. 8. *Be it further ordained,* That all tenements within the city, that are or may be used as dwelling houses, shall be furnished with suitable vaults or privies, which shall be sunk under ground, and shall be of sufficient capacity, in proportion to the number of inhabitants of each tenement or building. And if the Mayor and Aldermen shall be satisfied, that any such tenement is not provided with a suitable vault or privy, they shall give notice in writing to the owner thereof, or to his agent, if either be an inhabitant of the city, or if otherwise, public notice in two newspapers, printed in Boston, requiring such owner or agent, as soon as may be, to cause proper and sufficient vaults to be constructed and provided for such tenement or building; and in case of neglect or refusal to obey such notice, within a reasonable time, the Mayor and Aldermen shall have power to cause such vaults or privies to be made for such tenements, the expense of which shall be paid by such owner or agent.

Swine and goats.

SEC. 9. *Be it further ordained,* That no swine or goats shall be kept within the limits of the city without the license of the Mayor and Aldermen, and in such manner as they shall direct.

Livery Stables.

SEC. 10. *Be it further ordained,* That the owners and occupants of Livery and other stables within the city, shall not wash or clean their carriages or horses, nor cause them to be washed or cleaned, in the streets, or public ways, nor otherwise incumber the same; they shall keep their stables and stable yards clean, and shall not permit more than two cart loads of manure to accumulate and remain in or near the same, at any one time between the first day of May, and the first day of November; nor shall they, within that period, remove any manure, nor cause or suffer the same to be removed, except between the hours of twelve at night, and two hours after sunrise.

SEC. 11. *Be it further ordained*, That no person shall land on any wharf or other place, or shall otherwise bring into the city, any damaged grain, rice or coffee without a permit therefor from the Mayor and Aldermen, and in such manner as they shall direct. Damaged grain.

SEC. 12. *Be it further ordained*, That whenever any person shall have been duly notified to remove any nuisance, or to cleanse, alter or amend any vault, or drain, or to perform any other act or thing which it may be his duty to perform, in obedience to the laws of the Commonwealth, or the rules, orders, regulations, by-laws or ordinances for the preservation of the health of the city, which are now, or which hereafter shall be made by lawful authority, and the time limited for the performance of such duty shall have elapsed, without a compliance of such notice, the City Marshal shall issue new notice from time to time, to such delinquents, until the duty shall be executed, and the nuisance remedied or removed. And the Mayor shall cause all persons who shall violate or disobey the said health laws and regulations to be forthwith prosecuted and punished. And in case, in the opinion of the Mayor and Aldermen, it shall be for the health or comfort of the inhabitants, that any particular nuisance should be forthwith removed, and without delay it shall be their duty to cause the same to be removed accordingly. Nuisance. Notices to be issued.

[Passed June 24, 1824.]

Ordinance passed Oct. 7, 1853 superseding.

An ordinance establishing and regulating the Quarantine of vessels, and for repealing a former ordinance upon that subject.

SEC. 1. *Be it ordained by the Mayor, Aldermen and Common Council of the City of Boston, in City Council assembled,* That on and after the fifteenth

23

day of June, annually, and until the fifteenth day of September, in each year, a quarantine shall be had of all vessels, their officers and crews, passengers and cargoes, that come within the harbour of Boston, on board of which any person shall have died, or been sick of any infectious or contagious disease, during the passage to Boston, or which are from, or have brought their present cargo, or part thereof, from any port or place in the West India Islands, or from any port or place within the tropics, except any port or place beyond the Cape of Good Hope or Cape Horn, or from any port or place within the Straits of Gibraltar, or from any port or place where infectious or contagious disease doth prevail, or recently hath prevailed : *Provided, however*, that in the latter case, public notice shall first be given by the Mayor and Aldermen of such fact of the prevalence of contagious or infectious disease : *And provided, also*, that any vessel, at any other season of the year, having on her passage to Boston, any person die of any infectious or contagious disease, or having on her arrival, any person sick of such disease, or being found to be foul or infected after her arrival, shall be liable to quarantine, though coming from any port or place in the United States, or elsewhere.

SEC. 2. *Be it further ordained*, That the said quarantine, shall be had and performed at an anchorage ground, near Rainsford Island, under the direction of the Resident Physician of the City of Boston, and shall continue on every such vessel, until the master shall receive a certificate from such Resident Physician, that he may be discharged : *Provided, however*, that in case of unreasonable delay, by the Resident Physician, to grant such certificate, the owner, agent or consignee of such vessel, or of any part of her cargo, may apply to the Mayor and Aldermen, who may, on being satisfied of the propriety of discharging such vessel from quarantine, issue such certificate ; and any passenger in such vessel, may be discharged by said Physician, from quarantine, at any time.

SEC. 3. *Be it further ordained*, That in the month of June, annually, and as much oftener as the good of the city may require, a Resident Physician shall be chosen, by concurrent vote of the City Council, whose duty it shall be, to reside at Rainsford Island from the fifteenth day of June to the fifteenth day of September, in each year, and at such other times as the Mayor and Aldermen shall direct; to visit every vessel arriving, liable to quarantine; to deliver a copy of these regulations to the master, and a flag to be carried by his vessel; to direct in what manner she shall be cleansed, if necessary, and what articles from her shall be landed, washed, buried or destroyed, and what articles of cargo may be unladened ; to direct the care and attendance of the sick ; for whom he shall prescribe and supply medicine, according to his best skill ; to report every day to the Mayor and Aldermen, the situation of every sick person, or once a week if no person be sick ; to direct the pilots where and in what particular place, vessels shall be anchored—who are hereby required to obey such directions, and to grant a certificate to any passenger by him discharged from quarantine, at any time before the discharge of the vessel, in which such passenger arrived, and to give a certificate to the master of each vessel, when in his discretion, he shall think proper, that such vessel be discharged from quarantine.

Resident Physician to be appointed,—power and duty.

SEC. 4. *Be it further ordained*, That the sole and complete control of said Rainsford Island, and of all vessels lying at quarantine there, and of all persons employed on said Island, in whatever capacity, the same may be, or on board said vessels at quarantine, shall be, and hereby is vested in said Resident Physician, during his residence on said Island ; subject, however, to the superior control, in all cases, of the Mayor and Aldermen. And in addition to the several duties of said Resident Physician, enumerated in the preceeding section of this ordinance, it shall also be the further duty of said Resident Physician, to report to the Mayor and Aldermen, the state and condition of said Rainsford Island, of the buildings thereon, of the vessels lying there, and of the accommodations provided and existing at said Island, for the ease and comfort of the sick, or of

Rainsford Island to be under control of Resident Physician.

To report to Mayor and Aldermen.

the quarantine of vessels, whenever he shall be thereunto required, by the Mayor and Aldermen, or whenever the said Resident Physician shall deem it expedient to make such report; and, also, to recommend, from time to time, such measures as he may deem expedient, for the better execution of the ordinances of the city, relative to the quarantine of vessels, or for the convenience and comfortable accommodation of persons under quarantine; and if, in any case, or at any time, the City Council, or either branch thereof, shall request of the said Resident Physician, any information or advice, relative to the better preservation of the health of the city, it shall be his duty to furnish the same gratuitously.

SEC. 5. *Be it further ordained*, That said Resident Physician shall receive such salary as the City Council may grant and authorize,—to be paid quarter yearly; and he may also be allowed to charge sick persons for his attendance and medicine, in extraordinary cases, such reasonable sums, respectively, as the Mayor and Aldermen may approve; and the said Resident Physician shall hold his office during the pleasure of the City Council.

SEC. 6. *Be it further ordained*, That the master of every vessel discharged from quarantine, shall, within twenty-four hours after such discharge, deliver at the Mayor's office, the certificate and flag he shall have received of the Resident Physician, and pay the sum of ten dollars, for which he shall be entitled to a certificate from the City Clerk, to authorize his entry at the Custom House.

SEC. 7. *Be it further ordained*, That the keeper of Rainsford Island shall be appointed by the City Council, and be, in every respect, under the direction and control of the Resident Physician; subject, however, to the superior control and order of the Mayor and Aldermen, and shall be allowed such compensation for himself and his assistants, as the City Council may direct and authorize.

SEC. 8. *Be it further ordained*, That the Mayor and Aldermen, may permit any person to visit Rainsford Island, during the time of quarantine, carrying a certificate from the Mayor or City Clerk: *Provided,*

Marginal notes:
Resident Physician's salary.
Masters of Vessels to deliver certificate and flag.
Island keeper to be appointed.
Permits to visit the Island.

that such certificate shall be in force only on the day of its date, and the succeeding day. And without such permit, no person shall visit said island, or any vessel lying there, during the time of quarantine.

SEC. 9. *Be it further ordained*, That in June, annually, five physicians shall be appointed by concurrent vote of the City Council, on whom, in case of any alarm of Small Pox, or other contagious or infectious or dangerous disease, occurring in the city or neighbourhood, the Mayor may call for consultation and advice ; and that the Mayor and Aldermen shall have power to remove or cause to be removed from any dwelling house or other place within said city, any person or persons, sick with any contagious or infectious disease, or any person who may have been exposed to such contagious or infectious disease, to any hospital or place within the city, or on any island within the harbour, proper for the reception of such sick and exposed persons : *Provided*, a majority of the said consulting physicians shall give their opinion in writing, to said Mayor and Aldermen, that such removal is necessary and expedient, for the safety of the inhabitants, and in case any person sick with such contagious or infectious disease, in any house or other place within said city, cannot in the opinion of said physicians, be removed, then the Mayor and Aldermen shall have power to cause any house or tenement contiguous thereto, to be vacated, by the removal of the occupants thereof, for such time as said physicians or a majority of them shall think expedient, and the safety of the inhabitants may require.

Consulting Physicians to be appointed.

Persons sick may be removed.

Proviso.

Houses may be vacated.

SEC. 10. *Be it further ordained*, That skins, furs, rags, hair, carpets, and goods of woolen or cotton fabric, and feathers, arriving at the port of this city, after the fifteenth day of September and before the fifteenth day of June, in any year, from any port or place within the Straits of Gibraltar, or any port or place on the Atlantic coast of Africa, shall not be landed in this city, or be permitted to be removed from the vessel in which either of them shall be brought, before the same have been examined by the Resident Physician, or such other person as the Mayor and Aldermen shall appoint for that purpose, and

Skins, furs, rags, &c. to be examined.

purified in such manner as said physician, or such other person as shall be appointed by the Mayor and Aldermen, as aforesaid, shall direct, and a permit granted for the same, by the said physician or other person, appointed as aforesaid. And the said physician shall be entitled at any season of the year, to demand and examine the bill of health issued to any vessel arriving from any port where such documents are usually granted, to enable him the better to decide on the situation and purification of such vessel and her cargo.

Former ordinances repealed.

SEC. 11. *Be it further ordained*, That an ordinance made and passed on the third day of June, in the year of our Lord, one thousand eight hundred and twenty four, entitled an ordinance establishing and regulating the quarantine of vessels and also such parts of the third section of another ordinance, made and passed on the thirty-first day of May, in the year last aforesaid, entitled " an ordinance relative to the police of the City of Boston," as are inconsistent with the provisions of this ordinance, be, and the same are hereby repealed.

[Passed Dec. 25, 1826.]

Ordinance passed Aug. 1, 1833.

An ordinance relative to the Burial of the Dead.

SEC. 1. *Be it ordained by the Mayor, Aldermen, and Common Council of the City of Boston, in City Council assembled*, That the Superintendent of burying grounds and cemeteries in the City of Boston,

Superintendent of burial grounds.

shall give such bonds for the faithful performance of his duties, as shall be satisfactory to the Mayor and Aldermen ; and that it shall be the duty of the said Superintendent, to keep the fences, walls, and gates of the several burying grounds and cemeteries in the city, in good and sufficient repair, and that the said burying grounds and cemeteries shall be sufficiently secured by locks and bolts ; to point out the place, depth, and width of every grave to be dug therein ;

to cause the said graves to be dug in exact ranges,
parallel with, and as near to each other as the said
superintendent shall think fit and proper; and to take
care that the said graves be so filled and elevated,
that water may not remain and stagnate thereon; to
cause the tombs which may be opened in the respec- *Burial grounds & cemeteries.*
tive cemeteries between the first day of July, and
the thirtieth day of September, to be closed and
pointed with lime within twenty-four hours after the
deposite of bodies therein; and to order and direct
the Wardens, or other proper officer or officers, of
the several Churches to which cemeteries belong, to
cause at least three bushels of good stone lime to be
slacked therein, on the first, and fifteenth days of *Deaths, &c. to be recorded.*
July, August and September; and also to record in
a book to be kept for that purpose, the name, age
and sex of each person interred; the family to which
the deceased belonged; the disease of which he or
she died; and whether citizen or stranger; the
time when interred; the number of the grave, and
the number of the range where buried, or the tomb
where deposited.

SEC. 2. *Be it further ordained*, That the said
superintendent shall permit the family of any person
hereafter buried in any grave in the north or south *Graves.*
burial grounds, to place, within one month after the
burial of such person, a stone of the following dimensions, to wit: length four and a half feet, breadth
one foot ten inches, thickness three and a half
inches, having the persons name and age, the number of the grave, and the number of the range cut
thereon, and placed perpendicularly six inches from
the head of the grave, and settled in the earth
eighteen inches, from a level surface; which facts
being recorded by the said superintendent, such
grave shall be reserved for the use of the same family twenty years; and graves may be reopened for
members of the same family: *Provided*, the top of
any coffin placed therein, be not within three feet
of the surface of the ground. The bottom of the
first coffin buried in any grave, in the north burying
ground shall be at least eight feet from the surface
of the ground, and the bottom of the first coffin

buried in any grave in the south burying ground, shall be at least six feet six inches, from the surface of the ground.

New ranges of graves.

SEC. 3. *Be it further ordained,* That no new range of graves shall be commenced, until the preceding range shall be taken up by the deposite of one or more bodies therein.

Funeral Cars.

SEC. 4. *Be it further ordained,* That all funeral Cars, used in this city, shall be under the care of said superintendent, and shall be deposited for safe keeping in places provided for that purpose. And it shall be the duty of said superintendent to cause them to be kept clean and in good repair; and that he shall permit no person to use the same, except the funeral undertakers licensed as such, by the Mayor and Aldermen; and that the said superintendent shall

Superintendent to account.

account monthly to the Auditor of Accounts, for all fees.

SEC. 5. *Be it further ordained,* That a sufficient number of funeral undertakers shall be appointed and licensed by the Mayor and Aldermen; who shall

Funeral undertakers.

be responsible for the decent, orderly and faithful management of the funerals undertaken by them, and for a strict compliance with the ordinances of the city in this behalf. Each undertaker may employ por-

Porters.

ters of a discreet and sober character to assist him, and shall be accountable to the Mayor and Aldermen for their conduct; and all persons not licensed as undertakers, are hereby forbidden and prohibited to undertake the management of any funeral, under a penalty of a sum not less than two dollars, and not more than twenty dollars for each offence.

SEC. 6. *Be it further ordained,* That no person shall bury or inter, or cause to be buried or interred, any dead body at any other time of the day than between sun-rising and sun-setting, except when otherwise ordered by the Mayor and Aldermen, or superintendent of burying grounds, in cases of the prevalence of contagions and malignant diseases; and all

Funerals regulated.

funerals shall be conducted through or into at least one of the principal streets. No bell shall be tolled in the City of Boston, at any funeral, without a special permit therefor from the Mayor or one of the

Aldermen. The corpse of every person of ten years of age and upwards, shall be conveyed to the grave or tomb in a funeral car, to be drawn by not more than two horses : *Provided, however,* that on extraordinary occasions, permission may be obtained from the Mayor and Aldermen, on application for that purpose, to dispense with any of the provisions of this section. — Proviso.

SEC. 7. *Be it further ordained,* That the central, chapel, and granary burying grounds, so called, shall be so far closed, as that no new graves shall be opened or dug, nor tombs built therein, until the further order of the Mayor and Aldermen ; and that the old part of the north burying ground, shall be so far closed, as that no new graves shall be opened or dug therein ; but any person may obtain permission from the Mayor and Aldermen, to erect tombs in the new part of the north burying ground, and in the south burying ground, under the direction, and upon such terms and conditions as shall or may be prescribed by the said Mayor and Aldermen. — Burying grounds to be closed.

SEC. 8. *Be it further ordained,* That if the said superintendent shall be guilty of any violation of duty required of him by this ordinance he shall forfeit and pay for each offence, a sum not less than two dollars and not more than twenty dollars ; that if any undertaker shall be guilty of any violation of duty required of him by this ordinance, he shall forfeit and pay for each offence, a sum not less than two dollars and not more than twenty dollars ; and that all other persons who shall be guilty of any violation of the provisions of this ordinance, shall forfeit and pay for each offence, a sum not less than two dollars and not more than twenty dollars. And the said superintendent and funeral undertakers and porters, shall at all times be removeable, at the pleasure of the Mayor and Aldermen. — Superintendent, undertakers and porters. See statute 1816, chap. 44, sec. 11.

SEC. 9. *Be it further ordained,* That the following fees shall be collected and paid for services in the execution of this ordinance, to wit : to the city, seventy five cents, for each person buried, and one dollar per mile, for any distance that a funeral car may be sent out of the city, which, together with the — Fees.

24

fees for graves, and tombs, are to be collected from the families of the persons interred. *To the undertakers*, for digging a grave eight feet deep, and covering the same, *two dollars and fifty cents*; for digging a grave six feet six inches deep, *one dollar and fifty cents*; for digging a grave five feet deep, *one dollar and twenty five cents*; and for one four feet deep *one dollar*. For opening and closing a tomb, *seventy five cents*. For attendance and service at the house of a person deceased, in collecting and returning chairs, and other service, *one dollar*. For every family notified by request, *five cents*. For tolling a bell by special permission, *fifty cents*. For placing a corpse in a coffin, when requested, and removing the same down stairs, *one dollar*. For the use of one horse in the car, and leader, *one dollar and fifty cents*, and for each additional horse, *seventy five cents*. For carrying a corpse from the house to the car, and from the car to the grave, tomb, or vault, and placing the same therein and closing the same, including the assistance of the funeral porters, *three dollars*; and the same fees shall be allowed and paid in all cases of removing a corpse from any public vault, and reburying or entombing the same, as are allowed and paid for burying or entombing a corpse in any grave, vault, or tomb, as aforesaid. *For the burial of children*, under ten years of age, to wit: diging a grave three and a half feet deep, *seventy five cents*; for service at the house, *one dollar*; tolling a bell by special permission, *fifty cents*; carrying the corpse to the carriage, and from the carriage to the place of deposite, *fifty cents*; for the use of a Pall, *twenty five cents*. And when a corpse shall be carried into a church for a funeral service, the undertaker may make an additional charge of *two dollars*; and when the ground shall be frozen, the charge of digging graves may be augmented at the discretion of the Mayor and Aldermen. And it shall be the duty of the several undertakers to pay over, monthly, to the superintendent the fees received by them on account of the city, provided for and established in this section.

Fees for burial of children.

Removal of bodies out of the city.

SEC. 10. *Be it further ordained*, That if any person should be desirous to remove out of the city, the body of a deceased person for interment, it may be lawful so to do, on application to the Superintendent of burial grounds, whose duty it shall be to attend at the time and place of removal : *Provided*, no cause should appear to withhold the permission : The applicant to pay the city twenty-five cents for the permit.

SEC. 11. *Be it further ordained*, That no person shall remove any bodies, or the remains of any bodies, from any of the graves or tombs in this city, without the special permission of the Superintendent of burying grounds.

Bodies not to be removed without a permit.

SEC. 12. *Be it further ordained*, That no grave or tomb shall be opened from the first day of June to the first day of October, except for the purpose of interring the dead, without the special permission of the Mayor and Aldermen, or Superintendent of burying grounds.

No grave or tomb to be opened without a permit.

SEC. 13. *Be it further ordained*, That all by-laws, orders, rules and regulations, heretofore made and established by the Selectmen, or Board of Health, or Inhabitants of the town of Boston, relative to the burying grounds, cemeteries, funerals, and the burial of the dead, be, and the same are hereby repealed.

By-laws, orders, &c. repealed.

[Passed Dec. 25, 1826.]

ordinance passed Sept 26. 1843 suspending

An ordinance regulating the sale of Fresh Fish.

SEC. 1. *Be it ordained by the Mayor, Aldermen and Common Council of the City of Boston, in City Council assembled*, That Fresh Fish of every kind, before they shall be brought into this city, shall be made perfectly clean ; and (excepting such as are hereinafter named,) shall not be offered for sale, between the first day of June and the first day of October, unless kept in covered stalls, fish boxes, or other houses situated over the salt water, or in Faneuil Hall Market, subject to the regulations from time to time, made by the Mayor and Aldermen.   And fresh fish offered for sale in the streets of the city, before the first day of June and after the first day of October, shall be kept clean in covered carts or boxes.

SEC. 2. *Be it further ordained*, That Salmon, Shad, Bass, Mackerel, Eels, Flounders, Smelts, and other small fish, may be sold at all times, at any part of the city, provided they be kept secure from the rays of the sun : *Provided, however*, that no Salmon, or Bass, brought to the city by sea, shall be sold or landed therein, until the same shall have been cleansed of their entrails ; which entrails shall be kept on board of the vessels or boats in which the fish were brought, in a safe manner, and removed below low water mark, at every flowing of the tide.

SEC. 3. *Be it further ordained*, That no Oysters shall be offered for sale within the limits of this city, between the fifth day of July and the first day of September.

Horns or trumpets not to be sounded.

SEC. 4. *Be it further ordained*, That no horns, trumpets, or other wind instruments, shall be blown or sounded by any fishermen or other persons within the City of Boston, to call the attention of the people to their occupation, and business.

Penalty.

SEC. 5. *Be it further ordained*, That whoever shall offend against any of the provisions of this ordinance, shall forfeit and pay for each offence, a sum not less than one dollar, nor more than twenty dollars.

Former orders repealed.

SEC. 6. *Be it further ordained*, That so much of an order of the Board of Health of the town of Boston, passed on the thirtieth day of July, A. D. 1816, as relates to fresh fish, salmon, and small fish, and the sale of oysters, be, and the same is hereby repealed.

[Passed Dec. 18, 1826.]

CHAP. XXVII.

House of Correction.

ACT OF THE LEGISLATURE.

An act concerning the regulation of the House of Correction in the City of Boston, and concerning the form of actions commenced under the by-laws of said city, and providing for filling vacancies in the board of Aldermen.

SEC. 1. *Be it enacted by the Senate and House of Representatives, in General Court assembled, and by the authority of the same,* That the City of Boston shall be entitled to the same remedies in order to recover the expenses of supporting any poor person maintained in the House of Industry of said city, that towns in this Commonwealth are entitled to for the recovery of the expenses of persons for whom support or relief is provided by overseers of the poor, or under their direction.

Supporting poor persons.

SEC. 2. *Be it further enacted,* That the House of Correction within the City of Boston, shall be the House of Correction* for the County of Suffolk ; and that the City Council of said city shall have power, from time to time, to appoint such a number of overseers of the House of Correction in said City of Boston, not exceeding nine, as they shall deem expedient ; who shall have, use and exercise, all the powers and authority in regulating and governing said House of Correction, and the inhabitants thereof, subject to the control of the Mayor and Aldermen of the said city, that are granted to the overseers of Houses of Correction in and by an act, entitled " An act for suppressing and punishing of rogues, vaga-

Appointment of overseers.

*See post. act concerning juvenile offenders 5, 6 & 7 sections.

bonds, common beggars, and other idle and lewd persons," passed on the twenty sixth day of March in the year of our Lord one thousand seven hundred

Rules by which they are to be governed.

and eighty eight, and the several acts additional thereto ; and the said overseers so appointed, or the major part thereof, shall, from time to time, make, ordain and establish, such rules and orders, not repugnant to the constitution and laws of this Commonwealth, for the governing and punishing of persons committed to the said house, as they shall find needful and proper ; which, within one month after they shall have been made, shall be submitted to the said

Persons may be discharged.

City Council, and shall be in force until repealed by the said overseers, or until disapproved of by the said City Council, and the power of discharging persons committed to the said House of Correction, by the Justices of the Police Court of said city, or by any Justice of the Peace for the County of Suffolk, before the expiration of their term of commitment, upon the recommendation of the overseers of said house, shall be and hereby is vested in any one or

City Council power.

more of the Justices of the Police Court of said city.

SEC. 3. *Be it further enacted,* That the City Council shall have power, from time to time, to appoint a master of the said House of Correction, who shall be under the direction and control of the said overseers, and shall be compensated in such manner as the said City Council shall direct. And the said City of Boston shall bear and defray all the expenses of the said House of Correction, and shall be entitled to the same remedies to recover the charges of maintaining any person therein, that the masters or overseers of the several Houses of Correction throughout the Commonwealth, or that towns or counties are now entitled to by law.

[Passed June 12, 1824.]

NOTE. The other sections of this statute relate to the recovery of fines and penalties accruing under the Health laws of the city, to the prosecutions by complaint before the police court of the city, and to the appointment of Aldermen, in case of resignation ; but why these provisions *should be put into the House of Correction,* is best known to those, by whom it was done.

CHAP. XXVIII.

House of Industry.

ACTS OF THE LEGISLATURE.

An act concerning the House of Industry in the City of Boston.

SEC. 1. *Be it enacted by the Senate and House of Representatives, in General Court assembled, and by the authority of the same,* That the City Council of the City of Boston shall choose annually, in the month of May, by ballot, nine discreet and suitable citizens, to be Directors of the House of Industry in said city. *Directors.*

SEC. 2. *Be it further enacted,* That the said directors shall have and exercise the like authority and power, in using, regulating and governing said House of Industry, as are had and exercised by overseers of the poor within this Commonwealth, and may send such persons to said house, and for such purposes, as overseers of the poor are by law authorized to do. *Powers of directors.*

SEC. 3. *Be it further enacted,* That the Justices of the Police Court in the City of Boston, in the County of Suffolk, shall have and exercise the like authority and power, in ordering commitments to said House of Industry, as are now vested in Justices of the Peace, as to commitments to Houses of Correction, according to the provisions of an act, entitled " An act for suppressing and punishing of rogues vagabonds, common beggars, and other idle disorderly and lewd persons," passed on the twenty sixth day of March in the year of our Lord one thousand seven hundred and eighty eight. *Vagabonds may be committed.*

SEC. 4. *Be it further enacted,* That the said directors shall, in the month of April, in every year, make report in writing to the City Council of the persons who shall have been resident in said House of In- *Annual report of directors.*

dustry, during the next preceeding twelve months,—and the manner in which such persons shall have been employed during their residence therein; and the said directors shall also render to the City Council in the month of April, annually, an account of all moneys received and paid on account of the said House.

SEC. 5. *Be it further enacted,* That all rules and orders for the governing and managing said House of Industry, shall, within two months after the same shall have been made, be submitted to the City Council; and such rules and orders shall be in force until repealed or altered by said directors, or until disapproved of by vote of the said City Council.

Rules & orders.

SEC. 6. *Be it further enacted,* That no rules or orders shall be established for the governing and managing said House of Industry, by the directors thereof, unless at a meeting at which five or more of said directors are present.

Limitation of power.

SEC. 7. *Be it further enacted,* That the City Council of the City of Boston, be, and the same hereby is authorized and empowered, as soon after the passing of this act as they may see fit, to choose nine directors of said House of Industry, to continue in office until the election of directors which may be made pursuant to this act in the month of May in the year one thousand eight hundred and twenty-four, any thing in this act to the contrary notwithstanding.

Choice of directors.

[Passed Feb. 3, 1823.]

An act, in addition to the act, entitled "An act concerning the House of Industry in the City of Boston."

Be it enacted by the Senate and House of Representatives, in General Court assembled and, by the authority of the same, That the directors of the House of Industry in the City of Boston, shall have and exercise all the powers and perform all the

duties relative to paupers, and the binding out of
children and other persons committed to said House
of Industry for support as the overseers of the poor
of the several towns in this Commonwealth now have
and exercise in relation to paupers and the binding
out of children and other persons under and by virtue of the several laws of this Commonwealth; and
all acts of said directors shall impose the same duties, liabilities and obligations in all judicial tribunals
on the City of Boston aforesaid, and on the several
towns and individuals of this Commonwealth, as the
same acts would impose, if done and performed in
the same manner by the overseers of the poor of the
several towns in this Commonwealth.

[Passed March 5, 1827.]

Abstract passed Mar 16, 1833

CHAP. XXIX.

Intelligence Offices.

An ordinance relative to Intelligence Offices.

SEC. 1. *Be it ordained by the Mayor, Aldermen, and Common Council of the City of Boston, in City Council assembled,* That the Mayor and Aldermen of said city for the time being, may, from time to time grant licenses to such persons as shall produce to them satisfactory evidence of their good character, to keep intelligence offices in the said city ; and that each license shall designate the house in which the person licensed shall keep his or her office ; and such license shall continue in force until the first day of May after the date thereof, unless sooner revoked by the Mayor and Aldermen (which they shall have authority to do) and no longer.

SEC. 2. *Be it further ordained,* That no person shall keep any intelligence office in the City of Boston, without such license as aforesaid, or after the same shall have been revoked, or at any other house or place than the one designated in such license, under a penalty of a sum not less than five dollars, nor more than twenty dollars.

[Passed Sept. 14, 1826.]

Mayor and Aldermen to grant licenses, &c.

No person to keep an office without license.

CHAP. XXX.

Juvenile Offenders.

An act concerning Juvenile Offenders in the City of Boston.

SEC. 1. *Be it enacted by the Senate and House of Representatives, in General Court assembled and by the authority of the same,* That the City Council of the City of Boston, be, and hereby are authorized to erect a building in said city, for the reception, instruction, employment and reformation of such Juvenile Offenders, as are hereinafter named; or to use for these purposes the House of Industry, or Correction, at South Boston, or any other House or building belonging to said city, that the City Council may appropriate to these uses.

SEC. 2. *Be it further enacted,* That the Directors of the said House of Industry, or such other persons as said City Council shall appoint Directors of said house, for the employment and reformation of Juvenile Offenders, shall have power, at their discretion, to receive and take into said house all such children who shall be convicted of criminal offences Powers granted. or taken up and committed under and by virtue of an act of this Commonwealth, "for suppressing and punishing of rogues, vagabonds, common beggars, and other idle, disorderly and lewd persons," and who may, in the judgment of any Justice of the Supreme Judicial Court, sitting within and for the County of Suffolk, or of the Judge of the Municipal Court of the City of Boston, or of any Justice of the Police Court, within and for the City of Boston, be proper objects therefor; and upon the conviction or commitment aforesaid, of any child, in the judgment of such Judge or Justice a proper object for the said house of employment and reformation, the said Judge or Justice, previous to declaring the sentence of the law on such child, shall cause notice to be given to the Directors of the said house; and in case the said Directors shall declare their assent to the admission of such child into said house, the said Judge or Justice shall sentence him or her to be committed to said house of employment and reformation, subject to the control of the Directors thereof, in conformity with the provisions of this act.

Notice to be given.

SEC. 3. *Be it further enacted,* That any Justice or Judge of either of the said Courts respectively, on the application of the Mayor, or of any Alderman of the City of Boston, or of any Director of the House of Industry, or house of Reformation, or of any Overseer of the Poor, of said city, shall have power to sentence to said house of employment and reformation all children who live an idle or dissolute life, whose parents are dead, or if living, from drunkenness, or other vices, neglect to provide any suitable employment, or exercise any salutary control over said children. And the persons thus committed, shall be kept governed and disposed of, as hereinafter provided, the males till they are of the age of twenty-one years, and the females of eighteen years.

Mayor, &c. may sentence.

SEC. 4. *Be it further enacted,* That the Directors of said House of Industry, or such other persons as said City Council shall appoint Directors of the institution, authorized by this act, may receive the persons sentenced and committed as aforesaid, into said institution; and they shall have power to place the persons committed to their care, the males until they arrive at the age of twenty-one years, and the females until they arrive at the age of eighteen years, at such employments, and to cause them to be instructed in such branches of useful knowledge, as shall be suitable to their years and capacity; and they shall have power to bind out said minors as apprentices or servants, until they arrive at the ages aforesaid, to such persons, and at such places, to learn such arts, trades, and employments, as in their judgment will be most for the reformation, amendment, and future benefit and advantage of such minor. And the provisions of an act, entitled an act providing for the relief and support, employment and removal of the poor and

Authorized to place at service.

for repealing all former laws made for these purposes, passed the twenty-sixth day of February, in the year of our Lord one thousand seven hundred and ninety-four, contained in the fourth, fifth, and sixth sections thereof, so far as they relate to binding out children as servants or apprentices, are adopted as a part of this act ; and the Directors specified in this act shall have all the powers, and be subject to all the duties, of the Overseers of the Poor, as set forth in the sections aforesaid, of the act aforesaid ; and the master or mistress, servant and apprentice, bound out as aforesaid, shall have all the rights and privileges, and **Rights, &c.** be subject to all the duties, set forth in the sections aforesaid, of the act aforesaid.

SEC. 5. *Be it further enacted*, That whenever said Directors, Overseers, or Managers, shall deem it expedient to discharge any minor, committed to their charge as aforesaid, and not bound out as a servant **Discharge.** or apprentice, and shall recommend the same in writing to the court by whom such minor was committed, said court shall have power to discharge him or her from the imprisonment or custody aforesaid.

SEC. 6. *Be it further enacted*, That the said Judge or either of the said Justices, on the application of either of the persons mentioned in the third section of this act, shall have power to order the transfer of **Transfer.** any child committed to the common gaol, or the House of Correction, and inmates of the same at the time of passing this act, to the said house for the employment and reformation of Juvenile Offenders, to be received, kept, or bound out by the Directors thereof in conformity with the provisions of this act.

SEC. 7. *Be it further enacted*, That it shall be lawful for the said City Council, at their discretion, to establish within said city, two or more Houses of **Number of Houses.** Correction, to be Houses of Correction for the County of Suffolk ; and it shall be lawful for the Mayor and Aldermen of said city to transfer persons held under sentence in either of said houses, to any other of said houses, when, in their opinion, the health, moral improvement, or beneficial employment of such persons will be promoted thereby.

[Passed March 4, 1826.]

CHAP. XXXI.

Lamps.

An act for the regulation of Lamps in the City
of Boston.

SEC. 1. *Be it enacted by the Senate and House of
Representatives, in General Court assembled, and by
the authority of the same*, That from and after the
publication of this act, it shall be lawful for the May-
or and Aldermen of the City of Boston, for the time
being, to cause to be set up and affixed, such and so
many Lamps in the streets and other places in the
said city, for the purpose of lighting the same, as they
may determine to be convenient and necessary. And
the said Mayor and Aldermen are hereby empowered to make all necessary contracts, rules, orders, and
regulations, respecting the said lamps, and the lighting and keeping the same in repair, and the regulation and preservation of the same, as they may deem
most for the benefit of said city.

Empowered to make contracts, &c.

SEC. 2. *Be it further enacted*, That whoever shall
wilfully, maliciously, carelessly or wantonly break,
throw down, extinguish, or otherwise injure any of
the said lamps, or the posts, irons, or other furniture
to the same belonging, shall be liable to the fines,
penalties, and forfeitures which are provided in and
by an act, entitled " An act to prevent the wanton
destruction of lamps," made and passed on the eighteenth day of February, in the year of our Lord, one
thousand eight hundred and twenty-four, to be recovered and appropriated in the manner provided in
said act.

Fines, penalties, &c.

SEC. 3. *Be it further enacted*, That the act, entitled " An act for regulating lamps already set
up, or that may hereafter be set up, for enlight-
ening the streets, lanes, alleys, or passage-ways in

Repeal of act.

the town of Boston and to prevent the breaking or otherwise damnifying the same, and also establishing the method for paying the expenses that may arise in supporting or maintaining said lamps," be, and is hereby repealed : *Provided*, the said act shall remain in force as to all fines, penalties, and forfeitures which have been incurred prior to the passing of this act, in and by virtue thereof.

[Passed June 16, 1825.]

CHAP. XXXII.

Licensed Houses.

An act in addition to an act, entitled "An act for the due regulation of Licensed Houses."

Sec· 1. *Be it enacted by the Senate and House of Representatives in General Court assembled, and by the authority of the same,* That from and after the first day of April, which will be in the year of our Lord one thousand eight hundred and seventeen, no person shall presume to be a Confectioner, within the

Regulation of Confectioners.

town of Boston, in the County of Suffolk, except such persons be first duly licensed according to law, by the Justices of the Court of Sessions of the same county, in court assembled, on pain of forfeiting the sum of

Transferred to the Mayor and Aldermen. See City Charter, Sec. 13.

fifty dollars; and if any person shall presume to be a confectioner within the town of Boston, without license therefor, duly had and obtained according to law; or if any confectioner in said town shall presume to sell any spirituous liquors, or any mixed liquors, part of which is spirituous, or shall suffer any person to be drinking spirituous liquors in his or her house, store, or other place of business; or if any confectioner or victualler, as hereinafter described, shall keep open his or her house, store, or other place of business, and entertain any persons therein, after ten of the clock of the evening of any working day, or on any part of the Lord's day or evening, such confectioner or victualler, in any wise so offending, shall on conviction thereof, forfeit and pay for each offence, a fine of ten dollars, with costs of prosecution.

Sec. 2. *Be it further enacted,* That it shall be the

Altered by City Charter, Sec. 13.

duty of the selectmen of the town of Boston, to certify from time to time, to the said Court of Sessions,

what number of victuallers the said selectmen judge
necessary in the said town of Boston, for the public
convenience; who shall not be required to furnish
accommodations for horses or cattle, or lodgings for
travellers or other persons, and shall make return to the
said court of the names and places of business of all
persons who may be so approved by them, as victual- Victuallers.
lers of the description aforesaid; and the said Court
of Sessions may thereupon license such persons as
victuallers as aforesaid, in the manner and for the
term of time as set forth with respect to innholders
and other licensed persons, in the act to which this
is in addition.

SEC. 3. *Be it further enacted,* That no person shall
presume to exercise the trade or business of a confectioner, within the said town of Boston, unless he
or she shall have been first recommended as a suitable person therefor, by the selectmen of the said town
of Boston, to the Court of Sessions, and shall have Altered by City
Charter, Sec. 12.
been licensed by the said Court of Sessions therefor, in
like manner, and for the same term of time as is provided in the act to which this is in addition, for innhold-
ers and retailers. And in all licenses hereafter to 1786. Chap. 68.
Licenses.
be granted to any victualler, confectioner, innholder,
or retailer of spiritous liquors, within the said town of
Boston, the street, lane, alley, or other place, within
the said town, shall be specified, where such licensed
person shall carry on and exercise his or her respective employment. And such license shall not pro-
tect such person for carrying on and exercising his
or her said employment, in any place which is not
therein so specified. And every person, so as aforesaid
licensed, shall, before he or she shall commence, or
carry on and exercise his or her employment, cause Sign.
a sign to be fixed upon a conspicuous place, on the
front of his or her house, shop, or other place of
business, with his or her name painted, and with the
business of innholder, retailer, common victualler, or
confectioner, for which he or she shall have been so licensed, thereon expressed; and no license shall pro-
tect any person in the exercise of his or her said employment, until he or she shall have complied with
this provision.

26

SEC. 4. *Be it further enacted*, That the selectmen of the town of Boston, be, and hereby are authorized and empowered to appoint, from time to time, so many prudent and judicious persons, as Tythingmen of the said town, as in their opinion the public good may require, and for such term of time as they may think fit, and the same to remove from office at their pleasure. And the said tythingmen, so appointed, shall be sworn to the faithful discharge of the duties of their said office, before they shall enter upon the same : and it shall be the duty of the said tythingmen at all times carefully to inspect all licensed houses, shops, or other places within the said town of Boston, and of all offences against this act, and of all disorders or offences which shall at any time come to their knowledge, to have been committed therein, duly to inform, so that prosecutions may be thereupon duly commenced ; and such tythingmen are hereby authorized and empowered, to enter into any licensed house, shop, or other place, and into any rooms or apartments of the same, upon the Lord's day, to the end that they may ascertain whether the laws regulating the same, are duly observed ; and in case any person having a license, or any other person under him or her, or having charge of such licensed house, shop, or other place, shall refuse to admit any such tythingman into the same, or into any rooms or apartments therein, such licensed person, or other person under him or her, so refusing, shall upon con-

Fines and forfeitures. viction thereof, forfeit and pay a fine of ten dollars, with costs of prosecution ; and the license of such person shall thereupon be forfeited. Nor shall a license to such person be renewed, except upon the recommendation of the selectmen to the Court of

Transferred to Mayor and Aldermen. City Charter, Sec. 13. Sessions, who may thereupon renew the same, if they shall think fit so to do.

SEC. 5. *Be it further enacted*, That all fines and penalties which are specified in this act, or forfeitures

Fines and penalties in this act appropriated half to the city, and half to informer. See Stat. 1817, Chap. 50, Sec. 5. incurred under the same, or under the act to which this is in addition, within the town of Boston, shall be prosecuted for, and recovered by indictments in the Municipal Court for the town of Boston ; and all moneys so paid and received, shall be for the use of the County of Suffolk ; and the clerk of the said court, and likewise of the Supreme Judicial Court, to which any judgment of the said Municipal Court may be carried by appeal, shall certify to the selectmen of the town of Boston, within ten days after any conviction shall be had in the same, against any person for any breach of this act, or of the act to which this is in addition, and of final judgment rendered thereon, the names and offences of all persons so convicted, and in all cases of such convictions as aforesaid, and of judgments rendered thereon, the person so **Forfeit of licen; ses.** convicted shall, in addition to the fine or penalty incurred thereby,likewise forfeit his or her said license : which however may be renewed upon the recommen- **Transferred to Mayor and Aldermen.** dation of the selectmen, by the Court of Sessions, in manner as is herein before provided : *Provided, how-* **Proviso** *ever*, that nothing herein contained,shall be considered as affecting in any degree, the force and validity of any existing license, or the right of persons to receive and accommodate boarders and lodgers ; but the law respecting the same is to continue as though this act had not passed.

[Passed Dec. 14, 1816.]

[See also 1807, Chap. 127, additional act to that of 1786, Chap. 68, and 1818, Chap. 65.]

CHAP. XXXIII.

Markets.

An ordinance for the due regulation of the Markets.

SEC. 1. *Be it ordained by the Mayor, Aldermen, and Common Council of the City of Boston, in City Council assembled,* That the limits of Faneuil Hall Market shall be the lower floor and porches of the building recently erected and called Faneuil Hall Market, and the streets on each side thereof, called North Market Street, and South Market Street.

Limits of Faneuil Hall Market See City Charter, sec. 16.

SEC. 2. *Be it further ordained,* That no person shall keep his or her wagon, cart, chaise or other carriage, ox, horse, mule, cow or calf within said North Market street or South Market street, for any longer space of time, or shall range them in any other manner or form than such as may be directed by the Clerk of Faneuil Hall Market, in conformity to the rules and regulations for that purpose made and published by the Mayor and Aldermen, and which they are hereby authorized from time to time to make and publish.

North and South Market streets not to be incumbered.

SEC. 3. *Be it further ordained,* That all carts or other carriages with provisions of any kind for sale, which shall stand within said North and South Market streets, shall be under the direction of the Clerk of Faneuil Hall Market.

Carts and carriages under direction of clerk of F. Hall Market.

SEC. 4. *Be it further ordained,* That no cart, wagon, or other carriage, containing beef, mutton or lamb, shall be allowed to stand within said North and South Market streets, except such as shall be owned by farmers bringing the produce of their own or their neighbours farms for sale.

Farmers bringing the produce of their farms.

SEC. 5. *Be it further ordained,* That all horses shall be taken from the carts or other carriages with provisions of any kind for sale, which shall stand

Horses to be removed from carts and carriages.

within either of the streets aforesaid, and conducted to a stable, or otherwise removed from the said streets by the owner or driver ; and it shall be lawful for the Clerk of the said Market, and he is hereby authorized and empowered, whenever he shall find any wagon, cart, chaise or other carriage, ox, horse, mule, cow or calf, standing or being within either of the streets abovementioned, in a manner, place, or for a time not authorized by law, or contrary to the regulations made in that respect as aforesaid, and without a driver or owner, forthwith to cause such wagon, cart, chaise or other carriage, ox, horse, mule, cow, or calf, to be conducted to some stable or other *Carts and carriages to be carried to stabling, &c.* safe and proper place ; and the owner or the person having the care or keeping thereof shall be liable to pay before the redelivery thereof into his possession the entire cost and expense thereof, during the time it shall be in the said stable, or other safe and suitable place, together with such further sum to the city, not exceeding one dollar, for the trouble arising in that behalf, as the clerk of said market shall demand, the same to be paid to, and accounted for by said clerk.

SEC. 6. *Be it further ordained,* That carriages containing any kind of provisions, excepting beef, *Washington street in front of Boylston market.* mutton or lamb, shall be allowed to stand in Washington street, in front of the Boylston Market house, in one line, on the west side of said street, leaving two spaces for the entrances to the said market house, to be designated and limited by the clerk of the market ; that no cart, wagon, sled or other carriage with beef, mutton or lamb for sale, shall be allowed to stand in Washington street, Boylston street or Essex street, and that no carriages of any kind, nor any empty carriages shall be allowed to stand in Boylston, Essex or Beach streets.

SEC. 7. *Be it further ordained,* That no person shall be allowed to stand in Cambridge street, or *Cambridge street &c.* either of the streets branching therefrom, State street, Dock square, or the square between Ann street, Elm street and Faneuil Hall, Elm street, Ann street, Union street, Brattle street, Market street, Exchange street, Washington street as far south as Court street,

Merchant's Row, or in the street or wharf running from Long Wharf by the east end of the said Faneuil Hall Market to Mill Creek, with their wagons, carts, sleds or horses having meat, poultry, vegetables or other articles of provision for sale, nor shall any person be allowed to place any stall, bench or block in either of said streets, squares or spaces on which to exhibit any such provisions for sale.

Sec. 8. *Be it further ordained*, That no Inhabitant of the City of Boston, or of any town in the vicinity thereof, not offering for sale the produce of his own farm or of some farm in his neighbourhood, shall at any season of the year, without the permission of the Clerk of the Faneuil Hall Market be suffered to occupy any stand, with cart, sleigh or otherwise, for the purpose of vending commodities in either of the streets mentioned in the first section of this ordinance, and every such person, on being ordered so to do by the said clerk, shall forthwith remove from and out of said streets.

Persons not offering for sale the produce of their farms to stand in streets.

Sec. 9. *Be it further ordained*, That no person shall at any time hereafter sell any butter or other commodity, the same, or any separate portion of which, shall be of less weight or measure than that for which he shall undertake to sell the same, or shall practice any species of fraudulent dealing in the market, and no person who shall be convicted of either of the offences or acts aforesaid, or either of the offences enumerated in this ordinance shall be permitted to use, or hire a stall, or have and occupy any stand in either of the public markets in this city, or in any of the streets leading thereto, for the purpose of offering for sale any article of provisions, usually sold in said market, for the term of one year, from and after such conviction.

Butter, &c. fraud in sale of.

Sec. 10. *Be it further ordained*, That whoever shall be guilty of a breach of any of the provisions of this ordinace shall forfeit and pay for each offenc, a sum not less than one dollar, nor more than twenty dollars, and that all by-laws, rules, orders and regulations, made and passed by the town of Boston on the subjects of this ordinance be, and the same are hereby repealed.

Forfeitures.

Sec. 11. *Be it further ordained*, That the clerks of the market appointed and qualified according to law, shall have power, and it shall be their duty to preserve order in the several markets in the city, and to execute and carry into effect all the regulations, orders and ordinances, which may be duly made and established from time to time, by the City Council, or either branch thereof, for the due regulation of the markets, and the said clerks of the market shall be compensated for their services in such manner, and to such amount as shall from time to time, be provided by the city government.

Clerks of markets duty.

[Passed Nov. 13, 1826.]

ordinance passed Sep. 3, 1833 superseding

CHAP. XXXIV.

Marshal of the City.

An ordinance authorizing the election, and prescribing the duties of the City Marshal.

SEC. 1. *Be it ordained by the Mayor, Aldermen, and Common Council of the City of Boston in City Council assembled,* That the Mayor and Aldermen shall forthwith, and forever hereafter, in the month of May annually, appoint a City Marshal, who shall remain in office until the next annual election, unless removed as hereinafter provided.

See City Charter, Sec. 16.

SEC. 2. *Be it further ordained,* That said City Marshal shall be appointed to the offices of Tythingman and Constable ; and during his continuance in the office of City Marshal, shall have precedence and command over the other constables and tythingmen, whenever engaged in the same service, or when directed thereto by the Mayor and Aldermen.

To be also appointed Tythingmen and Constables.

SEC. 3. *Be it further ordained,* That the said City Marshal, before entering upon the duties of his office, shall take before the Mayor and Aldermen, the oaths of office, as by law provided for constables and tythingmen ; and he shall give bond in the sum of one thousand dollars, with surety, to be approved by the Mayor and Aldermen, for the faithful performance of his said office.

Take Oaths of office and give bond.

SEC. 4. *Be it further ordained,* That the City Marshal shall, whenever authorized by the Mayor and Aldermen, employ one or more deputies, who shall be approved by the Mayor and Aldermen ; who shall also, in like manner, take the said oaths of office : whereupon such deputy shall have power and authority to assist the City Marshal, in the execution of his

Deputy Marshals.

office ; or, on any occasion when the City Marshal is not present, to officiate for him in his stead ; but no deputy shall remain in office longer than during the approbation of the Mayor and Aldermen. And the City Marshal shall be responsible for the conduct of each of his deputies.

SEC. 5. *Be it further ordained*, That it shall be the duty of the City Marshal, from time to time, to pass through the streets, alleys, and courts of the city ; to observe nuisances, obstructions, and impediments therein, to the end that the same may be removed or prosecuted, according to law ; to notice all offences against the laws and orders in being, taking the names of offenders, to the end that the same may be prosecuted ; to aid the clerks of the Market in the execution of their duty ; and to receive all complaints of the inhabitants, made against any breach of the laws ; and for this purpose, shall attend daily at some stated hour, in some central and public place. It shall also be his duty to enforce and carry into effect to the utmost of his power, all and every of the city ordinances, according to the true intent and meaning of the same ; as well those which now are, as those which hereafter shall or may be in force ; to obey and execute all the commands and orders of the Mayor and Aldermen, in relation to any matter or thing in which the city may be in any wise concerned or interested ; to be vigilant in detecting any violation or breach of any law or city ordinance ; and for that purpose to pass through every street, lane, alley, or open court of the city, not less than twice a week ; to furnish the Mayor, once a week, with a detailed report, in writing, of all such offences against the laws or the city ordinances, or any of them, as he or his deputies may have detected ; to prosecute all offenders against the laws or city ordinances, if possible, within one week after detecting or ascertaining the offence or offences by them respectively committed ; to attend regularly and punctually, on all trials of offenders prosecuted on behalf of the city ; and to use all lawful ways and means, for the effectual prosecution, and final conviction of offenders ; to lay before the Mayor and Aldermen a cor-

Duty of City Marshal.

27

rect statement of all prosecutions by him instituted before the Municipal or Police Court, within one week after their final determination ; and further to perform all such other and additional duties, and to comply with all such regulations, as may at any time be prescribed to him, by the Mayor and Aldermen.

Sec. 6. *Be it further ordained,* That the Mayor and Aldermen may, at any time, by vote, remove from office the said City Marshal ; and thereupon, or in case of his death or resignation, proceed to appoint a successor, for the residue of the year. And the said City Marshal and his deputies, shall be compensated in like manner, as the Superintendent of Police and his assistants, are now by law authorized to be compensated.

Sec. 7. *Be it further ordained,* That the office of Superintendent of Police, be, and the same is hereby abolished.

[Passed June 18, 1823.]

CHAP. XXXV.

Officers and Office Hours.

Mayor, chosen by the citizens in Ward meetings second Monday of Dec. see City Charter, Sec. 5. Stat. amendment of charter, January 27, 1825.— This last law altered the time of election from the second Monday in April.

City and County Treasurer, chosen annually by City Council in convention, City Charter, Sec. 18.

City Clerk, chosen by City Council in convention first Monday of January, City Charter, Sec. 10, altered from first of May, amendment of charter January 27, 1825.

Clerk of Common Council, chosen by Common Council first Monday of January, City Charter, Sec. 11, altered from first of May, amendment of charter January 27, 1825, and ex officio, assistant City Clerk by virtue of an order of City Council, June 10, 1822.

Auditor of Accounts, chosen by concurrent vote of City Council, in the month of May. Ordinance, December 22, 1825, Sec. 2.

City Marshal, chosen by Mayor and Aldermen, in month of May. Ordinance, June 18, 1822, Sec. 1, and City Charter, Sec. 13.

Superintendent of Burial Grounds, chosen by concurrent vote of City Council, in the month of May or June. Ordinance, May 31, 1824, Sec. 2.

Resident Physician, chosen by concurrent vote of City Council, in month of June. Ordinance, December 25, 1826, Sec. 3.

Island Keeper, chosen by concurrent vote of City Council. Ordinance, December 25, 1826, Sec. 7.

Street Commissioners, chosen by concurrent vote of City Council in January or February, to be first acted upon by the Mayor and Aldermen. Ordinance, April 23, 1827.

Messenger, chosen by Mayor and Aldermen.— City Charter, Sec. 13.

Five Assessors, chosen by concurrent vote of City Council, in the month of March. Ordinance, April 9, 1827.

Clerk of Faneuil Hall Market, chosen annually by Mayor and Aldermen. City Charter, Sec. 13.

Captain of City Watch and Superintendent of Lamps, chosen annually by Mayor and Aldermen. City Charter, Sec. 13.

ORDINANCE OF THE CITY.

An ordinance for regulating the Office hours of the the public Officers of the City.

Treasurer.

SEC. 1. *Be it ordained by the Mayor, Aldermen and Common Council of the City of Boston, in City Council assembled,* That the public office hours of the City Treasurer shall be from 9 o'clock A. M. until 2 o'clock P. M.

City Clerk.

SEC. 2. *Be it further ordained,* That the office hours of the City Clerk shall be, from the first day of April to the first day of October, from 8 o'clock A. M. until 2 o'clock P. M. and from half past 3 o'clock until 6 o'clock P. M. and the remainder of the year 9 o'clock A. M. until 2 o'clock P. M. and from half past 3 o'clock until 5 o'clock P. M. and also to attend and keep the records at all meetings of the Mayor and Aldermen, and of the City Council.

Auditor, Health Commissioner, Superintendent of burying grounds.

SEC. 3. *Be it further ordained,* That the office hours of the Auditor of Accounts, Commissioners of Health and Superintendent of Burying Grounds, shall be the same as are prescribed for the City Clerk.

Clerk of Common Council.

SEC. 4. *Be it further ordained,* That the office hours for the Clerk of the Common Council shall be the same as are prescribed for the City Clerk, and he shall also attend and keep the records at all meetings of the Common Council.

Assessors.

SEC. 5. *Be it further ordained,* That the office hours of the Assessors shall be the same as those appointed for the City Clerk; except such portion of the year as they may be necessarily absent for the purpose of appraising the real and personal property and obtaining the number of polls for taxation.

SEC. 6. *Be it further ordained,* That each of the officers above named shall attend the duties of their several offices at such other times as the interest of the city may require.

[Passed Jan. 10, 1825.]

CHAP. XXXVI.

Porters and Handcartmen.

ACT OF THE LEGISLATURE.

An act for the better regulating Porters employed within the town of Boston.

SEC. 1. *Be it enacted by His Excellency the Governor, Council and Representatives in General Court assembled, and by the authority of the same,* That the Selectmen of the town of Boston for the time being, shall have full power and authority to order what number, and who shall be employed, and take upon them the business of carrying goods, wares and merchandize for pay or wages, as common porters within said town ; and what rate or price such persons shall ask, receive and take for their labour, service and attendance, according to the distance of place or other circumstances, the Selectmen shall order and ascertain ; all which persons, so admitted by the Selectmen, shall at all times when in the service or doing the business of porters wear a badge or ticket with the figure of a pine tree marked thereon, on some part of his upper garment or girdle ; which badge or ticket shall be numbered, and a fair entry of each porters ticket made in the Selectmen's book, also the wages they are to ask and receive, within ten days after the approbation of the Selectmen as aforesaid.

Transfered to the Mayor and Aldermen by city charter.

Porters to be appointed by selectmen to wear badges.

Porters wages.

SEC. 2. *Be it further enacted by the authority aforesaid,* That whosoever shall presume to take up the business and employ of a common porter, and convey or carry goods and merchandize from place to place, within the town of Boston, for hire or wages, without being admitted by the Selectmen, as aforesaid, shall forfeit and pay the sum of twenty shillings, for every time he shall be convicted thereof, before any one of his Majesty's Justices of the Peace, within the county of Suffolk, at Boston aforesaid ; the one half of which fine or forfeiture, shall be disposed of to and for the use of the poor of the town of Boston, the other half to him or them that shall inform and sue for the same.

SEC. 3. *Be it further enacted by the authority aforesaid,* That whosoever being admitted as a porter as aforesaid, shall ask, take, and receive any more than what the selectmen shall allow, for any work or service, shall for every such exaction, forfeit and pay the sum of twenty shillings, to be recovered and disposed of as by this act is already directed ; and if any person admitted and approved of as aforesaid, as a common porter, shall officiate or concern himself in the business of transporting goods or merchandize, not having his badge or ticket, shall, for every such breach of this act, forfeit and pay the sum of twenty shillings, to be recovered and disposed of as aforesaid.

Penalty for appearing without badge, or asking more than the established wages.

SEC. 4. *Be it further enacted by the authority aforesaid,* That the selectmen shall require and take bond of each one of the porters, admitted as aforesaid with sufficient surety, in a sum not exceeding fifty pounds, for their orderly and faithful acting in the business ; more especially, their safe conveying and delivering such goods, as shall be committed to them ; and that upon complaint made to the selectmen, that any whom they may have admitted as aforesaid, do not behave and conduct themselves orderly, peaceably and quietly towards their employers, it being made to appear, the party accused being seasonably notified thereof, such person may be removed, and other meet and orderly person admitted in his room : *Provided,* this act be in force, and so continue for the space of seven years, from the publication thereof, and no longer.

Selectmen to take security for porter's fidelity.

Disorderly to be removed.

Limitation.

[Passed 1741, and made perpetual by an act passed in 1797 —See Vol. I, Mass. Laws, 523.]

An ordinance for the regulation of public Porters and Handcartmen.

SEC. 1. *Be it ordained by the Mayor, Aldermen and Common Council of the City of Boston, in City Council assembled,* That no person shall follow the business of a public Porter or Handcartman in *To be licensed.* the City of Boston, without being licensed as such by the Mayor and Aldermen for the time being, under a penalty of five dollars for every such offence.

SEC. 2. *Be it further ordained,* That the Mayor and Aldermen of said city, for the time being, may *Duration of license.* from time to time, grant licenses to such persons as shall produce to them satisfactory evidence of their good character, to follow the business of public porter or handcartmen in this city; and such license shall continue in force until the first day of May, after, the date thereof, unless sooner revoked by the Mayor and Aldermen, (which they have authority to do,) and no longer.

SEC. 3. *Be it further ordained,* That the Mayor and Aldermen be, and they are hereby authorized *Stands to be assigned.* and empowered to appoint, from time to time, as occasion may require, such and so many stands for handcarts and wheelbarrows, as to them shall appear requisite, and no owner or person using such handcart or wheelbarrow, (the same being intended to carry for hire,) shall stand in any other place with his handcart or wheelbarrow, than such as has been, or shall be directed and established by the Mayor and Aldermen, in pursuance of this ordinance, unless such owner shall first obtain the consent of the Mayor and Aldermen of the city so to place the same; and whoever shall offend against any provision of this section shall forfeit and pay for each offence, a sum not less than one dollar, nor more than three dollars.

SEC. 4. *Be it further ordained,* That every handcart, wheelbarrow, or handbarrow belonging to any *Handcarts and barrows to be marked with name and number.* individual of the city, and intended to carry for hire shall be marked with the initials of the christian, and

the whole of the surname, of the owner or owners of
the same, and the number of his license strongly and
legibly in paint, upon a plate of tin or iron, which
names shall be placed upon some conspicuous part of
every handcart, wheelbarrow, or handbarrow, so as
to be clearly visible and discernable to all persons
passing and repassing the streets during the daytime,
and the names and numbers herein required, to be
marked and painted upon all handcarts, wheelbarrows, and handbarrows, shall be renewed as often as
they become defaced, or indistinct ; and whoever
shall offend against any provision of this section shall
forfeit and pay for each offence, a sum not less than
one dollar, nor more than three dollars.

Sec. 5. *Be it further ordained,* That no public
porter or handcartman shall ask, demand, or receive
any exorbitant, unreasonable, or unusual rate or price
for transporting any article or articles ; and no public porter or handcartman shall neglect or refuse to
Duty of porters, transport any article for a reasonable and customary
&c. not to re- price, when required, unless he shall be actually
fuse to transport otherwise engaged or employed, or unless the dis-
articles. tance he shall be required to go shall exceed two
miles ; and no public porter or handcartman shall
practice or be guilty of any deceit, fraud, or imposi-
tion whatsoever ; and whoever shall offend against
any provision of this section, shall forfeit and pay for
each offence, a sum not less than one dollar, nor
more than five dollars.

Sec. 6. *Be it further ordained,* That no public
porter or handcartman, shall permit or suffer any
No persons ex- other person, except one of good character and reg-
cept licensed to ularly employed by him, to carry any article or arti-
carry for hire. cles in his handcart, wheelbarrow, or handbarrow,
under the penalty of two dollars for each offence.

Sec. 7. *Be it further ordained,* That all orders
Former by-laws, and by-laws heretofore made and passed by the in-
&c. repealed. habitants of the town of Boston ; and all orders and
ordinances heretofore made and passed by the City
Council of the City of Boston, on the subjects of
this ordinance be, and the same are hereby repealed.

[Passed Sep. 18, 1826.]

CHAP. XXXVII.

Provisions.

An ordinance to prevent the sale of Unwholesome Provisions.

Be it ordained by the Mayor, Aldermen, and Common Council of the City of Boston, in City Council assembled, That if any person shall sell or offer for sale, in any of the markets of this city, any unwholesome, stale or putrid articles of provisions; or any meat that has been blown, raised or stuffed; or any diseased or measly pork, knowing the same to be such, he shall for each offence, forfeit and pay a sum not less than two dollars nor more than twenty dollars.

[Passed Dec. 18, 1826.]

NOTE—The statute of 1784, Chap. 50, " against selling unwholesome provisions," embrace, the principal objects of this ordinance. Prosecutions upon this statute are not unfrequent; and if the offences committed in our markets come within its provisions, the prosecutions ought to be carried to the Municipal Court, that the severest penalties of the statute may be inflicted, for this *foul* offence.

28

CHAP. XXXVIII.

Pumps and Wells.

An ordinance for the repair and keeping in order Wells and pumps.

SEC. 1. *Be it ordained by the Mayor, Aldermen, and Common Council of the City of Boston, in City Council assembled,* That it shall be the duty of the Mayor and Aldermen, to keep supplied with suitable pumps, all wells belonging or which have or may belong to the city; and to keep the same in good order and repair; and to cause the expense of providing such pumps, as well as keeping them in repair, and also a reasonable charge for the use of the same, to be annually assessed upon the owners of real estate in the vicinity of such well, and whose tenants make use of the same; and where such owners are absent or out of this Commonwealth, or unknown, then they shall assess his or their proportion of the same, upon the tenants of such real estate, said assessment to be charged on said estate.

SEC. 2. *Be it further ordained,* That the owner or tenant of such real estate, as the case may be, being assessed as aforesaid, shall pay the amount thereof into the City Treasury within ten days from the time of delivery of such notice; and in case of neglect thereof for the space of ten days, it shall be the duty of the City Treasurer to prosecute for the same.

SEC. 3. *Be it further ordained,* That if the said owner or tenant being assessed, as aforesaid, shall make it appear to the satisfaction of the Mayor and Aldermen, that he has, upon his own estate, a good and sufficient well of water, and that neither he, nor any tenant or occupant of his estate, has made any use of, or has any necessity to resort to such public pump or well, that in such case it shall be in the power of the Mayor and Aldermen to release such

[Marginal notes:]

Wells to be supplied with pumps the owners of real estates to be assessed therefor.

City Treasurer to prosecute persons who neglect to pay.

Owners not making use of the water not to be assessed.

owner or tenant from the payment of such assessment : *Provided, always,* that in such case if it shall be made satisfactorily afterwards to appear, that any tenant or occupant of such estate, hath made use of said public well or pump, that such owner or tenant shall be liable to pay double the amount of that, and of all other assessments, which may have been made upon such estate, if from the circumstances of the case, the Mayor and Aldermen shall see fit to demand the same.

SEC. 4. *Be it further ordained,* That in case of any well or pump being in any street, alley, court or other open place, the proprietors whereof are unknown, or who unreasonably neglect to keep the same in good order and repair, it shall be lawful for the Mayor and Aldermen (in case they consider the interest of the city, or the convenience of the neighbourhood requires it) to take possession of such well or pump, and to cause the same to be put into, and to be kept in suitable order and repair, and to assess the same, either upon the proprietors thereof, or upon the owners or tenants of such real estate, in the vicinity, in the manner, on the principles, and under the restrictions provided in the second and third sections of this ordinance, in the case of public wells and pumps.

SEC. 5. *Be it further ordained,* That the Mayor and Aldermen may, if they see fit, annually appoint one or more superintendents of public wells and pumps, and allow him or them for his or their services, in each case, such compensation as they may deem just, and reasonable, to be charged, and to make a part of the assessment against the owners or tenants of the estate in the vicinity as aforesaid.

SEC. 6. *Be it further ordained,* That all pumps belonging to the inhabitants of this city, shall be kept in constant good order and sufficient repair, at all times ready to deliver water for extinguishing any fire. And whosoever shall permit the pump or pumps, of any of his, her or their house or houses, tenement or tenements, to be out of order, and so to remain for the space of ten days together, shall forfeit and pay the sum of four dollars. And further if any such person or persons, shall refuse or neglect to put his, her, or their pump or pumps, into good order and proper repair, after having so incurred and forfeited such penalty of four dollars, as aforesaid, every such person so refusing or neglecting, shall be deemed to be guilty of a new offence every week after; and shall for such new offence, forfeit and pay the sum of four dollars for every such week that the same shall be permitted to continue out of order or repair as aforesaid.

City Marshal to inspect pumps.

SEC. 7. *Be it further ordained,* That the City Marshal shall visit and inspect, or cause to be visited and inspected, all the pumps belonging to the city, or to any inhabitant or inhabitants of the city four times in each year, to wit, on the first days of March, June, September, and December; to the intent that thorough information may be obtained of the state thereof and of the regular and speedy repair of the same.

By-law and order repealed.

SEC. 8. *Be it further ordained,* That all orders and by-laws coming within the purview of this ordinance, be, and the same are hereby repealed.

[Passed July 10, 1823.]

ordinance passed Dec 30. 1831. superseding

CHAP. XXXIX.

Seal of the City.

An ordinance to establish the City Seal.

Be it ordained by the Mayor, Aldermen, and Common Council of the City of Boston, in City Council assembled, That the design hereto annexed, as sketched by John R. Penniman, giving a view of the city, be the devise of the city seal ; that the motto be as follows, to wit: " Sicut patribus, sit deus nobis ;" and that the inscription be as follows, to wit: " Bostonia condita A. D. 1630. Civitatis regimine Donata, A. D. 1822."

[Passed Jan. 2, 1823.]

CHAP. XL.

South Boston.

ACT OF THE LEGISLATURE.

An act to set off the north east part of the town of Dorchester, and to annex the same to the town of Boston.

Boundaries of land set off.

See ante as to buildings in South Boston

Proviso respecting taxes.

SEC. 1. *Be it enacted by the Senate and House of Representatives, in General Court assembled, and by the authority of the same,* That all that part of Dorchester, lying north east of the following line, to wit : Beginning at a stake and stones at Old Harbour, so called, at the southwest corner of land formerly belonging to John Champney, running north thirty-seven and one half degrees west, to a large elm tree marked P. on the southwest side, and B. on the north east, standing on land belonging to the heirs of Thomas Bird, deceased ; then running the same course to a heap of stones on the south east side of the road ; thence across the road, the same course, to a heap of stones on the north west side ; thence on the same course to a black oak tree, standing on a small hummock marked D. on the one side, and B. on the other, upon land of Ebenezer Clapp, Jr. ; thence the same course until it comes to Boston harbour, with the inhabitants thereon, be and they are hereby annexed to the town of Boston in the County of Suffolk, and shall hereafter be considered and deemed to be a part of the town of Boston : *Provided,* That the said tract of land and the inhabitants thereon, set off as aforesaid, shall be holden to pay all such taxes as are already assessed, or ordered to be assessed by said town of Dorchester, in the same manner as they would have been, if this act had not been passed.

SEC. 2. *Be it further enacted,* That the proprietors of the said tract, shall assign and set apart three lots of land on the same, for public use, viz: one lot for the purpose of a public market place ; one lot for a school house ; and one lot for a burial ground, to the satisfaction and acceptance of the Selectmen of the said town of Boston ; or in case the said selectmen and proprietors shall not agree upon the said lots, it shall be lawful for the Supreme Judicial Court at any session thereof in the said County of Suffolk, upon application of the said selectmen, to nominate and appoint three disinterested freeholders within the Commonwealth, and not inhabitants of the said town of Boston, to assign and set off the three lots of land aforesaid, by metes and bounds ; and the report of the said freeholders, or any two of them, being made and returned to, and accepted by the said Court, at any session thereof in said county, shall be final and binding on all parties ; and the lots of land by them assigned and set off as aforesaid, shall thenceforth vest in the said town of Boston forever, without any compensation to be made therefor by the town ; but if the person or persons whose land shall be assigned and set apart as aforesaid, shall demand compensation therefor, the same shall be appraised by three freeholders to be appointed as aforesaid, who shall also assess upon the other proprietors, the sum or sums which each shall be holden to pay to the person whose lands may be thus assigned for public use ; and the report of said freeholders or any two of them, being made and returned to, and accepted by said court, judgment thereon shall be final, and execution awarded as in case of reports of referees under a rule of court.

SEC. 3. *Be it further enacted*, That the select- men of said town shall be, and hereby are authorized to lay out such streets and lanes through the said tract, as in their judgment may be for the common benefit of the said proprietors and of the said town of Boston ; a reasonable attention being paid to the wishes of said proprietors ; and in case of disagreement between the selectmen and said proprietors, or either of them, the same proceedings shall be had as are provided by law in other cases for laying out town ways : *Provided, only,* that no damages or compensation shall be allowed to any proprietor for such streets and lanes as may be laid out within twelve months from the passing of this act: *And provided also,* that the town of Boston shall not be obliged to complete the streets laid out by their selectmen pursuant to this act, sooner than they may deem it expedient so to do.

Proviso.

[Passed March 6, 1804.]

CHAP. XLI.

Schools.

An ordinance providing for the election and compensation of Instructors of the public schools.

Be it ordained by the Mayor, Aldermen and Commom Council of the City of Boston in City Council assembled, That the School Committee be, and they are hereby authorized to elect all such Instructors for the public schools, as they may think necessary, and to fix and determine the amount of their respective salaries, and also to remove any instructor from said schools, whenever in their discretion they shall deem it necessary or proper ; and generally to execute all the powers, which Selectmen or School Committees in the several towns in this Commonwealth are by law authorized to execute in relation to public schools.

See city charter, Sec. 19. Choice of School Committee.

[Passed May 24, 1822.]

CHAP. XLII.

Streets.

ACTS OF THE LEGISLATURE.

Add act March 4, 1805.

An act to regulate the paving of streets in the town of Boston, and for removing obstructions in the same.

SEC. 1. *Be it enacted by the Senate and House of Representatives in General 'Court assembled and by the authority of the same,* That all streets shall hereafter be paved in the town of Boston agreeable to the following regulations, viz. The foot path or walk on each side of every street, shall be of the breadth of one sixth part of the width of the whole street, and shall be laid or paved with bricks or flat stones, and secured with a beam or cut stone along the out side thereof; and the middle or remaining four sixths of every street, shall remain as a passage-way for carriages of burden or pleasure; and shall have a gutter on each side thereof, or otherwise as the surveyors of high ways in the said town shall determine; and shall be paved with good and sufficient paving stones : *Provided, always,* that if in any street so to be paved, the sides shall not exactly range, the gutter or out side of the foot walk shall be laid out as nearly in a straight line, as the street will admit of ; and in all squares, and other large open spaces, and in all streets the breadth of which shall not conform to this law, the breadth of the foot walk, and the ascent and descent, and the crowning of the pavement in every street, shall be regulated by the surveyors of high ways.

SEC. 2. *Be it further enacted,* That where the cartway in any public street, shall be hereafter or-

Foot walk, width of, and manner of paving.

Provision for squares and narrow streets.

dered to be paved, every owner of the lot or lots of ground upon such street, shall, without delay, at his own cost, cause the footway in front of his ground to be paved with bricks or flat stones, and supported by [timber or] hewn stones, and kept in repair; the same to be done under the direction of, and to the approbation of the surveyors of highways; and if the owner or owners of such lots shall neglect to pave with bricks or flat stones, and to support the footway, for the space of twenty days after he or the tenant of such lot, or the attorney of the said owner or owners, shall have been thereto required by any of the surveyors of highways, then it shall be lawful for the said surveyors of highways, and they are hereby enjoined and required to pave the said footways with brick or flat stones, and to support and to defend the same, and to repair the same; and shall recover the whole amount thereof by action of the case to be brought by the surveyors of highways, before any court proper to try the same: *Provided, nevertheless,* that in all cases where applications may be made for new paving of streets, any individual who may be affected thereby, may make their objections to the selectmen, or surveyors of highways, who are directed to take them into consideration while deliberating upon the expediency of said application, and to pave the same at the expense of said town whenever they shall think it expedient: *Provided, also,* that where there are any vacant lots of land in any such streets, the surveyors of highways may, at their discretion, allow the owner or owners thereof to cover the foot-path with planks, which shall be removed, and the brick, or flat stone pavement shall be completed, whenever it may become necessary in the judgment of said surveyors.

SEC. 3. *Be it further enacted,* That the Selectmen of the said town of Boston, for the time being, whenever in their opinion the safety and convenience of the inhabitants of said town shall require it, shall be, and they are hereby empowered, to lay out or widen any street, lane, or alley of said town; and for that purpose, to remove any building or buildings of what nature soever; and the owner or owners of such

Marginal notes:

Foot walk to be paved when the cartway is.

Repealed as to timber. 1809, Chap. 29, Sec. 1.

Owners neglecting to pave.

Provision for persons aggrieved.

Planks may be used before vacant lots.

Selectmen empowered to widen streets.

building, shall be entitled to receive compensation for the damages which he or they may sustain by such removal, which damages shall be ascertained, determined, and recovered in the way and manner pointed out in the act of this Commonwealth, entitled "An act directing the method of laying out highways."

SEC. 4. *Be it further enacted*, That no canopy, balcony, platform of cellar door, or step in any street, lane, or alley in the town of Boston, shall project into such street, more than one tenth part of the width of the street, and in no case more than three feet; and all cellar doors hereafter to be made or repaired, shall be built with upright cheeks, and shall not project from the line of the house, more than six inches; and if any proprietor or owner of any such canopy, balcony, platform, or cellar door, or steps, shall refuse or neglect to remove or take down the same, within five days after notice and direction given him or them by the surveyors of highways, or any person empowered by them to that purpose, such owner or proprietor, shall forfeit and pay the sum of two dollars, for each and every day the same shall remain after the expiration of the said five days.

Balconies, cellar doors, &c.regulated.

SEC. 5. *Be it further enacted*, That no post shall be erected or set in any of the streets of the said town of Boston, except at the corner or intersection of two streets, and in such other places as the surveyors of highways may authorize and direct, and the said surveyors may remove the same; and no person shall plant any tree in any street in the said town of Boston, without leave first obtained from the surveyors of highways, who shall have power to remove the same : And if any person shall drive any horse or cart, or any wheel carriage of burden or pleasure, or wheel any wheelbarrow on the footwalk of any street in said town of Boston, such person shall forfeit and pay the sum of one dollar, for every such offence, to be recovered by action of debt, in the name of the surveyors of highways, before any Justice of the Peace in the County of Suffolk; and no person shall in future make, erect, or have any portico or porch any bow window, or other window, which shall project into the streets of the said town of Boston, more

Posts and trees not to be put in streets without consent of the surveyors of highways.

Penalty for wheeling barrows, &c. on sidewalks.

Direction respecting bow windows, &c.

than one foot beyond the front of his or her house ; or hang any sign, or any goods, wares, or merchandize, which shall project into the street more than one foot beyond the front of his or her house or lot : And if any person shall hereafter offend against this provision, every person so offending, shall forfeit and pay the sum of one dollar for each and every day such portico or porch, bow-window, or other window shall be continued, after notice given to him by the surveyors of highways, or by any person by them authorized to that purpose.

SEC. 6. *Be it further enacted*, That if any person or persons shall continue to place in the street, contrary to the meaning of this act, any goods, wares, or merchandizes, it shall be lawful for the surveyors of highways of the said town of Boston, or any person empowered by them, to remove such goods, wares, and merchandizes, and to keep them in safe custody ; and the proprietor or owner of such goods, wares, and merchandizes, shall not have the same goods restored, until he or they shall have paid to the person or persons so removing them, all expenses of removing and storing them, and a reasonable compensation for the time so employed in their removal, as well as the fine aforesaid : And if any person shall place or pile any empty boxes, barrells, hogsheads, or other conveniency capable of containing goods or merchandize, or that may have contained goods or merchandize, in any part of the streets of the said town of Boston, more than five minutes after notice given to remove the same, such person shall forfeit and pay the sum of two dollars, for each and every such offence, to be recovered by action of debt, by the surveyors of highways, before any Justice of the Peace in said county.

Merchandize not to be placed in the streets.

SEC. 7. *Be it further enacted*, That if any driver, owner, or person having the ordering or care of any cart, wagon, stage, or hackney coach, stage wagon, or other carriage, new or old, finished or unfinished, shall suffer the same to be and remain in any street, lane, or alley, of said town, more than one hour after the same shall have first been placed there, unless by the permission of the surveyors of highways,

Carriages not to be left in the streets.

every such owner, driver, or person having the care or ordering of such carriage as aforesaid, shall forfeit and pay the sum of one dollar, for each and every such offence, to be recovered as above directed : *Provided, nevertheless,* that no prosecution shall be commenced against any driver of any cart or wagon coming from the country, unless by the particular direction and order of the Selectmen.

Proviso.

SEC. 8. *Be it further enacted,* That all the forfeitures and fines which may be recovered in pursuance of this act, shall go and be distributed, one moiety thereof to the poor of the town of Boston, and the other moiety to the surveyors of the highways.

Disposal of fines.

[Passed June 22, 1799.]

An act in addition to an act, entitled " An act to regulate the paving of Streets in the town of Boston, and for removing obstructions in the same."

Be it enacted by the Senate and House of Representatives in General Court assembled, and by the authority of the same, That the Selectmen of the town of Boston for the time being, whenever in their opinion the safety or convenience of the inhabitants of said town shall require it, shall be, and they are hereby empowered to lay out any new street, or to widen any street, lane or alley of said town, and for that purpose to take any land that may be required for the same, and to remove any building or buildings of what nature soever ; and the same street, lane or alley being recorded in the town's books, shall be thereby established as such ; and the owner or owners of the land or buildings that shall be so taken or removed, shall receive such recompense for the damages which he or they may thereby sustain, as the party interested and the Selectmen shall agree upon, to be paid by the town, or the individual person or persons, for whose use such street, lane or

New streets may be laid out.

Owners of land, &c. to indemnified.

alley is laid out or widened, or as shall be ordered by the Justices of the Court of General Sessions of the peace, upon an enquiry into the same by a Jury to be summoned for that purpose ; who shall be drawn out of the Jury box of the Supreme Judicial Court of the town of Boston, by the Selectmen of said town, upon the application of the Sheriff of the County of Suffolk ; and if by accident or challenge, there should happen not to be a full jury, said officers shall fill the pannel, *de talibus circumstantibus*, as in other cases ; or by a special committee, if the parties agree thereto.

[Passed March 4, 1805.]

An act in addition to the several acts now in force to regulate the paving of Streets in the town of Boston and for removing obstructions in the same.

SEC. 1. *Be it enacted by the Senate and House of Representatives in General Court assembled, and by the authority of the same,* That in paving or repairing the pavement in any street in the town of Boston, in future, no person shall place timber or wood in front of his or her house or lot, to support the foot walk, but the same shall be supported with hammered or cut stone, any thing in the second section of the act to which this is in addition, passed the twenty second day of June in the year of our Lord one thousand seven hundred and ninety nine, to the contrary notwithstanding. *(Stone, curb stones.)*

SEC. 2. *Be it further enacted,* That the Selectmen* of the town of Boston, shall be, and they are hereby empowered to appoint suitable places in the streets or squares of said town, in which all wagons, carts, sleds or other carriages, shall be directed to stand. *(Places may be appointed for teams, &c.)*

---

* Mayor and Aldermen.

Sec. 3. *Be it further enacted*, That the said Se-lectmen* shall have power from time to time, to make and adopt such rules and orders for the due regulation of all such carriages in the streets of the said town of Boston as to them shall appear neces-sary and expedient ; which rules and orders shall be published, at least one week, in two of the newspa-pers p inted in said town ; and any owner or driver of any carriage, who shall offend against any such rule and order so adopted and published, shall forfeit and pay a sum not exceeding five dollars, to be re-covered upon complaint of either one of the Select-men of said town of Boston before any one of the Justices of the Peace for the County of Suffolk ; and all such fines and forfeitures shall be paid for the use of the person prosecuting for the breach of any such rule or order.

Rules and regu-lations respect-ing carriages.

[Passed June 19, 1809.]

An act in further addition to an act, entitled " An act to regulate the paving of Streets in the town of Boston, and for removing obstructions in the same."

Sec. 1. *Be it enacted by the Senate and House of Representatives in General Court assembled and by the authority of the same*, That the Selectmen† of the town of Boston, for the time being, whenever in their opinion the safety or convenience of the Inhabitants of said town shall require it, shall be and they hereby are empowered to discontinue any street, lane or alley of the said town, or to make any alteration in the same, in part or in whole ; reserving however, in all cases, to individuals who may sustain damage thereby, recompense for the same, to be ascertained and allowed in the same manner as is provided in the act, entitled " An act entitled an act, in addition to an act, entitled " an act to regulate the paving of

Power to discon-tinue streets, &c.

streets in the town of Boston, and for removing obstructions in the same."

SEC. 2. *Be it further enacted,* That all orders votes and determinations of the said Selectmen of the town of Boston, heretofore had and passed for the discontinuance of any street, lane or alley of the said town, or respecting any alteration in the same, in whole or in part, shall be held and considered as good and valid to all intents and purposes, as if the said act to which this is in addition, had explicitly vested said authority in the said Selectmen ; reserving always to i ndividuals recompense for damages sustained thereby as is provided in the said act. *Orders, votes, &c. valid.*

SEC. 3. *Be it further enacted,* That the Selectmen of the town of Boston shall keep a record of all the streets, lanes and alleys of the said town, and of all votes and proceedings relative to the same ; and that copies thereof, certified by the town Clerk, shall be valid to all intents and purposes. *Record of streets.*

SEC. 4. *Be it further enacted,* That from and after the passing of this act, no person shall raise up from any street, wharf, or place of public resort, within the town of Boston, for the purpose of storing the same, any cask, bale of goods, or other articles of merchandize, into the second or any higher story of an house, store, or other building upon or adjoining the same, and on the out side of such buildings ; and that no person shall deliver, from the second or any higher story of any house, store, or other building on the out side of the same, which shall adjoin upon any street, wharf or place of public resort, within the said town of Boston, any cask, bale of goods, or other article of merchandize, except at such times and places, and under such restrictions and limitations, as the Selectmen* for the time being shall, by writing authorize and direct. And every person who shall offend in manner aforesaid, shall forfeit and pay to the Commonwealth, for each and every such offence, a sum not exceeding one hundred dollars, nor less than ten dollars, to be recovered by indictment in the Municipal Court for the town of Boston, with costs of prosecution : *Provided,* that this shall not *Prohibitions.* *Penalties.* *Proviso.*

* Mayor and Aldermen.

be construed to extend to the raising any materials or other articles which may be necessary in erecting, repairing or taking down any building within the said town of Boston, or for the convenience thereof, or for removing any merchandize or other article in case of danger by fire, or other inevitable casuality.

[Passed Dec. 13, 1816.]

Act passed June 13, 1831 - Mar. 5, 1830
Mar. 5, 1833
Mar. 26, 1833

ORDINANCES OF THE CITY.

An ordinance changing the names of sundry streets therein named.

Be it ordained by the Mayor, Aldermen and Common Council of the City of Boston, in City Council assembled, That from and after the passing of this ordinance, the main street leading from Faneuil Hall Market, through Cornhill, Marlborough, Newbury, Orange and Washington streets, over the neck to the line between Boston and Roxbury, and heretofore called and known by those several names, shall be called and known by the name of Washington street only. And that the street running from Faneuil Hall Market, through Ann, Fish, and Ship streets, to North street, shall be called and known by the name of Ann street only. And that the street leading from the main street easterly by the old south meeting house to India street, and heretofore called Milk and Commercial streets, shall be called and known by the name of Milk street only. And the street running from State street across Liberty Square to Milk street, and now called Kilby and Adams streets, shall be called and known by the name of Kilby street only. And that the street running from Court street, through Hanover, Middle and North streets, to the ferryways, shall be called and known by the name of Hanover street only. And that the street running from Beacon street through Bowdoin and Middlecot streets to Cambridge street, shall be called and known by the

Streets.
Washington.

Ann.

Milk.

Kilby.

Hanover.

name of Bowdoin street only. And that the street Bowdoin. running from Charles street to Temple street, and now known and called Olive and Sumner streets, shall be known and called by the name of Sumner Sumner. street only. And that the street now called Temple street, leading from Cambridge street to Sumner street, and that part of Sumner street which runs east of the State House, to Beacon street, shall be called Temple. and known by the name of Temple street only. And that the street running from Court street to the main street, and heretofore called Tremont, Common and Nassau streets, shall be called and known by the Common. name of Common street only. And that the streets called Back and Salem streets, leading from Hanover street to Charter street, shall hereafter be known by the name of Salem street only ; and that the street Salem. called Richmond street and Proctor's lane, leading from Back street to Fish street, be hereafter called Richmond street only ; and that the street called Richmond Rainsford and Front streets, leading from Essex street to South Boston bridge, be hereafter called Front Front. street only.

[Passed July 6, 1824.]

An ordinance to prevent unlawful and injurious practices in the streets of the city.

SEC. 1. *Be it ordained by the Mayor, Aldermen and Common Council of the City of Boston, in City Council assembled,* That no person shall break or dig Streets not to be broken up without a permit. up the stones or ground in any of the streets, lanes, alleys, public squares or other public places in this city for the purpose of laying or repairing of any drain, or for or upon any occasion whatever, without the leave or license of the Mayor and Aldermen, in writing, or some person by them authorized for that purpose, first had and obtained, on pain of forfeiting for each offence a sum not less than three dollars and not more than twenty dollars.

SEC. 2. *Be it further ordained*, That whosoever shall, by virtue of such leave or license, break up the pavement, or dig, or cause to be dug and broken up, any part of the pavement, or any of the ground of any street, lane, alley, public square or place in the city, shall, within such time as the Mayor and Aldermen shall grant or order, after the same is broken or dug up, cause the same to be sufficiently repaired and amended from time to time to the satisfaction of the Mayor and Aldermen, on pain of forfeiting for such offence a sum not less than three dollars, nor more than twenty dollars, and also a sum not less than one dollar and not more than twenty dollars for each and every week, until the same be properly and duly amended and repaired as aforesaid.

Streets to be repaired after drains have been laid.

SEC. 3. *Be it further ordained*, That when any drain or aqueduct shall be opened or laid, and the dirt gravel or other material therefrom, shall be laid in any street, lane, alley, public square or other public place in the city, the person or persons by whom the said drain or aqueduct shall be opened or laid, shall cause a rail or other sufficient fence to be placed and fixed, so as to inclose such drain or aqueduct, and the dirt, gravel, or other material thrown into the street, and other places as aforesaid; and such fence shall be continued during the whole time such drain or aqueduct shall be open for the purposes aforesaid. And that a lighted lantern, or some other proper and sufficient light, shall be fixed to some part of such fence or in some other proper manner, over such open drain or aqueduct, and the dirt, gravel or other material taken from the same, and so kept from the beginning of the twilight of the evening, through the whole of the night, and shall be continued every evening or night, during all the time such drain or aqueduct shall be open, or in a state of repair; and that whoever shall be guilty of a breach of any part of this section, shall forfeit and pay for each offence a sum not less than three dollars, and not more than twenty dollars.

Drains and Aqueducts—laying of.

Fence and lights to be kept.

SEC. 4. *Be it further ordained*, That whenever any person shall intend to erect any building upon his, her, or their land abutting on any of the streets, lanes, alleys, or other public places or squares in this city, or shall intend to repair any building so abutting, he, she or they, or his, her or their agent, shall make the same known to the Mayor and Aldermen, or any person or officer by them empowered, who shall have power and authority to set off or allot such part or portion of the street, or other public places aforesaid, thereto adjoining, as they in their discretion shall think necessary and sufficient for the purpose; observing nevertheless to do the same with as little detriment as possible; and so as to leave, in all parts where it can be done, sufficient room for carts and carriages to pass therein. And the part or portion so set off or allotted, shall be used for laying all the materials for any such building or repairing, and for receiving the rubbish arising therefrom. And all the rubbish arising therefrom or thereby, shall be fully and entirely removed and carried away, at the expense of the person or persons so building or repairing, which shall be done in such convenient time as the Mayor and Aldermen may direct and limit. And all persons offending against any of the provisions of this section, shall forfeit and pay for each offence, a sum not less than three dollars, and not more than twenty dollars : *Provided, nevertheless,* that the time granted for any allotment shall not be extended beyond the period of thirty days on one application.

Buildings or lots in streets to be set off on erecting.

SEC. 5. *Be it further ordained,* That neither the purchaser nor seller of any cord wood, or other firewood, shall permit or suffer such wood unnecessarily to be and remain in any of the streets, lanes, alleys, or other public places in this city, after dark in the evening ; nor shall any greater quantity than two loads of such wood in any case, be permitted either by the purchaser or seller thereof, to lay or continue in any street, lane, alley, or other public place. And in case the same must of necessity remain after dark, the purchaser thereof shall cause a sufficient light to be kept or placed over or near the same, throughout the whole of the night, so as to give sufficient notice to all the inhabitants, and thereby prevent injury to all persons passing in the places where

Cord wood not to remain in streets.

such wood may be laid and deposited ; nor shall any person whatever suffer or permit any such wood, at any time, by day or by night, to lay or remain in any street, lane, alley, or other public place or square in the city, so as unnecessarily to obstruct the passage in the same ; and whoever shall be guilty of a breach of any of the provisions of this section, shall forfeit and pay for each offence, a sum not less than one dollar, and not more than twenty dollars.

Sec. 6. *Be it further ordained,* That no person
Wood not to be sawed or piled on sidewalks, &c. hereafter shall saw any firewood, or pile the same, upon the foot or sidewalks of any of the streets or lanes of this city ; and that no person shall stand on any such foot or sidewalk, with his woodsaw or horse, to the hindrance or obstruction of any foot passenger, under a penalty of a sum not less than one dollar, and not more than twenty dollars.

Sec. 7. *Be it further ordained,* That whosoever
Foot-ball, throwing stones and snowballs. hereafter shall, at any time, use the exercise of playing at foot ball ; or whoever shall be guilty of throwing stones or snow-balls within any of the streets, squares, lanes, or alleys of this city, shall forfeit and pay, for each offence, a sum not less than fifty cents, and not more than two dollars, to be paid by each offender respectively.

Sec. 8. *Be it further ordained,* That no person
Gambling or games of chance prohibited. shall expose in any of the streets, lanes, alleys, squares, or other public places in this city, or on the common, any table or device of any kind whatever, upon, or by which, any game of chance or hazard can be played ; and no person shall play at any such table or device, in any street, lane, alley, or square aforesaid, or on the common, under the penalty of a sum not less than three dollars, and not more than twenty dollars for either of the said offences.

Sec. 9. *Be it further ordained,* That whoever shall
Coursing or coasting in streets prohibited. exercise the dangerous practice of coursing or coasting upon sleds in any of the streets, or upon any of the sidewalks in this city, shall forfeit and pay for each offence a sum not less than one dollar, and not more than twenty dollars, to be paid by each offender respectively.

SEC. 10. *Be it further ordained,* That in future no step in front of any house or other building, or lot of land, shall be permitted to project into any street, lane, alley, public square or place, in the city, more than one foot from the front of said house or other building, nor shall any cellar door platform rise above the even surface of the sidewalk, under a penalty of four dollars, and the like penalty for every week it shall be continued, after the same shall be ordered to be removed by the Mayor and Aldermen.

SEC. 11. *Be it further ordained,* That if any person shall, for any purpose whatever, intentionally place, or cause to be placed ; or shall suspend or cause to be suspended, from any house, shop, store, lot, or place, on or over any public street, lane, court, or alley in this city, any goods, wares, or merchandize whatever, so that the same shall extend or project from the wall or front of said house, store, shop, lot, or place, more than one foot towards, or into the street, lane, alley, court, or other public place aforesaid, the person or persons so offending shall forfeit and pay the sum of two dollars for every such offence.

SEC. 12. *Be it further ordained,* That if any person shall place, or cause to be placed, any trunk, bale, box, crate, cask, or any package, article, or thing whatsoever, containing, or capable of containing, or which may have contained any goods, wares, or merchandize, on or over any part of any public street, lane, court, or alley in this city, except as is provided in the last preceeding section, whether the same shall be exposed for sale there, or otherwise, and shall suffer the same to remain more than three hours after it is first placed there, or more than ten minutes after notice to remove the same, given by the Mayor, or some person by him authorized, the person or persons so offending, shall forfeit and pay the sum of two dollars for every such offence : *Provided,* that nothing herein contained, shall be deemed to extend to any goods, wares, or merchandize, placed in any street, lane, alley, or court, for the purpose of being sold by auction : *And provided, also,* that the proceedings in placing the same, and vending thereof shall conform to the regulations which shall be made by the Mayor and Aldermen on that subject ; and all laws, orders, and regulations, restricting such sales, shall remain unaffected by this ordinance.

SEC. 13. *Be it further ordained,* That no person shall take any quantity of street dirt or manure whatsoever, collected from any street, lane, alley, or public place of the city, without the license of the Board of Aldermen first obtained, under the penalty of four dollars for any quantity thus taken.

Street dirt and manure.

SEC. 14. *Be it further ordained,* That from and after the passing of this ordinance, the tenant, occupant, and in case there shall be no tenant, the owner of any building or lot of land bordering on any street, lane, court, or public place within the city, (excepting that part of the city called South Boston,) where there is any footway or sidewalk, shall, after the ceasing to fall of any snow, if in the daytime, within six hours, and if in the night-time, before two of the clock in the afternoon succeeding, cause the same to be removed therefrom ; and in default thereof shall forfeit and pay a sum not less than one dollar, and not more than four dollars ; and a further sum not less than one dollar, and not more than four dollars, for every day that the same shall afterwards remain on such footway or sidewalk.

Snow to be removed from sidewalks.

SEC. 15. *Be it further ordained,* That every person who shall lay or throw, or cause to be laid or thrown, any ice or snow into any street, lane, alley, court or public place within the city, shall cause the same to be broken into small pieces, and spread evenly on the surface of such street, lane, alley, court and public place ; and in default thereof, shall forfeit and pay a sum not less than one dollar, nor more than four dollars for every such offence.

Ice or snow not to be thrown into streets, unless, &c.

SEC. 16. *Be it further ordained,* That it shall be lawful for any person to place and fix awnings or shades, made of cloth, before his or her house, shop, or store, in any street in the city, conforming as near as may be to the outer line of the side walk ; and to cause such awnings or shades, to be safely fixed and supported, and in such a manner as not to interfere with passengers, which awnings or shades shall

Awnings and shades.

always be so fixed and placed, that the lowest part thereof shall be seven feet in height, above the side walk or street under the same.

SEC. 17. *Be it further ordained,* That no person shall swim or bathe in the waters surrounding the city, which are adjacent to any of the bridges or avenues leading into the same, so as to be exposed to the view of spectators, under a penalty of four dollars for each offence.

Swimming and bathing.

SEC. 18. *Be it further ordained,* That all orders and by-laws, heretofore made and passed by the inhabitants of the town of Boston, on the subjects of this ordinance, and such parts of all the orders and ordinances heretofore made and passed by the City Council on the subjects of this ordinance, as are inconsistent with the provisions thereof, and also the order of the City Council, passed June the ninth, A. D. 1825, concerning the side walks, be and the same are hereby repealed.

Former orders & by-laws repealed.

[Passed Dec. 18, 1826.]

CHAP. XLIII.

Suits at Law.

ACTS OF THE LEGISLATURE.

An act regulating the commencement of certain actions, in which the Inhabitants of the town of Boston, in the County of Suffolk, shall be a party.

SEC. 1. *Be it enacted by the Senate and House of Representatives, in General Court assembled, and by the authority of the same,* That all actions to be commenced hereafter, wherein the inhabitants of the town of Boston, in the County of Suffolk, in their corporate capacity, shall sue, or be sued, and which cannot now by law be brought in any other county than the County of Suffolk, may and shall be brought in the County of Norfolk,* any law to the contrary notwithstanding.

Writs, &c. service of.　SEC. 2. *Be it further enacted,* That the Sheriff of the County of Suffolk, or his deputy, be, and he hereby is authorized to serve and execute within the said County of Suffolk, all writs and precepts to the said Sheriff, or his deputy, legally directed, wherein the said inhabitants of the town of Boston may be a party, notwithstanding the said Sheriff or his deputy may be an inhabitant of the said town.

[Passed June 10, 1808.]

* May now be brought in Middlesex or Essex. 1815, Chap. 103.

An act in addition to an act, entitled, " An act regulating the commencement of certain actions, in which the Inhabitants of the town of Boston, in the County of Suffolk, shall be a party."

SEC. 1. *Be it enacted by the Senate and House of Representatives, in General Court assembled, and by the authority of the same,* That all actions to be commenced hereafter, wherein the inhabitants of the town of Boston, in the County of Suffolk, in their corporate capacity, shall sue or be sued, may be instituted and prosecuted in either of the Counties of Norfolk, Middlesex, or Essex, any thing in the law to which this is in addition to the contrary notwithstanding.

Actions may be brought in Norfolk, Essex, or Middlesex.

SEC. 2. *Be it further enacted,* That any Coroner of the County of Suffolk be, and he hereby is authorized to serve and execute all writs and precepts to him directed, wherein the inhabitants of the town of Boston shall sue or be sued, by the Sheriff of said county, or either of his deputies, notwithstanding the said Coroner may be an inhabitant of said town.

Coroner of Suffolk may serve writs, &c.

SEC. 3. *Be it further enacted,* That whenever an execution which has been issued on the judgment of any Court within this Commonwealth, in which judgment, the inhabitants of the said town of Boston shall be a party, shall be in the hands of an officer having authority to serve the same, and the said officer shall be directed to extend the said execution on real estate of the debtor, situated in the said town of Boston, then the said officer shall cause three discreet men, being freeholders in the said County of Suffolk, to be chosen and sworn to appraise such real estate, in the manner prescribed in the second section of an act of this Commonwealth, passed the seventeenth day of March, in the year of our Lord one thousand seven hundred and eighty-four, and entitled " An act, directing the issuing, extending, and serving of Executions," and the appraisment so made, shall be valid, notwithstanding the appraisors so chosen, or any of them, may be an inhabitant of said town.

Freeholders in Boston may appraise real estate, &c. 11 Mass. Rep. 468.

1783, Ch. 47.

[Passed Feb. 13, 1816.]

CHAP. XLIV.

Surveyors of Highways.

ACT OF THE LEGISLATURE.

An act concerning Surveyors of Highways in Boston.

Be it enacted by the Senate and House of Representatives, in General Court assembled, and by the authority of the same, That the City Council of the City of Boston, shall have the power and authority of electing, if they see fit, the Mayor and Aldermen of said city, Surveyors of Highways for said city, any thing in the act establishing the City of Boston to the contrary notwithstanding.

[Passed June 10, 1823.]

CHAP. XLV.

Taxes.

See Assessors and Assessments, ante Chap. 2.

An ordinance upon the subject of Taxes.

Sec. 1. *Be it ordained by the Mayor, Aldermen and Common Council of the City of Boston, in City Council assembled,* That the Assessors of the City of Boston, be, and they hereby are required to assess upon the owners of real estate within the City of Boston, the amount of taxes for which such estates may be respectively taxed : *Provided,* that in cases where the assessors may think it to be more for the public interest to assess the tenant or occupant, instead of the owner, they may so assess : *Provided, also,* that nothing in this ordinance contained, shall affect the right, which owners and tenants may have between themselves respectively, by reason of any contract or agreement between them.

Owners of real estate to be assessed.

Proviso.

Sec. 2. *Be it further ordained,* That the permanent assessors may transfer the amount of taxes assessed on real estates not owned at the time of assessment by the person or persons charged with such taxes, to the person or persons by whom the same may have been owned at the time of such assessment ; that they may abate all taxes for the payment of which the person or persons assessed are not legally liable, by reason of non residence, and may abate poll taxes, in all cases where they are satisfied that the individual assessed is unable, or not legally liable to pay the same.

Assessors may transfer amount of taxes assessed on real estate.

Poll taxes may be abated.

Sec. 3. *Be it further ordained,* That in all cases where the tax does not exceed the sum of sixteen dollars, the same, or any part thereof, may be abated : *Provided,* that a majority of the permanent as-

Taxes may be abated, &c.

sessors, and both the assistant assessors who reside in the same ward with such person or persons applying for relief, are first fully satisfied that such person or persons are rated more than his or their proportion of the taxes, or are unable, from old age, infirmity, or poverty, to pay the taxes assessed against him or them.   But no abatement, (unless for reasons stated in the second section of this ordinance,) shall be made of any tax, when the same exceeds the sum of sixteen dollars, except by the assent of a majority of permanent assessors, and assistant assessors from the several wards of the city, expressed and declared in convention ; and every applicant for abatement shall state his claim in writing, and subscribe the same with his name, and address the same to the permanent assessors.

SEC. 4. *Be it further ordained*, That all abatements which shall at any time be allowed, shall be recorded by the permanent assessors, and the record thereof shall contain the names of all persons whose taxes shall be abated, in whole or in part, and the amount originally assessed, and the amount of abatements, and that all the reasons for abatement shall be stated on the said record, against the name of each person whose tax shall be abated ; and that this record shall be laid before the city government, as soon as may be, and in every year, before the election of assessors for the ensuing year.

Abatements to be recorded and the reason thereof.

SEC. 5. *Be it further ordained*, That all ordinances of the City Council, heretofore made, upon the subject of taxes, be, and the same are hereby repealed.

Former ordinances repealed.
Vide ante. p. 32 and 33.

[Passed Dec. 12, 1825.]

CHAP. XLVI.

Treasurer of the City and County.

ACTS OF THE LEGISLATURE.

An act directing the time and manner of appointing a treasurer for the County of Suffolk. (Rendered inoperative by the City Charter, Sec. 18.—And by Stat. 1821, Chap. 109, Sec. 12.)

Extract from the City Charter.

SEC. 18. *Be it further enacted,* That the Mayor and Aldermen of said city, and the said Common Council, shall, as soon as conveniently may be, after their annual organization, meet together in convention, and elect some suitable and trust-worthy person, to be the Treasurer of said city.

Treasurer, choice of.

Extract from an act to regulate the administration of Justice within the County of Suffolk, and for other purposes. 1821, Chap. 109.

SEC. 12. *Be it further enacted,* That the Treasurer of the City of Boston, shall be *ex officio* Treasurer of the County of Suffolk; and shall keep all such books as may be proper and necessary, as Treasurer of the City of Boston, and as Treasurer of the County of Suffolk.

Ex officio County Treasurer.

☞ See Chap. VIII, Buildings, where the Treasurer is to prosecute for injuries to public buildings.

An act to enable the Treasurer of this Commonwealth, and the Treasurers of Counties, Towns and
other corporations for the time being, to commence
and prosecute Suits at Law, upou securities given
to their predecessors.

*Be it enacted by the Senate and House
of Representatives, in General Court assembled, and
by the authority of the same,* That the Treasurer of
this Commonwealth, the Treasurers of Counties,
Towns, Parishes, and other corporations, for the time
being, be and hereby are authorized and empowered
in their own names and capacities, respectively, to
commence and prosecute to final judgment and execution, any suit or suits at law, upon any bonds,
notes or other securities, which have been or shall be
given to them or their predecessors in said capacity ;
and to prosecute to final judgment and execution,
any suits which have been or shall be commenced
by their said predecessors in said capacity, during
their continuance in office, and pending at the time
of their removal therefrom.

[Passed June 22, 1797.]

See Chapter II, title Assessors and Assessments, where the duty of the
Treasurer and Collector of the City is particularly set forth.

CHAP. XLVII.

Theatrical Exhibitions.

An ordinance to regulate Theatrical Exhibitions.

Be it ordained by the Mayor, Aldermen, and Common Council of the City of Boston, in City Council assembled, That if any person shall violate any of the provisions contained in the fourteenth section of the act, entitled " An act establishing the City of Boston," such person shall forfeit and pay for each and every offence against any of the provisions in said fourteenth section contained, a sum not less than five dollars nor more than twenty dollars.

[Passed Dec. 18, 1826.]

32

CHAP. XLVIII.

Ward Clerks pro tempore.

An ordinance to authorize the Inhabitants of the several Wards, within the city to choose Clerks pro tempore in certain cases.

Be it ordained by the Mayor, Aldermen, and Common Council of the City of Boston, in City Council assembled, That in all cases when the Clerk of any Ward shall be absent from any legal Ward meeting, it shall be lawful for the Inhabitants of said Ward to choose by ballot, a clerk pro tempore, who shall be a resident in said Ward, and shall serve until the standing clerk of said Ward shall resume the duties of his office, or until another shall be elected in his stead, and said Clerk pro tempore shall be sworn in like manner as is provided by law for the qualification of the standing Clerks of the Wards.

[Passed March 22, 1824.]

CHAP. XLIX.

Warrants.

An ordinance prescribing the form of Warrants, and of the service thereof.

SEC. 1. *Be it ordained by the Mayor, Aldermen, and Common Council of the City of Boston, in City Council assembled,* That the form of Warrants for calling meetings of the citizens of the several Wards, shall be as follows, to wit:

> L.S.　　City of Boston, ss.
> 　　To either of the Constables of the City of Boston. 　　　　　　　　　Greeting :
> 　　In the name of the Commonwealth of Massachusetts, you are hereby required, forthwith, to warn the Inhabitants of Ward No.　, qualified as the law directs, to assemble at　　　on the　　　day of　　　at　o'clock　M. then and there to give in their ballots for
> 　　Hereof fail not; and have you there then this Warrant, with your doings thereon.　Witness
> 　　　　Mayor of our said City of Boston the
> day of　　　in the year of our Lord one thousand eight hundred and
> 　　By order of the Mayor and Aldermen.
> 　　　　　　　　　　*City Clerk.*

SEC. 2. *Be it further ordained,* That all Warrants for calling meetings of the citizens of the several Wards, which shall be issued by the Mayor and Aldermen, shall be served by any constable of the city, and returned to the Wardens of the several Wards in said city, on or before the time of meeting of the citizens of said Wards, therein specified.

SEC. 3. *Be it further ordained,* That the form of Warrants for calling meetings of the Inhabitants of the said City of Boston, shall be as follows, to wit:

[Margin notes:] See City Charter Sec. 26. — Warrants for Ward meetings. — Warrants for Ward meetings, service of. — Form of Warrants for general meetings.

City of Boston ss.

To the Constables of the City of Boston.

Greeting :

In the name of the Commonwealth of Massachusetts, you are required forthwith to warn the Inhabitants of the City of Boston, qualified as the law directs, to assemble at Faneuil Hall, on the
day of   at   o'clock   M. then and there to

Hereof fail not ; and have you there then this Warrant, with your doings thereon.   Witness,
        Mayor of our City of Boston, the
day of   in the year of our Lord one thousand eight hundred and

By order of the Mayor and Aldermen.

City Clerk.

SEC. 4. *Be it further ordained,* That all Warrants which shall be issued by the Mayor and Aldermen, for calling meetings of the Inhabitants of the city, shall be served by any constable of the city, and returned to the Mayor and Aldermen on or before the meeting of the citizens therein specified.

SEC. 5. *Be it further ordained,* That it shall be the duty of the Mayor and Aldermen to fix the time when the poll shall close, as well as the time for the opening thereof, in the election of all officers, except ward officers, and insert the same in any warrant and notification to the Inhabitants, of such election.

[Passed Dec. 27, 1827.]

Service of Warrants.

Time of opening and closing the poll to be fixed.

CHAP. L.

Watch.

ACT OF THE LEGISLATURE.

An act to establish a Watch, for preserving the safety and good order of the town of Boston.

SEC. 1. *Be it enacted by the Senate and House of Representatives, in General Court assembled, and by the authority of the same,* That the Selectmen of the town of Boston, be, and they are hereby authorized from time to time, to appoint such a number of their Inhabitants, to be Watchmen by night, in the town of Boston, as they shall judge expedient; to be paid at the charge of that town ; and the said Selectmen are also further authorized, and empowered, from time to time, to appoint a head constable to superintend said Watch, as also a constable for each division thereof; and the several constables of divisions are required to report every morning an account of their doings, and of the state of the town during the night, to the said head constable, in order that the same may be communicated to the chairman of the Selectmen daily. *(margin: Watchmen to be appointed.)*

SEC. 2. *Be it further enacted,* That the head constable, the several constables of divisions, and the Watchmen appointed by virtue of this act, shall have the same powers, and shall be held and obliged to perform the same duties, as are required of Watchmen, by a law of this Commonwealth, passed March the 10th, 1797* entitled " An act for keeping Watches and Wards in towns, and for preventing disorders in streets and public places." *(margin: Powers, &c. of Watchmen.)*

SEC. 3. *Be it further enacted,* That the expenses that may be incurred, by reason of the establishment *(margin: Provisions for the expenses.)*

* 1796. Chap. 92.

of the Watch aforesaid, shall be raised, levied and collected, as other expenses of said town are or may be raised, levied or collected ; any law to the contrary notwithstanding.

[Passed Jan. 29, 1802.]

addition puisee mari 1853

CHAP. LI.

Weights and Measures.

ACT OF THE LEGISLATURE.

An act in further addition to an act, entitled, " An Act for the due regulation of Weights and Measures ;" and for the more easy recovery of fines and penalties within the town of Boston, in the County of Suffolk.

1749, Chap. 60.

SEC. 1. *Be it enacted by the Senate and House of Representatives, in General Court assembled, and by the authority of the same,* That it shall be the duty of the sealer of weights and measures, within and for the town of Boston, to be provided with a house, or office, and to which all persons using scale beams, steelyards, weights or measures within the town of Boston, in trade, for the purpose of buying or selling any article, shall be required, after notice thereof shall have been given in two or more of the newspapers published within the said town, to send annually their scale beams, steel yards, weights and measures, for the purpose of having the same tried, proved and sealed, as is provided in and by the act aforesaid to which this is in addition ; and the said sealer shall be entitled to demand and receive therefor, such fees as are allowed, in and by the said act.

Notice to be given.

SEC. 2. *Be it further enacted,* That the said sealer is hereby authorized and required, to go to the houses, stores and shops of all such merchants, inholders, traders, retailers, and of all other persons living or residing within said town of Boston, using beams, steelyards, weights or measures, for the purpose of buying and selling, as shall neglect to bring or send the same to the house or office of the sealer

Sealer authorized to examine weights and measures.

aforesaid : and there, at the said houses, stores and shops, having entered the same with the assent of the occupant thereof, to try, prove and seal the same, or to send the same to his said house or office, to be tried, proved and sealed, and shall be entitled to de-

Double fees.

mand and receive therefor, double the fees he would be entitled to demand and receive for the same, if such beams, steelyards, weights and measures, had been sent to his said house or office ; with all the expenses attending the removal and transportation of the same ; and if any such person or persons shall refuse to have his, her or their beams, steelyards, weights or measures, so tried, proved and sealed, the same not having been tried, proved and sealed, within one

Forfeitures.

year preceding such refusal, he, she or they shall forfeit and pay ten dollars for each offence ; the one moiety to the use of the said town of Boston, the other moiety of the same to the sealer.   And if any such person or persons shall use any beam, steelyard, weight or measure, which shall not conform to the public standard, the same not having been tried, proved and sealed, within one year preceding such use of the same, he, she or they shall forfeit and pay ten dollars for each offence ; the one moiety to the use of said town of Boston, and the other moiety of the same to the informer.   And if any such person or persons shall alter any beam, steelyard, weight or measure, after the same shall have been tried, proved and sealed, so as that the same shall, by such alteration be made not to conform to the public standard, and shall fraudulently make use of the same, he, she or they shall forfeit and pay fifty dollars for each offence, the one moiety to the use of the said town of Boston,

Forfeitures and penalties to be recovered by law.

and the other moiety of the same to the informer.

SEC. 3.   *Be it further enacted,* That all fines, forfeitures and penalties accruing within the said town of Boston under this act, or for the breach of any by-law of the said town, which is now in force, or which hereafter may be duly enacted and made, may be recovered by indictment, information or complaint, in the name of the Commonwealth, in any court competent to try the same ; and all fines so recovered and paid, shall be appropriated to the uses, for which the same are now by law ordered to be applied ;

reserving however, in all cases to the party complained of and prosecuted, the right of appeal to the next Municipal Court in the town of Boston, from the judgment and sentence of any Justice of the Peace, in which case the judgment of said Municipal Court shall be final; and to the next Supreme Judicial Court, to be holden within the County of Suffolk and for the Counties of Suffolk and Nantucket, from the judgment of the Municipal Court, where the indictment or information originated in the same; such party recognizing, with sufficient surety or sureties, to the satisfaction of the court, to enter and prosecute his, her or their said appeal, and to abide the final judgment thereon.

Sec. 4. *Be it further enacted*, That when a person, who, upon a conviction before a Justice of the Peace for any offence mentioned in this act, or for the breach of any by-law of the town of Boston, shall be sentenced to pay a fine, and shall not appeal from said judgment; or if upon claiming an appeal, shall fail to recognize as aforasaid, and upon not paying the fines and costs so assessed upon him, shall be committed to prison; there to remain until he or she shall pay such fines and costs, or otherwise be discharged according to law; and such person shall not be holden in prison for a longer time than ten days; and at the expiration of that term, the keeper of the said gaol is hereby authorized to release such person from confinement. *Appeals.*

Sec. 5. *Be it further enacted*, That all fines and penalties which shall hereafter be recovered for any offences which shall hereafter be committed against the act of this Commonwealth, which was made and passed on the fourteenth day of December, in the year of our Lord one thousand eight hundred and sixteen, entitled " An act in addition to an act, entitled an act for the due regulation of Licensed Houses," shall be appropriated, the one moiety to the town of Boston, and the other moiety of the same to the informer, any thing to the contrary in that act notwithstanding. *Appropriation of fines.*

Sec. 6. *Be it further enacted*, That the seventh section of the act aforesaid, to which this is in addi- *Repeal of act.*

33

tion, be and the same is hereby repealed, so far as respects the said town of Boston.

[Passed June 17, 1817.]

ORDINANCE OF THE CITY.

An ordinance providing for the appointment of two Sealers of Weights and Measures.

Be it ordained by the Mayor, Aldermen, and Common Council of the City of Boston, in City Council assembled, That two Sealers of Weights and Measures, shall be appointed within the City of Boston.

[Passed July 22, 1822.]

CHAP. LII.

Wood and Bark.

An ordinance regulating the admeasurement of Wood and Bark.

SEC. 1. *Be it ordained by the Mayor, Aldermen and Common Council of the City of Boston, in City Council assembled,* That hereafter there shall be three places for the measuring of Wood and Bark, brought into this city in carts, wagons, or sleds, from the country for sale, to wit : one at the southerly part of Washington street ; one at the westerly part of Cambridge street, near Cambridge bridge ; and one in Leverett street, near Canal bridge. *Places appointed for measuring.*

SEC. 2. *Be it further ordained,* That there shall be two stands for the sale of wood and bark brought into the city as aforesaid, to wit : the one in the southerly, and the other in the northerly part of the city, to be established by the Mayor and Aldermen. *Stands.*

SEC. 3. *Be it further ordained,* That there shall be three persons appointed annually, by the Mayor and Aldermen, as measurers of wood and bark, brought into the city as aforesaid, who shall be under oath, faithfully to perform the duties of their office, shall have all the powers, and perform all the duties of measurers of wood and bark, according to this ordinance, and the statutes of this Commonwealth relating to the measurement of wood and bark, and shall be furnished by the Mayor and Aldermen, with copies of the said statutes, and of this ordinance. And each person so appointed, shall deliver to the owner or driver of each load of wood or bark, a ticket, signed by the measurer, certifying the quantity of wood or bark the load contains, the name of the driver, and the town in which he resides ; and shall keep an accurate copy of said ticket, in a book to *Measurers appointed.* *Their duty.*

be furnished at their own expense, and kept for that purpose ; and it shall be the duty of the said measurers to make a return to the Mayor and Aldermen, on the first Monday of January annually, of the number of loads of wood and bark they have measured the preceeding year.

Sec. 4. *Be it further ordained.* That the Mayor and Aldermen shall establish all fees for measuring wood and bark brought into the city for sale as aforesaid.

Fees.

Sec. 5. *Be it further ordained,* That any person bringing wood or bark as aforesaid, into this city for sale, who shall, before or after the same has been duly measured, stand for sale thereof, in any other street or place than those appointed by the Mayor and Aldermen, shall forfeit and pay the sum of two dollars for each offence.

Penalty.

Sec. 6. *Be it further ordained,* That it shall be lawful for the Mayor and Aldermen to establish other places than those provided in the first section of this ordinance, for the measurement of wood and bark, and to appoint other measurers than those provided in the third section of this ordinance, whenever they may judge it necessary.

Other places may be appointed.

[Passed Dec. 27, 1826.]

INDEX

TO

The City Laws and Ordinances.

———

INDEX.

34

INDEX.

CPSIA information can be obtained
at www.ICGtesting.com
Printed in the USA
BVHW092208191118
533512BV00001B/330/P

9 780331 517316